DIAGRAM GRAPHICS 2

P·I·E BOOKS

DIAGRAM GRAPHICS 2

Printed in Hong Kong by Everbest Printing Co., Ltd.

P·I·E BOOKS
Villa Phoenix Suite 301, 4-14-6, Komagome,
Toshima-ku, Tokyo 170, Japan
Tel: 03-3949-5010 Fax: 03-3949-5650

ISBN 4-938586-74-6 C3070 P16000E

First published in Germany 1995 by:
NIPPAN / Nippon Shuppan Hanbai Deutschland GmbH
Krefelder Str. 85, D-40549 Düsseldorf, Germany
Tel: 0211-5048089 Fax: 0211-5049326

ISBN 3-910052-57-6

The designs used for the front cover were provided by
Eskind Waddel, Pentagram Design, and **Tetsuya Ohta**.

Contents

00042693890010

序 文

統計図表の目的は、事象を論理的に視覚化し、その内容を解り易く人々に伝える役割を果たすことである。その図表によって、私たちは全体の特性を知る事が出来るのである。図表の作成に当って大切な事は、まず正確なデータを使用しそれを上手に整理して簡潔でダイナミックな構成を試みる事である。もしそれを怠れば、何の感動も与えない月並みな図になるか、または事実を歪めて大げさに人々に伝える誤った図となる。

私達には印刷物に対するある種の信仰があり、一度印刷された統計図表は真実と錯覚され易い。その性質を悪用して統計図表が政治や経済の宣伝に悪用されたことも度々ある。ここまでは統計図表について説明した他の書物でも度々書かれていた。

しかし、ここで私達が最も求めているのは、一つの事象をどの様な方法で表現出来るかの可能性について知ることである。例えば、この図は如何に美しい形態で表現出来るのか。この図を説明するための文章には、どの様な書体が最もふさわしいのか。この図には如何なる配色が美しいのか。同時に、形態と色彩は論理的に整合されているのか。一点の図に盛り込む情報はどの程度が適切なのか。作られた図は一体誰に、どの様に見せるのか。統計図表をダイナミックに表現できるアイデアの鍵はどこに隠されているのか。

恐らく、この本の読者で統計図表専門のデザイナーは極く一部であろう。その人も、そしてそれ以外の人達をも含めて、ここに揚げられた全ての事柄を読者が問題にしているのである。その解決の方法とセンスまで、全てを知り尽くしたいのである。なぜならばそれらを解決した統計図表は、単に伝えるだけの手段に留まらず、芸術作品にまで到達することが出来るからなのである。そして、その様な統計図表を誰もが作ってみたいと思っている。

ピエ・ブックスから1992年に出版されたDIAGRAM GRAPHICS 1は、上記の主題をクリアーした素晴らしい出来ばえの作品を集めたものである。この度出版されたDIAGRAM GRAPHICS 2は更に内容を充実させている。世界中のトップ・グラフィック・デザイナーから集められた膨大な数におよぶ最近の作品を今回の出版目的にあった、特に優れた作品だけに厳選して、最も見易くする為に次の4つのジャンルに分類して掲載した。

1．比較統計グラフ・表 ／ 2．流れ図・組織図・機能図・主題図 ／
3．地図 ／ 4．建築・工業・科学イラストレーション

ここに掲載された作品は極く一部でしか無いが、集められた多くの作品は、ここ数年普及したパーソナル・コンピュータの導入によって大きく変化してきている。

以前には、非常に手間と時間がかかった表現や、完璧な印刷物に仕上げる為に必要だった熟練した作図技術、そして高度な印刷技術と多数の人々の犠牲的精神も必要だったのだが、パーソナル・コンピュータの導入で、これらの多くの難題が解決されていると思われる。もっとも個人の範囲内での集中した努力で図を完成させられるので、良い作品が出来る可能性も増えたことになる。私たちには頼もしい味方が現れたものである。

ともかく、過去には手間の掛かる割には報酬の少なかった作業が、この道具の出現で良い方向に進んでいるのは確かである。しかし、全てが良い訳でもない。例えば一つの警告として、表現したいイメージに合うソフトが開発されていない場合は、それが排除されるという事がある。つまり、ソフトによって発想が限定されるのであるから皆が同じ様な表現をする事になる。ここしばらく私たちは、人間の思考と手の技術がコンピュータと旨く共存する事を最善だと考えるべきだろう。

これ迄、古代からルネサンス・近代までの科学者や画家たちが図解のために惜しまなかった時間や労力に対して、現代社会は人々から時間の掛かる不経済な作業、または社会的意義だけの作業をことごとく取り上げてきた。過去には、これらの苦難を乗り越えた優れた図解が数多にある。

レオナルド・ダ・ヴィンチ、ヴェサリウスの人体解剖図、キルヒャーの著作に掲載された数多の図解、ディドーの図解百科。そして現代統計図表のスタイルを確立したバウハウスの人々。

カンディンスキーやイッテンの抽象形態及び色彩に関する基礎的分析。抽象形態に数値をあてはめ芸術的表現にまで高めたモホリ＝ナギの図解。思想の概念を見事に図解したクレー。バウハウスの思想をもとに1950年代に完成させたハーバート・バイヤーの世界地理地図帳のデザインなどの作品は、現代統計図の根元となるものである。

これ等の過去の偉大な作品と、この本に掲載された作品群を前にして、コンピュータを味方にした私達は果たして、それを越えることが出来るのであろうか。

中垣　信夫

FOREWORD

The purpose of statistical charts and diagrams is to express certain phenomena in a rational, visible form that people can readily grasp and understand. Charts and diagrams thus enable us to appreciate the significant features of such phenomena. What is important, when creating a chart, is to use accurate data, to arrange it intelligently, and to work towards a concise and dynamic composition. If these points are overlooked, the outcome will be either a very ordinary diagram that lacks impact, or else an imperfect one that distorts reality and exaggerates its message.

We all have a tendency to trust the printed word, and charts are highly persuasive once they are in print. Statistics can thus be easily abused, as frequently happens when graphs or charts are used to back up some political or economic message.

There are already plenty of books written on these aspects of charts and diagrams. What we want from this volume is to discover more about the potential for expressing a particular phenomenon in different ways. The issues involved here are, for example, what would be the most beautiful form for this diagram? what type face is suited to the diagram caption? what sort of colour scheme would look best? are the shapes and colours satisfactorily coordinated? of all the information to be shown in the diagram, how much is really appropriate? who will be seeing the finished diagram, and through what medium? and, where is the key to the ideas that will produce greater dynamic impact?

Most probably, graphic designers who specialize in charts and diagrams will form only one small part of the readership of this book. But the issues I've mentioned will concern every reader, whether professional designer or not. The reader wants to appreciate everything, including the designer's ideas and the techniques used to resolve problems. The reason is that once all the problems are satisfactorily resolved, the diagram is no longer simply a means of conveying information, but has the potential to become a work of art. And we would all like to be able to create diagrams like this.

DIAGRAM GRAPHICS, the first volume published by PIE Books in 1992, contained a collection of superb examples for which all the issues had been thoroughly resolved. This volume, DIAGRAM GRAPHICS 2, is even better. From a vast quantity of recent artwork submitted by the world's top graphic designers, a selection was made of the best of those fulfilling the objectives of this publication, and they have been divided into four sections for easier reference: **1 statistical graphs and tables, 2 flow charts, organization charts, functional diagrams and topic illustrations, 3 maps, and 4 architectural, industrial and scientific illustrations.**

The work in this book represents only a fraction of the total, but much of the artwork submitted for this project illustrates the significant changes that have occurred over the last few years through the widespread introduction of personal computers.

At one time design work required designs that took considerable time and trouble, the masterful drawing skills needed for perfect printing, sophisticated printing technology and the dedication of large numbers of people. But now the introduction of personal computers has eliminated many of the difficulties. Indeed, diagrams can now be completed through the concentrated efforts of a single individual, and this has increased the potential for work of a higher standard. Designers have gained a trustworthy tool.

At all events, the computer has brought about pleasing progress in this field of endeavour, which in the past was so poorly rewarded for all the effort it required. But the picture is not entirely rosy. One foreseeable problem area is that if there is no software available to produce the sort of image one wants to conjure up, the design concept will end up being scrapped. This means that everyone will gravitate towards the same sort of design, due to the fact that software places limitations on creative ideas. It seems to me that for the time being we should think it best that computers exist side by side with people's mental powers and manual dexterity.

All through the past, from ancient times to the renaissance and the modern era, scientists and artists lavished great time and effort on illustration, but modern society, by contrast, has robbed people of the opportunity to perform time-consuming, uneconomic tasks and those that have only social significance. Many superb illustrations in the past surmounted such difficulties: the anatomical drawings of Leonardo da Vinci and Vesalius, the many illustrations in the published works of Athanasius Kircher, Diderot's rich collection of illustrations. There were the artists of the Bauhaus, who set the style for contemporary chart and diagram design. Kandinsky's and Itten's fundamental analysis of abstract forms and colour also comes to mind, as do Moholy-Nagy's illustrations, in which he applied numerical values to abstract forms for his artistic expression. There is also Klee, who illustrated the concept of thought so well, and the design of Herbert Bayer's world atlas, completed during the 1950s and based on Bauhaus principles. Works such as these lie at the foundation of contemporary chart and diagram design.

Faced with this legacy of great works of art from the past, and the fine collection presented in this volume, we might well pause to wonder whether the use of computers will ever really help us enough to create work of even greater merit.

Nobuo Nakagaki

VORWORT

Der Zweck statistischer Schaubilder und Diagramme ist es, bestimmte Phänomene in einer rationalen, sichtbaren Form auszudrücken, sodaß Leute sie umgehend erfassen und verstehen können. Schaubilder und Diagramme versetzen uns in die Lage, die wesentlichen Eigenschaften solcher Phänomene zu würdigen. Was bei der Erstellung eines Schaubildes wichtig ist, ist die Verwendung akkurater Daten, sie intelligent zu arrangieren und eine in sich geschlossene und dynamische Komposition zu erarbeiten. Wenn diese Anforderungen nicht beachtet werden, ist das Ergebnis entweder ein sehr einfaches, wenig eindrucksvolles Diagramm beziehungsweise ein unzulängliches, das die Wirklichkeit verbiegt oder die Botschaft übertreibt.

Wir alle vertrauen tendenziell dem gedruckten Wort und gedruckte Schaubilder sind besonders überzeugend. Statistiken können deshalb leicht mißbraucht werden. Das kommt häufiger dann vor, wenn Diagramme und Tabellen benutzt werden, um eine politische oder wirtschaftliche Botschaft zu untermauern.

Es gibt bereits eine Reihe von Büchern über diese Aspekte von Schaubildern und Diagrammen. Was wir mit diesem Buch erreichen wollen, ist es mehr über das Potential zu entdecken, ein bestimmtes Phänomen auf verschiedene Art und Weise darzustellen. Die Fragen hier sind zum Beispiel: „Was wäre die schönste Form für dieses Diagramm?", „Welche Schrift würde am besten als Diagramm-Überschrift passen?", „Welche Art der Farbgebung wäre optimal?", „Sind Farben und Formen zufriedenstellend koordiniert?", „Welche der gezeigten Informationen sind wirklich notwendig?", „Wer wird das fertige Diagramm sehen und durch welches Medium?" und „Wo ist der Schlüssel zu den Ideen, durch die man einen noch dynamischeren Eindruck vermitteln kann?"

Sehr wahrscheinlich werden die auf Schaubilder und Diagramme spezialisierten Graphik-Designer nur einen kleinen Teil der Leserschaft dieses Buches ausmachen. Aber die oben beschriebenen Fragen gehen jeden an, gleich ob professioneller Designer oder nicht. Der Leser möchte alles verstehen, auch die Ideen des Gestalters und die Techniken zur Lösung der Probleme. Sind die Probleme zufriedenstellend ausgeräumt, dann ist das Diagramm nämlich nicht mehr nur ein einfaches Werkzeug zum Transport von Informationen, sondern hat auch das Potential, ein Kunstwerk zu sein. Und irgendwie möchten wir alle in der Lage sein, solche Diagramme zu schaffen.

DIAGRAM GRAPHICS, der von PIE Books 1992 herausgegebene erste Band, enthielt eine Sammlung von herausragenden Beispielen, bei denen alle Fragen sorgfältig gelöst waren. Dieser Band, DIAGRAM GRAPHICS 2, geht sogar darüber hinaus. Aus der großen Zahl von Einsendungen von weltweit führenden Graphik-Designern haben wir die ausgewählt, die den Zwecken dieses Buches optimal entsprachen. Sie sind in vier Kategorien eingeteilt: **1. Statistische Schaubilder und Tabellen, 2. Flußdiagramme, Organisationstafeln, Funktionsdiagramme und Themenillustrationen, 3. Karten und 4. Architektur-, Industrie- und Wissenschaftsillustrationen.**

Die Arbeiten in diesem Buch geben nur einen Ausschnitt wieder; die meisten eingereichten Arbeiten spiegelten jedoch den signifikanten Wandel in den letzten Jahren wider, der durch die weite Verbreitung von Personal Computern ausgelöst wurde.

In der Vergangenheit wurden für Diagramm-Designs beträchtliche Zeit und Mühe für die Gestaltung aufgewandt, besondere Zeichenkenntnisse gebraucht, sowie ausgefeilte Drucktechnik und die Aufmerksamkeit einer großen Zahl von Leuten. Jetzt jedoch hat die Einführung der Personal Computer viele der Schwierigkeiten ausgeräumt. In der Tat können heute Diagramme durch den konzentrierten Einsatz eines Einzelnen erstellt werden - und das hat das Potential für Arbeiten in einem höheren Standard verbessert. Designer haben jetzt ein vertrauenswürdiges, neues Werkzeug.

Der Computer hat bei alle dem einen erfreulichen Fortschritt in diesen Arbeitsbereich gebracht, der bisher für die dazu benötigten Anstrengungen eher wenig beachtet wurde. Aber das Bild wird zunehmend rosiger. Ein absehbares Problemfeld ist, daß bei Fehlen einer passenden Software zur Erstellung der gewünschten Diagramme, das Design-Konzept am Ende nicht durchgeführt wird. Das bedeutet, das jeder letztendlich bei der gleichen Art von Design anlangt, bedingt durch die Beschränkungen der Software für Umsetzung kreativer Ideen. Es scheint, daß man zur Zeit am besten den Computer Seite an Seite mit den persönlichen geistigen und manuellen Fähigkeiten sehen sollte.

Durch die Vergangenheit, vom Altertum bis zur Renaissance und der modernen Zeit, haben Wissenschaftler und Künstler viel Zeit mit Illustrationen verbracht. Im Gegensatz dazu hat die moderne Gesellschaft die Leute der Möglichkeit beraubt, zeitaufwendige, unökonomische Aufgaben auszuführen - auch solche, die nur soziale Bedeutung haben. Viele herausragende Illustrationen der Vergangenheit waren mit solchen Schwierigkeiten noch nicht konfrontiert: die anatomischen Zeichnungen von Leonardo da Vinci und Vesalius, die vielen Illustrationen in den Publikationen von Athanasius Kircher, Diderots reiche Sammlung von Illustrationen. Dann gab es die Bauhaus-Künstler, die den Stil für zeitgemäße Schaubilder und Diagramme begründeten. Kandinskys und Ittens fundamentale Analyse der abstrakten Formen und der Farben ist ebenso zu bemerken, wie auch Moholy-Nagys Illustrationen, in denen er als künstlerischen Ausdruck abstrakten Formen numerische Werte zuordnete. Dann sind noch Klee, der das Gedankenkonzept so hervorragend illustrierte, und Herbert Beyer, dessen in den 50er Jahren fertiggestellter Weltatlas auf den Bauhaus-Prinzipien aufbaute. Werke wie diese legten die Fundamente für das heutige, moderne Schaubild- und Diagramm-Design.

Angesichts des Vermächtnisses der großen Kunstwerke der Vergangenheit und der vorzüglichen Sammlung in diesem Band, möchte man gerne innehalten und fragen, ob der Gebrauch des Computers uns jemals wirklich so stark helfen wird, um Arbeiten mit noch größerer künstlerischer Qualität zu schaffen.

Nobuo Nakagaki

Editorial notes

Explanatory caption

ダイアグラム内容説明

Submittor's nationality / Year of completion

作品出品者国籍 / 制作年度

AD: Art director

CD: Creative director

CL: Client

CW: Copywriter

D: Designer

DF: Design firm

E: Editor

I: Illustrator

P: Photographer

1 Statistical graphs and tables

比較統計グラフ・表

Statistical graphs show in a simple form the relationship between two or more sets of figures, for an easy visual grasp of changes over time, comparative values and so on. Tables show figures organized into rows and columns so that they can be read off easily.

比較統計グラフは互いに関係のある２つ以上の数値を単純な図形におきかえて、その変化や大きさを比較しやすくしたものを指す。表はこみいった数値を整理して並べ、見やすいようにしたものである。

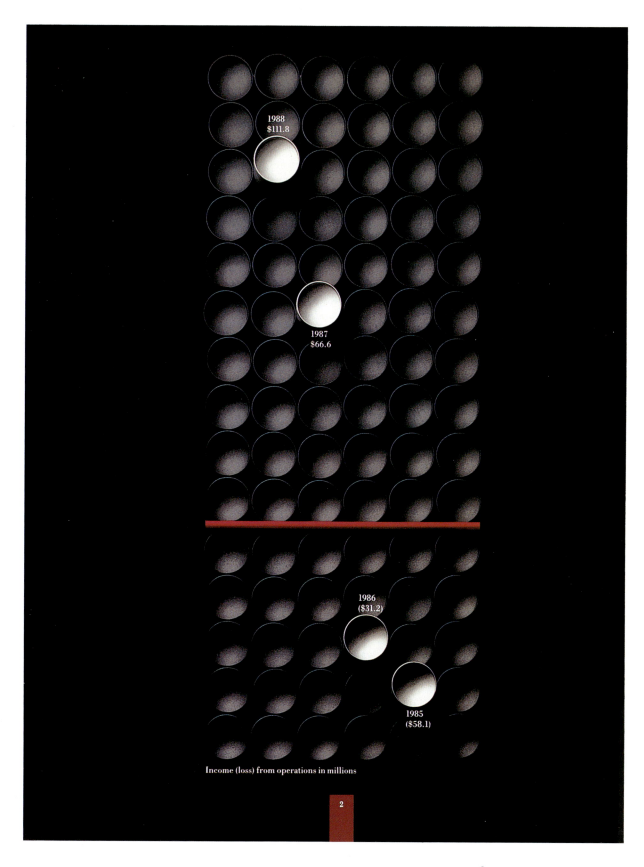

1988
$111.8

1987
$66.6

1986
($31.2)

1985
($58.1)

Income (loss) from operations in millions

2

Steel can bar graph illustrating financial results. From National Steel 1988 year-end report.

ナショナル・スチール社の1988年度末報告書より、決算結果に関するスチール缶をモチーフにした棒グラフ。

U.S.A.　1989
AD: Robert A. Adam
D: Ralph James Russini
P: Harry Giglio
DF: Adam Filippo & Associates
CL: National Steel

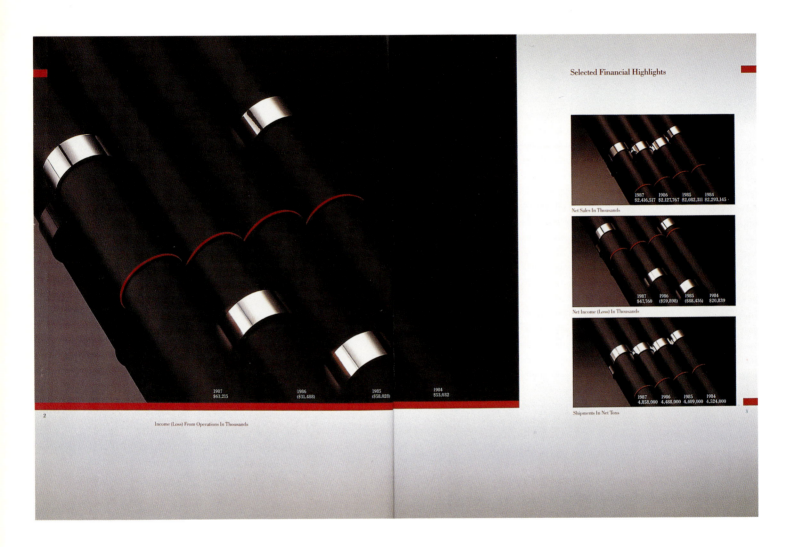

1987 1986 1985 1984
$2,416,517 $2,127,767 $2,082,311 $2,293,145
Net Sales In Thousands

1987 1986 1985 1984
$47,760 ($59,898) ($88,436) $20,839
Net Income (Loss) In Thousands

1987 1986 1985 1984
4,858,000 4,488,000 4,409,000 4,524,000
Shipments In Net Tons

1987 1986 1985 1984
$63,215 ($31,488) ($58,028) $53,032

Income (Loss) From Operations In Thousands

Coiled steel bar graphs illustrating
financial results. From National Steel
1987 year-end report.

ナショナル・スチール社の1987年度末報告
書より、決算結果に関するコイルをモチー
フにした棒グラフ。

U.S.A.　1988
AD: Robert A. Adam
D: Robert A. Adam
P: Harry Giglio
DF: Adam Filippo & Associates
CL: National Steel

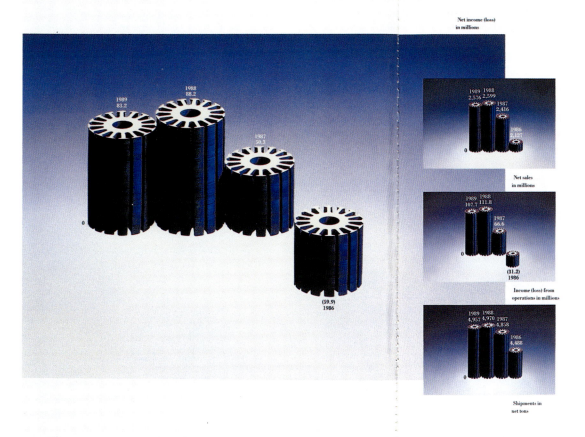

Net income (loss)
in millions

1989
83.2

1988
88.2

1987
50.3

0

(59.9)
1986

1989
2,576

1988
2,599

1987
2,416

1986
2,127

0

Net sales
in millions

1989
107.7

1988
111.8

1987
66.6

0

(31.2)
1986

Income (loss) from
operations in millions

1989
4,957

1988
4,970

1987
4,858

1986
4,488

0

Shipments in
net tons

D espite softness in the marketplace in the second half of the year, National Steel turned in a strong performance in 1989. Net income was within 6 percent of 1988, which was our best profit year since becoming a joint venture company. Sales approximated those of the previous year; production was a record 5,394,000 tons; and shipments were a near-record 4,957,000 tons.

Bar graphs illustrating financial results. From National Steel 1989 year-end report.

ナショナル・スチール社の1989年度末報告書より、決算結果に関する棒グラフ。

U.S.A.   1990
AD: Robert A. Adam
D: Ralph James Russini/Robert A. Adam
P: Harry Giglio
DF: Adam Filippo & Associates
CL: National Steel

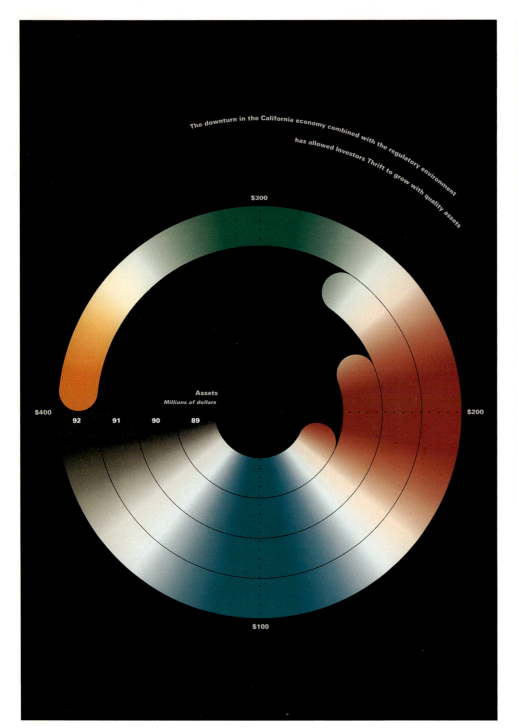

The downturn in the California economy combined with the regulatory environment has allowed Investors Thrift to grow with quality assets

Assets
Millions of dollars

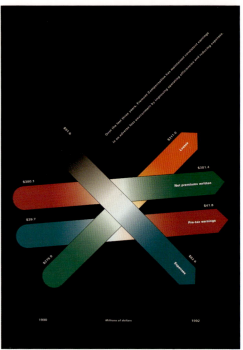

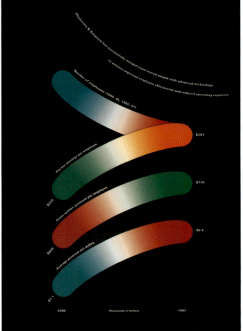

Charts illustrating financial results. From Fremont General Corporation 1992 annual report.

フリーモント・ジェネラル社の1992年アニ
ュアルレポートより、同社のいくつかの決
算内容を示したグラフ。

U.S.A.   1993
CD: Carl Seltzer
AD: Carl Seltzer
D: Carl Seltzer/Luis Alvarado
DF: Carl Seltzer Design Office
CL: Fremont General Corp.

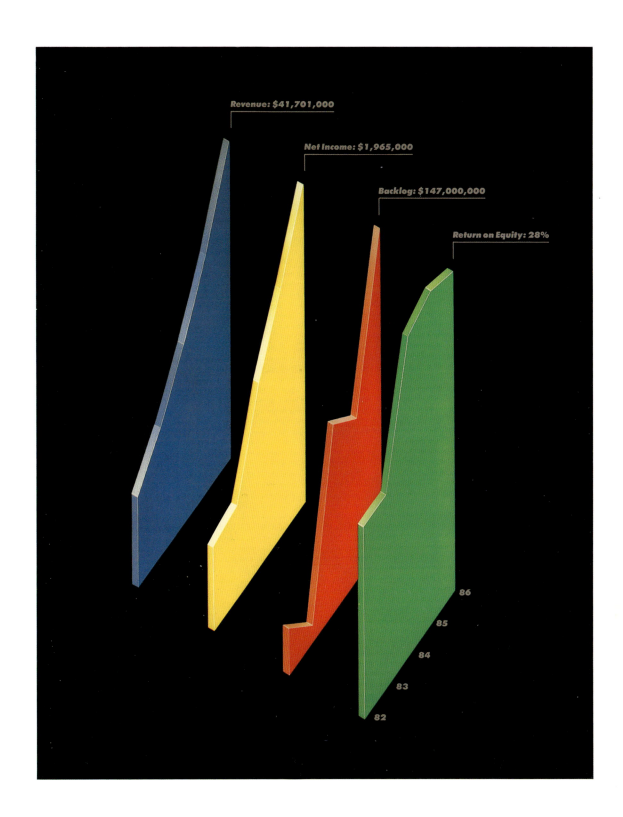

Revenue: $41,701,000

Net Income: $1,965,000

Backlog: $147,000,000

Return on Equity: 28%

86
85
84
83
82

Chart illustrating selected financial results, from Comarco 1986 annual report.

コマルコ社の1986年アニュアルレポートより、同社のいくつかの決算結果を表したグラフ。

U.S.A.   1986
CD: Carl Seltzer
AD: Carl Seltzer
D: Carl Seltzer
DF: Carl Seltzer Design Office
CL: Comarco

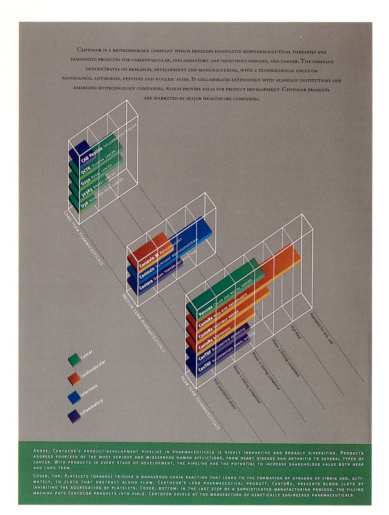

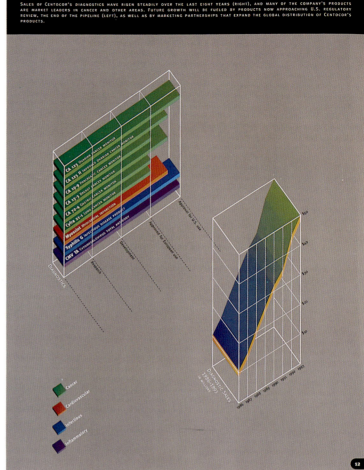

Charts showing product development progress in pharmaceuticals. From Centocor, Inc. 1993 annual report.

セントコー社の1993年アニュアルレポートより、同製薬会社の商品開発の進歩の様子を表したグラフ。

U.S.A.　1994
CD: Joel Katz
D: Joel Katz
I: Joel Katz/David Schpok/
Michael Richman
DF: Paradigm:design
CL: Centocor, Inc.

Charts showing product development progress in diagnostics and sales of diagnostic products. From Centocor, Inc. 1993 annual report.

セントコー社の1993年アニュアルレポートより、同社の病気診断業の開発過程と、商品の売上高を示すグラフ。

U.S.A.　1994
CD: Joel Katz
D: Joel Katz
I: Joel Katz/David Schpok/
Michael Richman
DF: Paradigm:design
CL: Centocor, Inc.

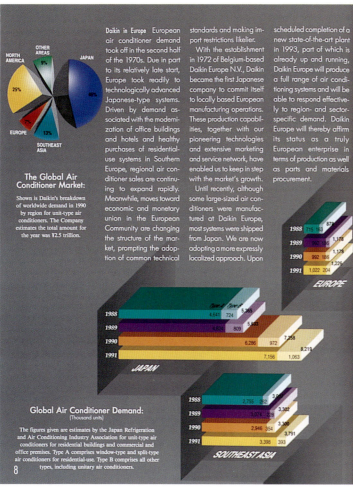
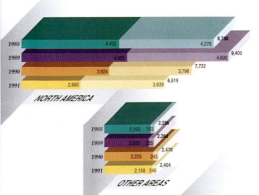

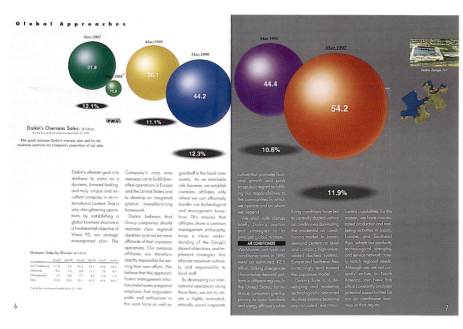

Graphs showing changes in global demand for air conditioners, and company's overseas sales turnover. From Daikin Industries, Ltd. annual report.

ダイキン工業社のアニュアルレポートより、空調機の需要と海外における同社の売上高の推移を表したグラフ。

Japan 1992
AD: Mari Sasaki
I: Tube Corporation
CL: Daikin Industries, Ltd.

メセナ活動の3年比を見る

当協議会が過去3年間にわたっておこなった調査によると、ご覧のとおり、メセナ実施企業の割合は年々増加傾向にあります。また、メセナ担当部署の設置も、専任部署とともに増加しています。担当部署が明確になってきていることは、企業が腰を据えてメセナ活動に取り組もうとしている姿勢のあらわれといえます。なお、資金援助総額は、91年が253億円、92年が236億円となっています。92年は、深刻な不況の影響が顕著になった年であり、減収減益を余儀なくされた企業も多かったことを思えば、この減少は微減というべきで、むしろ"メセナ健在"を裏づける数値と受け取りたいと思います。ただし、メセナ活動費を予算化している企業は43.6%と、まだ充分とはいえず、メセナ活動の活力を維持し継続性を確立させるためにも、予算を組む企業が今後増えることを期待したいと思います。

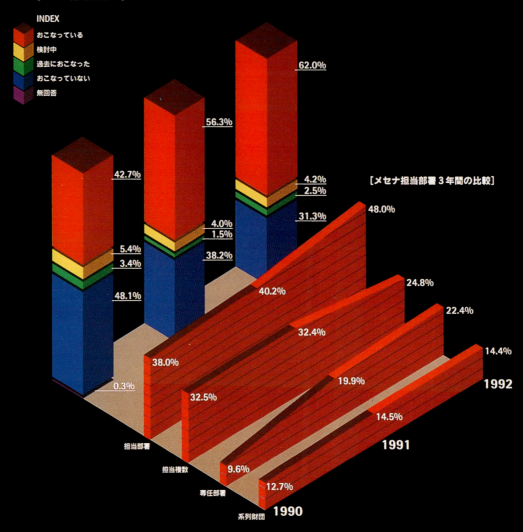

[メセナ活動実施状況]

INDEX
- おこなっている
- 検討中
- 過去におこなった
- おこなっていない
- 無回答

[メセナ担当部署3年間の比較]

資料：メセナ白書1993　Designed by NDC Graphics ⓒ1993

ヨーロッパの文化行政—中央政府＆地方政府の文化支出

ヨーロッパの文化行政というと、「国」が中心というイメージをお持ちではありませんか？でも下のグラフを見ると、中央政府のみならず地方政府も大きな役割を演じていることがわかります。特に連邦国家であるスイスやドイツでは、文化は明らかに州や市町村の仕事で、連邦政府の役割は非常に限定されたものです。中央集権で知られたフランスでさえ、地方分権化政策が推進され、文化行政はかなり地方に委譲されています。日本でも中央/地方の割合〔90年〕は、下のグラフのドイツと同じ。ただし、日本の地方文化支出は美術館やホールなど、「ハコ」の建設費ばかり大きいのが難点ですが、ともかく地方のほうが文化に積極的といえるでしょう。ここにさらに民間の力を加え、中央政府—地方政府—民間の三者が協力して文化を支える「三位一体」こそ、日本やヨーロッパがいま模索しつつあるメセナの未来像なのではないでしょうか。

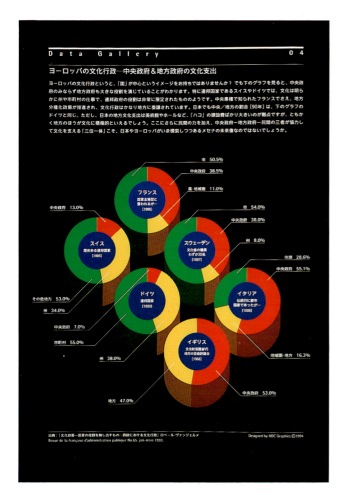

出典：「文化政策—国家の役割を無い出すもの—西欧における文化行政」ロベール・ヴァンジェルメ
Revue de la française d'administration publique no.65. jan-mars 1993.

Designed by NDC Graphics ©1994

地方自治体と企業はメセナのパートナーとなりうるか

地方自治体に「企業にメセナを要請したことがあるか」と尋ねた結果が下のグラフです。なぜ企業メセナを要請したのかという問いには、都道府県が主に財政困難による資金援助の必要性と答えているのに対して、市区は資金以外の経営資源の導入が重要だと答えています。逆に要請したことがない理由のトップは、都道府県が「特定の企業色がつく恐れがあったから」、市区が「これまで考えたことがなかった」。それでも、「企業との協力が必要」「どちらかというと必要」と答える都道府県はあわせて93.8%、市区は94%にのぼります。官民の協力が必要と痛感しつつも、不安や情報不足から躊躇と行動のあいだにはギャップがあるようです。しかし、地域文化に貢献したいという思いは、自治体も企業も市民も同じ。なんとか力を合わせてゆく方法を模索してほしいものです。

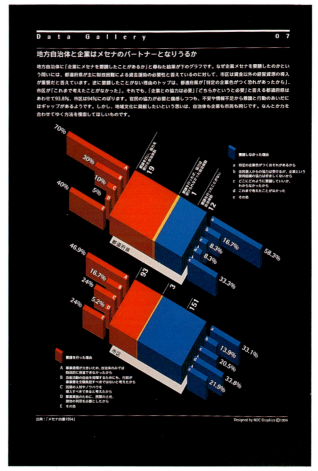

出典：「メセナ白書1994」

Designed by NDC Graphics ©1994

Graphs from 'Mésénat Quarterly', a publication of the Association for Corporate Support of the Arts. They illustrate the association's activities, compare central governments' and local governments' spending on the arts in selected European countries, detail requests for corporate support for the arts from local governments in Japan, and criteria for hiring art administrators in the US.

企業メセナ協議会が発行する「季刊メセナ」より、メセナ活動の発展状況、ヨーロッパ各国における中央政府と地方政府の文化支出の比較、日本の地方自治体による企業メセナの要請状況、アメリカにおけるアート・アドミニストレイターの採用基準の重要度を表したグラフ。

Japan   1993-94
AD: Kenzo Nakagawa
D: Satoshi Morikami/Norika Nakayama
DF: NDC Graphics Inc.
CL: Association for Corporate Support of the Arts

米国のアート・アドミニストレーターに求められる能力とは

アートマネージメント教育では、マーケティングや法律から芸術史まで、多岐に渡る領域を学習の対象とし、ゼネラリスト育成を目的としています。下のグラフは米国の芸術関連機関が求める主任アドミニストレーターの採用基準の重要度を表したものですが、これを見ても、芸術機関のスタッフが多方面の能力を発揮することを期待されていることがわかると思います。「マネージメント経験」「予算作成能力」といった具体的な実務能力などは、どの機関でも重視されている一方、劇場とオーケストラでは「作品評価能力」が、劇場と地域芸術機関では「公的資金獲得能力」が高い数値を示すなど、機関ごとに採用基準の優先順位も異なるようです。日本でもアートマネージメントへの関心がとみに高まっていますが、日本の文化状況に対応しうる多様な教養と能力を備えた人材の育成を望みたいと思います。

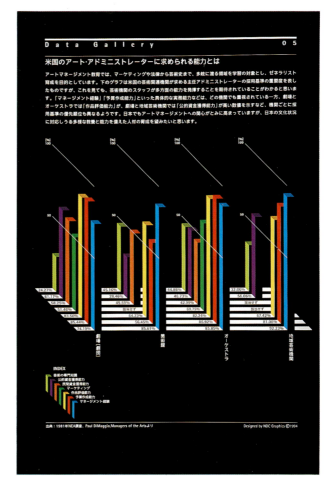

出典：1981年NEA調査、Paul DiMaggio,Managers of the Artsより

Designed by NDC Graphics ©1994

Bar chart showing expenses for 1989.
From nv PEN 1989 annual report.

PEN社の1989年アニュアルレポートより、
1989年の支出額を表す棒グラフ。

Netherlands   1990
D: Schil Schillemans Graphic
Designer bno/kio
I: Schil Schillemans Graphic
Designer bno/kio
DF: Schil Schillemans Graphic
Designer bno/kio
CL: nv PEN

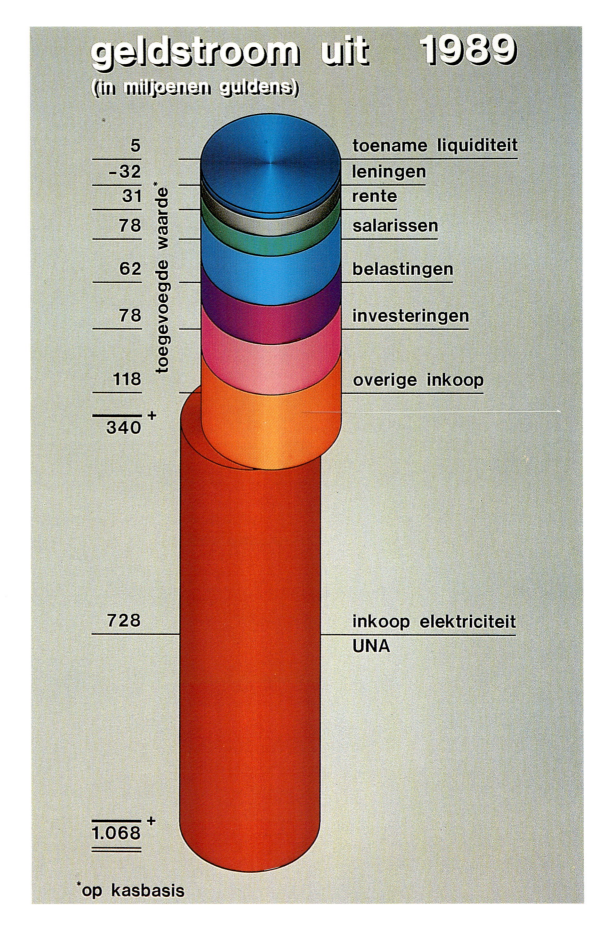

geldstroom uit 1989
(in miljoenen guldens)

5	toename liquiditeit
−32	leningen
31	rente
78	salarissen
62	belastingen
78	investeringen
118	overige inkoop
340 +	
728	inkoop elektriciteit UNA
1.068 +	

toegevoegde waarde*

*op kasbasis

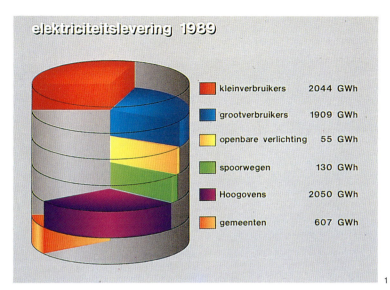

elektriciteitslevering 1989

kleinverbruikers	2044 GWh
grootverbruikers	1909 GWh
openbare verlichting	55 GWh
spoorwegen	130 GWh
Hoogovens	2050 GWh
gemeenten	607 GWh

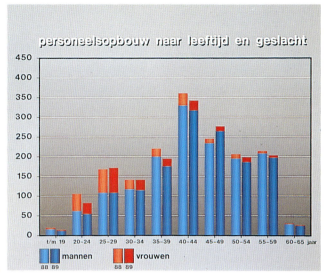

personeelsopbouw naar leeftijd en geslacht

1

2

1, 2
Charts showing electricity supplied in
1989 for various user categories,and
composition of company's personnel by
age and sex. From nv PEN 1989 annual
report.

PEN社のアニュアルレポートより、1989年
の利用者層別電気供給量の内訳と、同社の社
員構成を年齢、及び性別で表したグラフ。

Netherlands   1990
D: Schil Schillemans Graphic
Designer bno/kio
I: Schil Schillemans Graphic
Designer bno/kio
DF: Schil Schillemans Graphic
Designer bno/kio
CL: nv PEN

3, 4
Charts showing premiums in percentages and
absolute values, and numbers of insurance
policies in 1992 and 1993 for various lines of
insurance business. From Feuersozietät
Öffentliche Leben 1993 annual report.

Feuersozietät Öffentliche Leben社1993年
アニュアルレポートより、保険業界全般に
おける保険料の割合と絶対値、及び1992年
と1993年の保険証券数を表したグラフ。

Germany   1994
CD: Dieter Knoch
AD: Wladimir Perlin
D: Wladimir Perlin
I: Wladimir Perlin
DF: Dorland Advertising Agency
CL: Feuersozietät Öffentliche Leben
Assurance

Beiträge des selbst abgeschlossenen Versicherungsgeschäftes

Gesamt: 301 Mio. DM

- Verbundene Wohn-
  gebäudeversicherung
- Kraftfahrtversicherung
- Gebäude-Zwangs- und
  Monopol-Versicherung
- Feuerversicherung
- Haftpflichtversicherung
- Verbundene
  Hausratversicherung
- Sonstige

3

Anzahl der Versicherungsverträge

Gesamtes Geschäft: 507.407

- Sonstige Zweige
- Gebäude-Zwangs- und
  Monopol-Versicherung
- Glasversicherung
- Verbundene Wohn-
  gebäudeversicherung
- Verbundene
  Hausratversicherung
- Feuerversicherung
- Allgemeine
  Unfallversicherung
- Allgemeine
  Haftpflichtversicherung
- Kraftfahrtversicherung

4

Bar graph comparing a savings and loan bank's present assets with regulatory minimums, in percentages. From Collective Bancorp Inc. 1993 annual report.

コレクティヴ・バンコープ社の1993年アニュアルレポートより、貯蓄貸付銀行の現資産と最低規制基準をパーセンテージで比較した棒グラフ。

U.S.A.   1994
CD: Gil Roessner
D: Leslie Dawson
I: Scott MacNeill-MacNeill & Macintosh
DF: Roessner & Co.
CL: Collective Bancorp Inc.

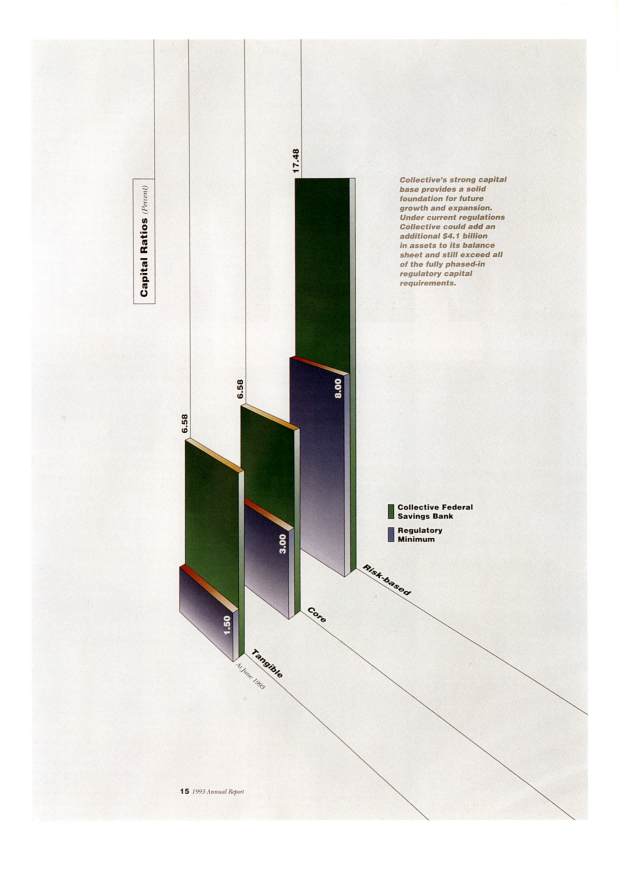

Capital Ratios *(Percent)*

17.48

6.58

6.58

8.00

3.00

1.50

Risk-based

Core

Tangible

At June 1993

■ Collective Federal
  Savings Bank
■ Regulatory
  Minimum

Collective's strong capital base provides a solid foundation for future growth and expansion. Under current regulations Collective could add an additional $4.1 billion in assets to its balance sheet and still exceed all of the fully phased-in regulatory capital requirements.

15 *1993 Annual Report*

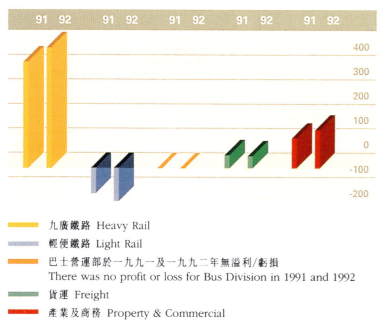

▮	九廣鐵路 Heavy Rail	
▮	輕便鐵路 Light Rail	
▮	巴士營運部於一九九一及一九九二年無溢利/虧損 There was no profit or loss for Bus Division in 1991 and 1992	
▮	貨運 Freight	
▮	產業及商務 Property & Commercial	

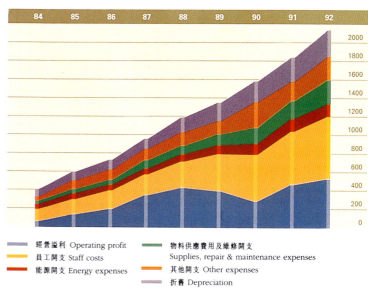

▮	經營溢利 Operating profit	▮	物料供應費用及維修開支 Supplies, repair & maintenance expenses
▮	員工開支 Staff costs	▮	其他開支 Other expenses
▮	能源開支 Energy expenses	▮	折舊 Depreciation

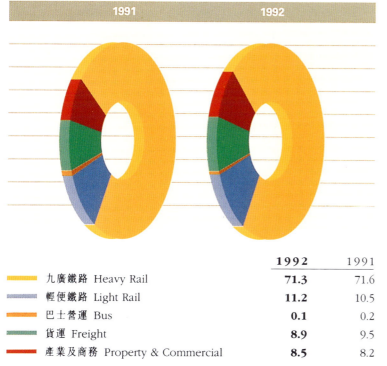

		1992	1991
▮	九廣鐵路 Heavy Rail	**71.3**	71.6
▮	輕便鐵路 Light Rail	**11.2**	10.5
▮	巴士營運 Bus	**0.1**	0.2
▮	貨運 Freight	**8.9**	9.5
▮	產業及商務 Property & Commercial	**8.5**	8.2

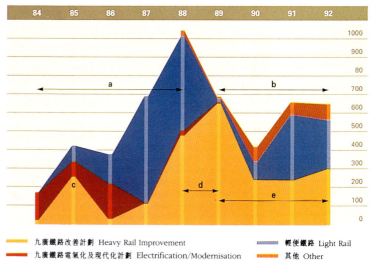

▮	九廣鐵路改善計劃 Heavy Rail Improvement	▮	輕便鐵路 Light Rail
▮	九廣鐵路電氣化及現代化計劃 Electrification/Modernisation	▮	其他 Other

Charts showing selected financial results. From Kowloon-Canton Railway Corporation 1992 annual report.

九龍広東鉄道会社の1992年アニュアルレポートより、主な決算結果を表すグラフ。

Hong Kong   1992
CD: Kan Tai-keung
AD: Eddy Yu Chi Kong
D: Eddy Yu Chi Kong
DF: Kan Tai-keung Design & Associates Ltd.
CL: Kowloon-Canton Railway Corporation

Chart illustrating worldwide sales spread over nine operating divisions. From The Black & Decker Corporation 1993 annual report.

ブラック・アンド・デッカー社の1993年ア
ニュアルレポートより、同社9部門の全世界
での売上高の割合を表した円グラフ。

U.S.A.　　1994
AD: Roger Cook/Don Shanosky
D: Cathryn Cook
I: Cathryn Cook
DF: Cook and Shanosky Associates, Inc.
CL: The Black & Decker Corporation

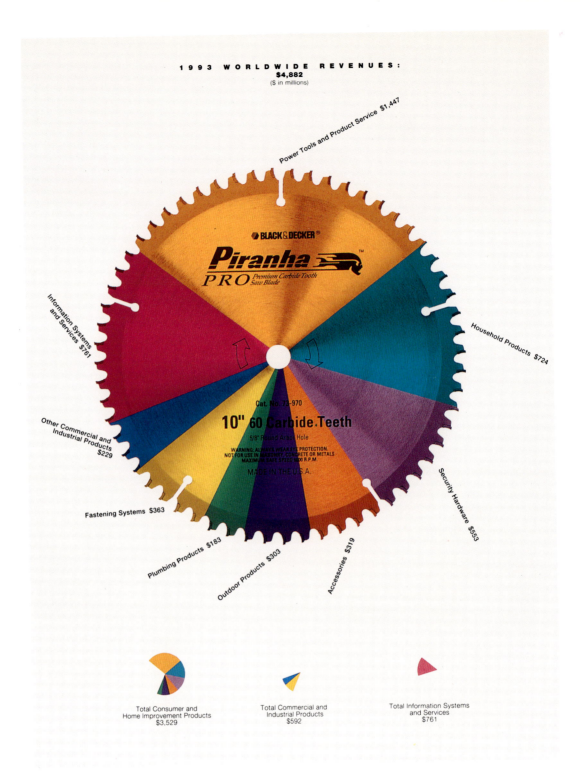

1 9 9 3 W O R L D W I D E R E V E N U E S :
$4,882
($ in millions)

Power Tools and Product Service $1,447

Household Products $724

Information Systems and Services $761

Other Commercial and Industrial Products $229

Fastening Systems $363

Plumbing Products $183

Outdoor Products $303

Accessories $319

Security Hardware $553

Total Consumer and Home Improvement Products $3,529

Total Commercial and Industrial Products $592

Total Information Systems and Services $761

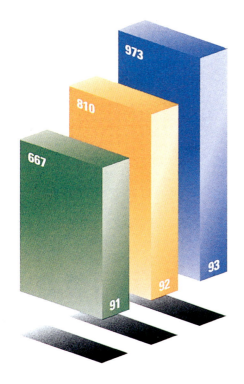

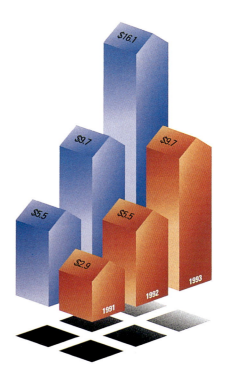

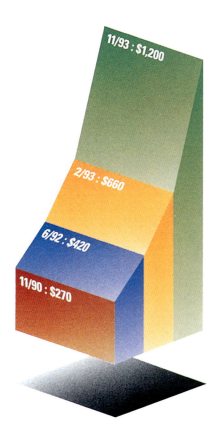

Charts showing financial data. From American Residential Holding Corporation 1993 annual report.

アメリカン・レジデンシャル・ホールディング社の1993年アニュアルレポートより、財務データを表すグラフ。

U.S.A.   1993
CD: Carl Seltzer
AD: Carl Seltzer
D: Carl Seltzer/Luis Alvarado
DF: Carl Seltzer Design Office
CL: American Residential Holding Corp.

Pie chart of revenues by region for fiscal 1994, using a close-up of a chip manufactured by the company. From international Rectifier Corporation 1994 annual report.

インターナショナル・レクティフィア社のア ニュアルレポートより、同社が製造するチップ の拡大図をモチーフに1994年度の総収入を 地域別に表した円グラフ。

U.S.A   1994
AD: Jim Berte
D: Maria Dellota/Jim Berte
DF: Runyan Hinsche Associates
CL: International Rectifier Corporation

north america
46.0%

europe
27.0%

asia
27.0%

Pie charts showing breakdowns of revenues. From The Reader's Digest Association, Inc. 1993 annual report.

リーダーズ・ダイジェスト・アソシエーション 社の1993年アニュアルレポートより、総収 入の内訳を表した円グラフ。

U.S.A.   1993
CD: Steve Ferrari
D: Sue Balle
I: Scott Walters
DF: The Graphic Expression
CL: The Reader's Digest Association, Inc.

**PERCENTAGE OF
REVENUES**

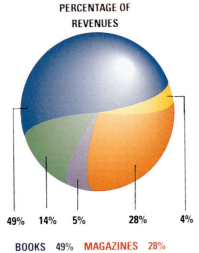

49%   14%   5%   28%   4%

BOOKS 49%   MAGAZINES 28%
MUSIC 14%   *Reader's Digest* 25%
VIDEO 5%   Special interest 3%
               OTHER 4%

**SOURCES OF
REVENUES**

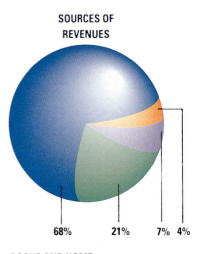

68%   21%   7% 4%

BOOKS AND HOME
ENTERTAINMENT 68%
MAGAZINE CIRCULATION 21%
MAGAZINE ADVERTISING 7%
OTHER 4%

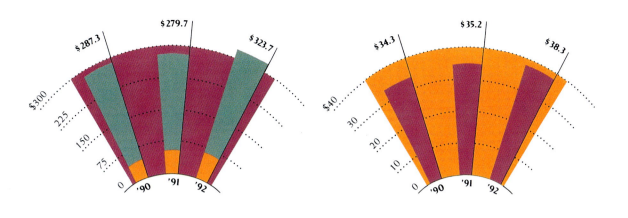

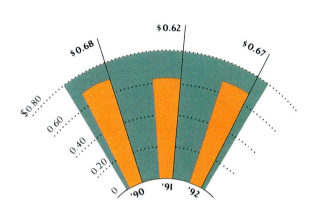

Graphs showing revenues, research and development expenses, and net income per share. From Advanced Technology Laboratories 1992 annual report.

アドバンスト・テクノロジー・ラボラトリーズ社の1992年アニュアルレポートより、収入、研究開発費、及び一株当りの純利益を表したグラフ。

U.S.A.　1993
AD: John Hornall
D: John Hornall/Julie Tanagi-Lock/
Mary Hermes
P: Darrell Peterson
I: Bruce Morser
DF: Hornall Anderson Design Works
CL: Advanced Technology Laboratories

INTERNATIONAL
Operations

BUSINESS SYSTEMS
& Other Capabilities

Graphs illustrating business data of Bell Atlantic's associated companies. From "Bell Atlantic 1992; A Year In Review".

ベル・アトランティック社「1992 ア・イヤー・イン・レビュー」より、同社の関連会社の企業データを表したグラフ。

U.S.A.　1993
CD: Steve Ferrari
I: Scott Walters
DF: The Graphic Expression
CL: Bell Atlantic

ACCESS LINES PER OPERATING COMPANY EMPLOYEE

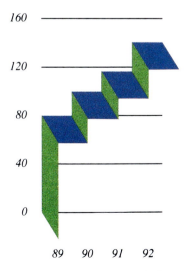

Telecom Corporation of New Zealand

COMPUTER EQUIPMENT NUMBER OF UNITS SERVICED

(In Thousands)

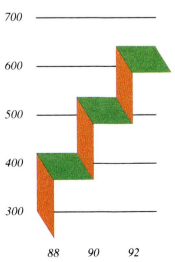

Bell Atlantic Business Systems Services, Inc.

*M*ax Planck, the father of quantum physics, once lamented that important innovations rarely win over opponents. Instead, he contended, opponents die out gradually, making way for generations who are open to new ideas. Fortunately, this is not always true in business. In only a few short years, our innovative "finite risk" concepts have gained widespread understanding and acceptance. That trend continued in 1991, further demonstrating Centre Re's viability as a company that exclusively writes finite risk reinsurance and insurance products.

As in previous years, our balance sheet remains the truest reflection of the size and quality of our reinsurance business. By year end 1991, our total assets reached $1.74 billion, a 62% annual increase from our initial capitalization of $250 million four years ago, and a 32% increase compared to 1990. Reinsurance liabilities exceeded $1.37 billion at December 31, 1991, a 35% increase over year end 1990. Net income continued to grow satisfactorily as our return on average GAAP equity reached 14.8% in 1991. Shareholders' equity increased to nearly $360.3 million from $291.8 million.

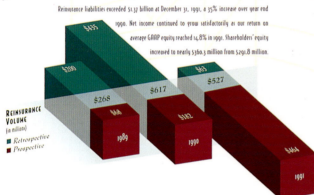

Reinsurance Volume (in millions)
- Retrospective
- Prospective

Consistent with our forecasts, reinsurance volume declined last year to $527 million from $617 million in 1990. Significantly, however, this does not include any Time and Distance contracts, which are now booked with our affiliate, CentreLine Reinsurance Limited (see financial statements beginning on page 36). Since our inception in 1988, Centre Re has written more than $1.7 billion in business, making us one of the fastest growing professional reinsurers in the world.

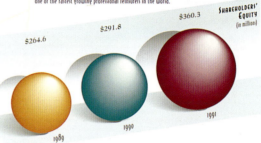

Shareholders' Equity (in millions)

Although aggregate reinsurance volume declined last year, revenues from prospective reinsurance increased dramatically from $182 million in 1990 to $464 million in 1991. We believe this reflects the growing trend of using finite risk products to control risk exposure for unknown or unforeseen events, and not merely to protect against historic exposures. Additionally, we improved the breadth and balance of our business last year. In 1990, our three largest contracts represented more than three-fourths of our volume; in 1991, the same percentage of volume comprised 11 transactions. Nonetheless, because of the relatively small number of contracts we write each year, our reinsurance volume is likely to remain reasonably variable from year to year.

Managing Losses

Losses, loss adjustment expenses, experience refunds and policy acquisition costs, as a percentage of premiums, increased from 101% in 1990 to 113% in 1991. Narrowing underwriting margins on new

Charts showing reinsurance company's reinsurance volumes and share holders' equity. From Centre Re 1992 annual report.

センター・リインシュランス社の1992年
アニュアルレポートより、同保険会社の保
険取引量、及び株価を示したグラフ。

U.S.A.   1992
CD: Frank Oswald
AD: Frank Oswald/David Dunkelberger
D: David Dunkelberger
DF: WYD Design Inc.
CL: Centre Reinsurance (Bermuda) Limited

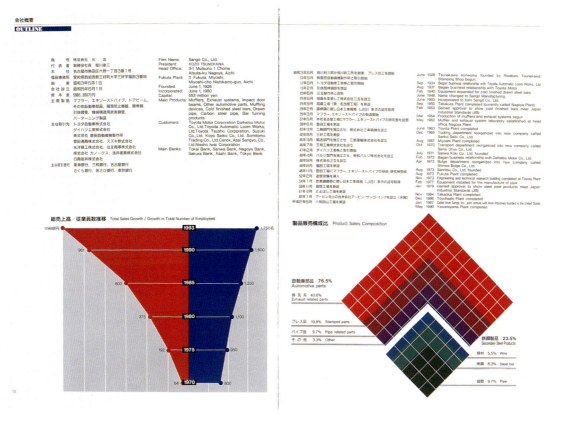

会社概要
OUTLINE

商　号	株式会社 三五	Firm Name: Sango Co., Ltd.
代表者	取締役社長 細川浩三	President: KOZO TSUNEKAWA
本　社	名古屋市熱田区大野一丁目3番1号	Head Office: 3-1 Mutsuno 1 Chome
		Atsuta-ku Nagoya, Aichi
福田事業所	愛知県西加茂郡三好町大字三好福田3番地	Fukuta Plant: 3 Fukuta Miyoshi,
		Miyoshi-cho Nishikamo-gun, Aichi
創　業	昭和3年6月1日	Founded: June 1, 1928
会社設立	昭和25年6月1日	Incorporated: June 1, 1950
資本金	5億5,300万円	Capital: 553 million yen
主要製品	マフラー、エキゾーストパイプ、ドアビーム、	Main Products: Mufflers, Exhaust systems, Impact door
	その他自動車部品、防音防止鋼板、冷間鋼、	beams, Other automotive parts, Muffling
	引抜鋼管、機械構造用冷間鋼鋼管、	devices, Cold finished steel bars, Drawn
	パターニング製品	pipe, Carbon steel pipe, Bar turning
		products
主な販売先	トヨタ自動車株式会社	Customers: Toyota Motor Corporation Daihatsu Motor
	ダイハツ工業株式会社	Co., Ltd.Toyoda Automatic Loom Works,
	豊田自動織機製作所	Ltd.Toyota Tsusho Corporation, Suzuki
	豊田通商株式会社、スズキ株式会社	Co., Ltd. Koyo Seiko Co., Ltd. Sumitomo
	光洋精工株式会社、住友商事株式会社	Trading Co.,Ltd.Canox, Asai Sangyo, Co.,
	株式会社 カノークス、浅井産業株式会社	
	日商岩井株式会社	
主な取引銀行	東海銀行、三和銀行、名古屋銀行	Main Banks: Tokai Bank, Sanwa Bank, Nagoya Bank,
	さくら銀行、あさひ銀行、東京銀行	Sakura Bank, Asahi Bank, Tokyo Bank

昭和3年6月	銀川町三郎が銀川鉄工所を創業、プレス加工を開始	June 1928	Tsunekawa Ironworks founded by Risaburo Tsunekawa. Stamping Shop begun.
9年9月	無償田自動織機製作所と取引開始	Sep 1934	Began business relationship with Toyoda Automatic Loom Works, Ltd
12年8月	トヨタ自動車工業株式会社との取引開始	Aug 1937	Began business relationship with Toyota Motor
15年2月	引抜鋼管部を設立	Feb 1940	Equipment expanded for cold finished drawn steel bars
25年6月	三五製作所と改称	June 1940	Name changed to Sango Manufacturing
25年6月	組織を変更し株式会社三五を設立	June 1950	Incorporated to form Sango Co., Ltd.
24年9月	高蔵工場（名古屋工場）を設立	Sep 1950	Takakura Plant completed (currently called Nagoya Plant)
28年2月	冷間鋼に関し日本工業規格（JIS）表示の認可取得	Feb 1953	Gained approval to show cold finished bars meet Japan Industrial Standards (JIS)
28年3月	マフラー、エキゾーストパイプの製造開発	Mar 1954	Production of mufflers and exhaust systems begun
37年5月	本社名古屋工場に設置、エキゾーストパイプの研究室を設置	May 1962	Muffler and exhaust system laboratory established at head office Nagoya Plant
38年6月	豊田工場を設置	June 1963	Toyota Plant completed
40年12月	工機部門を設立、株式会社三幸精機を設立	Dec 1965	Tooling department reorganized into new company called Sansu Seiki Co., Ltd.
42年8月	三好工場を設立	Aug 1967	Miyoshi Plant completed
46年10月	輸送部門を独立させ、三菱運輸株式会社を設立	Oct 1970	Transport department reorganized into new company called Sansu Unyu Co., Ltd.
46年7月	三和工業株式会社を設立	July 1971	Sanwa Koki Co., Ltd. founded
47年2月	ダイハツ工業株との取引開始	Feb 1973	Began business relationship with Daihatsu Motor Co., Ltd.
48年4月	バルジ部門を独立させ、神和バルジ株式会社を設立	Apr 1973	Bulge department reorganized into new company called Shiwa Bulge Co., Ltd.
48年6月	福田工場を設置	Aug 1973	Fukuta Plant completed
48年6月	豊田工場にマフラー、エキゾーストパイプの技術・研究棟を	Nov 1973	Engineering and technical research building completed at Toyota Plant
52年2月	造管設備を導入	Feb 1977	Equipment installed for the manufacture of pipe
54年11月	炭素鋼鋼管に関し日本工業規格（JIS）表示の認可取得	Nov 1979	Gained approval to show steel pipe products meet Japan Industrial Standards (JIS)
59年10月	高岡工場を設置	Aug 1984	Takaoka Plant completed
61年12月	とよはし工場を設置	Dec 1986	Toyohashi Plant completed
62年1月	アービン社との合併会社アービン・サンゴ・インクを設立（米国）	Jan 1987	Called Arvin Sango, Inc, joint venture with Arvin Industries founded in the United States
平成2年5月	八和田山工場を新設	May 1990	Yawatayama Plant completed

総売上高／従業員数推移 Total Sales Growth / Growth in Total Number of Employees

1993	1198億円	1,750名
1990	961	1,600
1985	800	1,350
1980	375	1,100
1975	192	950
1970	64	800

13

製品販売構成比 Product Sales Composition

自動車部品 76.5%
Automotive parts

排気系 43.6%
Exhaust related parts

プレス品 19.8% Stamped parts

パイプ品 9.7% Pipe related parts

その他 3.3% Other

鉄鋼製品 23.5%
Secondary Steel Products

線材 5.5% Wire

棒材 8.3% Steel bar

鋼管 9.7% Pipe

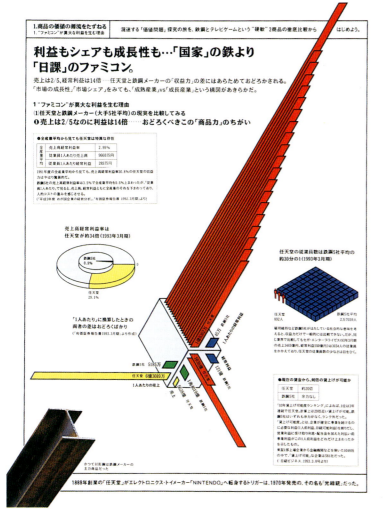

1.商品の価値の源流をたずねる
1.「ファミコン」が異大な利益を生む理由

混迷する「価値問題」探究の旅を、鉄鋼とテレビゲームという"硬軟"2商品の徹底比較から　はじめよう。

利益もシェアも成長性も…「国家」の鉄より「日課」のファミコン。

売上は2/5、経常利益は14倍…任天堂と鉄鋼メーカーの「収益力」の差にはあらためておどろかされる。「市場の成長性」「市場シェア」をみても、「成熟産業」vs「成長産業」という構図があきらかだ。

1 "ファミコン"が異大な利益を生む理由
①任天堂と鉄鋼メーカー（大手5社平均）の現実を比較してみる
●売上は2/5なのに利益は14倍……おどろくべきこの「商品力」のちがい

●全産業平均から見ても任天堂は特異な存在	
全産業平均 売上高経常利益率	2.99%
全産業平均 従業員1人あたり売上高	9660万円
全産業平均 従業員1人あたり経常利益	289万円

売上高経常利益率は
任天堂が約34倍（1993年3月期）

鉄鋼5社
0.9%

任天堂
29.1%

「1人あたり」に換算したときの
両者の差はおどろくばかり

鉄鋼5社 5185万
任天堂 6億3089万
1人あたりの売上

任天堂の従業員数は鉄鋼5社平均の
約30分の1（1993年3月期）

任天堂
892人

鉄鋼5社平均
2万7039人

かつて川形鋼は鉄鋼メーカーの
主力商品だった

●現在の賃金から、何倍の賃上げが可能か	
任天堂	約20倍
鉄鋼5社	余力なし

1889年創業の「任天堂」がエレクトロニクス・トイメーカー「NINTENDO」へ転身するトリガーは、1970年発売の、その名も「光線銃」だった。

Graphs of corporate data, from a Sango Co., Ltd. brochure.

三五社の業務案内より、会社概要を表すグラフ。

Japan　1993
AD: Mayumi Nishiyama
D: Mayumi Nishiyama
I: Mayumi Nishiyama
CL: Sango Co., Ltd.

Graphs comparing Nintendo Corporation's sales turnover and profits with those of five major Japanese steel makers. From Resumex 7, a Work Design Institute publication of Recruit Co., Ltd.

リクルート社ワークデザイン研究室の発行する「レジュメクス7号」より、任天堂社と鉄鋼5社の売上と利益を比較したグラフ。

Japan　1993
AD: Katsumi Asaba
CL: Recruit Co., Ltd.

Bar graphs illustrating data for various business sectors. From Seibu Saison Group annual report.

西武セゾングループのアニュアルレポートより、部門別の各データを表した棒グラフ。

Japan　　1987
CD: Tetsuya Ohta
AD: Tetsuya Ohta
D: Tetsuya Ohta
CL: Seibu Saison Group

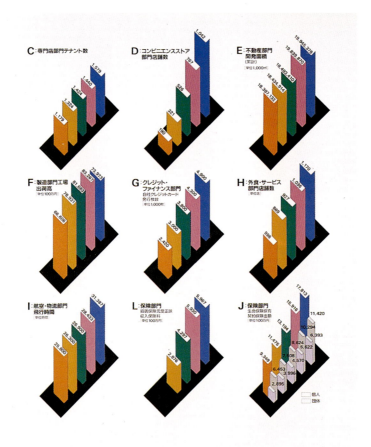

Growth in turnover by business sector. Seibu Saison Group annual report.

西武セゾングループのアニュアルレポートより、部門別に売上の推移を表したグラフ。

Japan　　1987
CD: Tetsuya Ohta
AD: Tetsuya Ohta
D: Tetsuya Ohta
CL: Seibu Saison Group

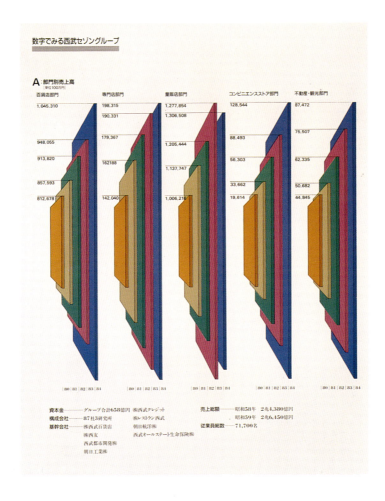

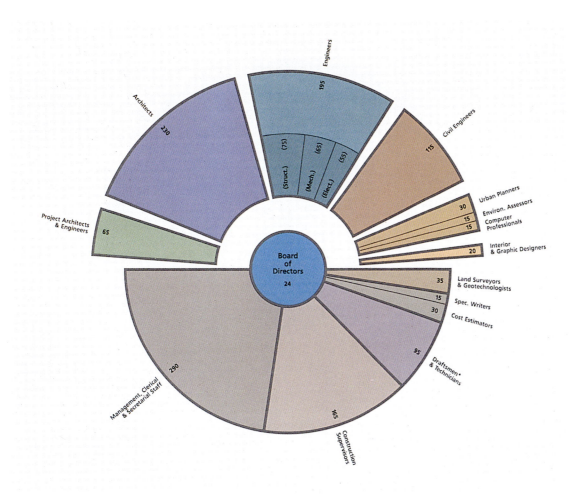

Engineers
195

Architects
230

Civil Engineers
115

(Struct.) (75)
(Mech.) (65)
(Elect.) (55)

Urban Planners
30

Environ. Assessors
15

Computer Professionals
15

Interior & Graphic Designers
20

Project Architects & Engineers
65

Board of Directors
24

Land Surveyors & Geotechnologists
35

Spec. Writers
15

Cost Estimators
30

Management, Clerical & Secretarial Staff
290

Draftsmen & Technicians
95

Construction Supervisors
165

Chart showing corporate structure and personnel. From Nikken Sekkei Corporation's corporate profile.

日建設計社の会社案内より、会社の組織構成とスタッフの状況を表したグラフ。

Japan   1986
CD: Tetsuya Ohta
AD: Tetsuya Ohta
D: Tetsuya Ohta
CL: Nikken Sekkei Corporation

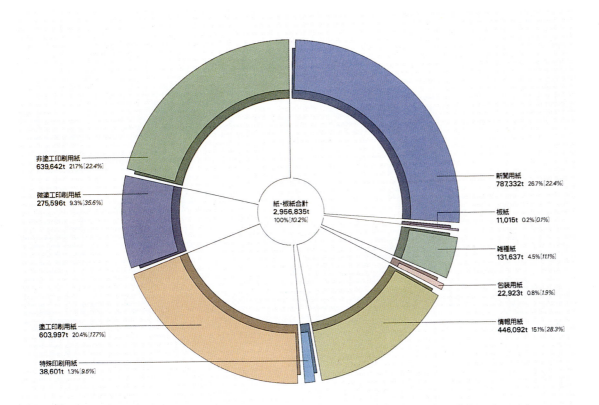

非塗工印刷用紙
639,642t 21.7% [22.4%]

微塗工印刷用紙
275,596t 9.3% [35.6%]

塗工印刷用紙
603,997t 20.4% [17.7%]

特殊印刷用紙
38,601t 1.3% [9.5%]

紙・板紙合計
2,956,835t
100% [10.2%]

新聞用紙
787,332t 26.7% [22.4%]

板紙
11,015t 0.2% [0.1%]

雑種紙
131,637t 4.5% [11.1%]

包装用紙
22,923t 0.8% [1.9%]

情報用紙
446,092t 15.1% [28.3%]

Graph showing production volumes of paper and paperboard products, from Nippon Paper Industries' corporate profile.

日本製紙社の会社案内より、紙と板紙の生産高を表したグラフ。

Japan   1993
CD: Tetsuya Ohta
AD: Tetsuya Ohta
D: Tetsuya Ohta
CL: Nippon Paper Industries

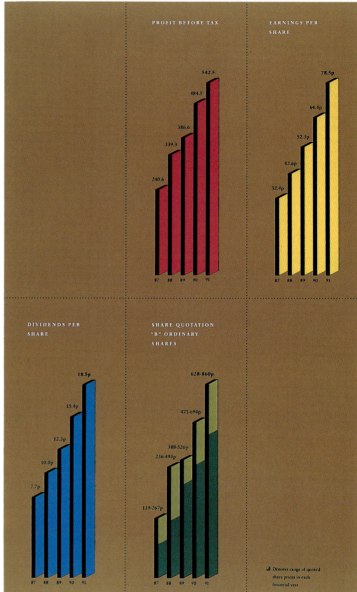

Bar graphs showing financial highlights.
From Rothmans 1993 annual report.

ロスマンズ社の1993年アニュアルレポート
より、主な財務実績を表す棒グラフ。

U.K.   1993
CD: Jonathan Davis
D: Jonathan Davis
DF: Michael Peters Limited
CL: Rothmans International

Bar graphs showing financial highlights.
From Rothmans 1991 annual report.

ロスマンズ社の1991年アニュアルレポー
トより、主な財務実績を表す棒グラフ。

U.K.   1991
CD: Jonathan Davis
D: Kin Ip Yu
DF: Michael Peters Limited
CL: Rothmans International

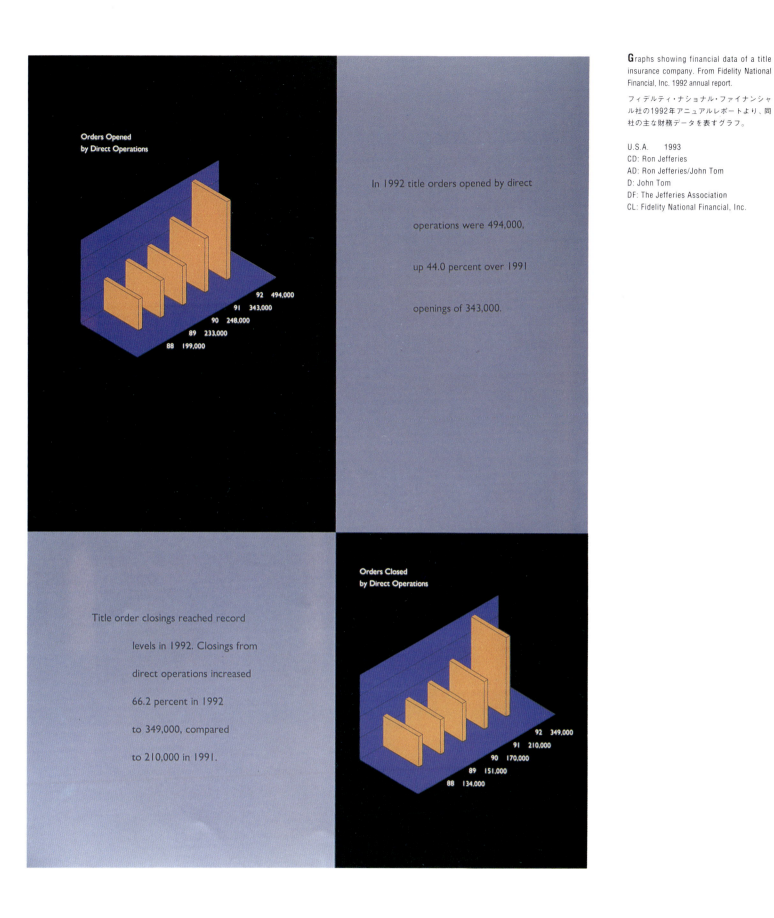

Orders Opened
by Direct Operations

92 494,000
91 343,000
90 248,000
89 233,000
88 199,000

In 1992 title orders opened by direct

operations were 494,000,

up 44.0 percent over 1991

openings of 343,000.

Title order closings reached record

levels in 1992. Closings from

direct operations increased

66.2 percent in 1992

to 349,000, compared

to 210,000 in 1991.

Orders Closed
by Direct Operations

92 349,000
91 210,000
90 170,000
89 151,000
88 134,000

Graphs showing financial data of a title insurance company. From Fidelity National Financial, Inc. 1992 annual report.

フィデルティ・ナショナル・ファイナンシャル社の1992年アニュアルレポートより、同社の主な財務データを表すグラフ。

U.S.A.   1993
CD: Ron Jefferies
AD: Ron Jefferies/John Tom
D: John Tom
DF: The Jefferies Association
CL: Fidelity National Financial, Inc.

The South East Essex
College of Arts & Technology

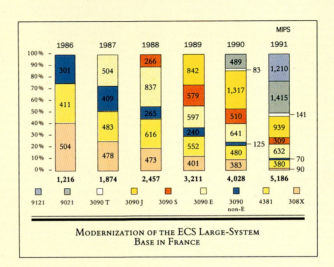

	1986	1987	1988	1989	1990	1991	MIPS
100%							
90%	301	504	266	842	489	1,210	83
80%							
70%			837		1,317	1,415	
60%	411	409	265	579			
50%				597	510		141
40%		483	616		641	939	
30%	504			240		309	
20%		478	473	552	480	632	125
10%				401	383	380	70
0%							90
	1,216	**1,874**	**2,457**	**3,211**	**4,028**	**5,186**	

Legend:
9121 · 9021 · 3090 T · 3090 J · 3090 S · 3090 E · 3090 non-E · 4381 · 308X

MODERNIZATION OF THE ECS LARGE-SYSTEM
BASE IN FRANCE

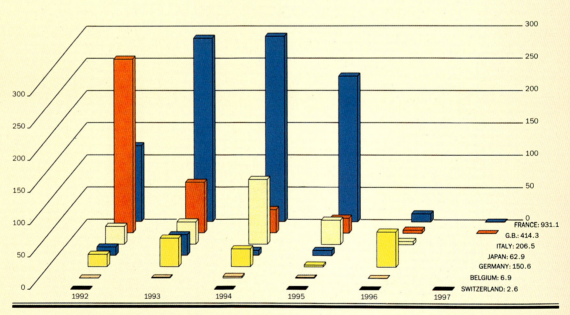

FRANCE: 931.1
G.B.: 414.3
ITALY: 206.5
JAPAN: 62.9
GERMANY: 150.6
BELGIUM: 6.9
SWITZERLAND: 2.6

END-OF-CONTRACT COST OF EQUIPMENT (UNADJUSTED AMOUNTS)
(in millions of French francs)

~ *F i n a n c i a l   A n a l y s i s* ~

— 28 —

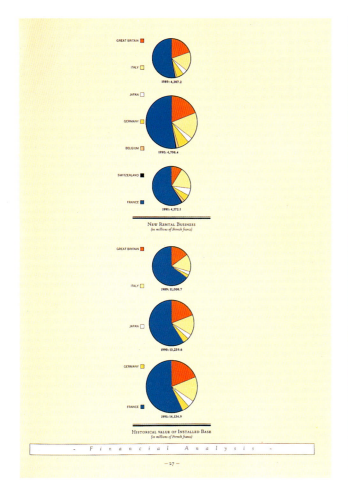

NEW RENTAL BUSINESS
(in millions of French francs)

HISTORICAL VALUE OF INSTALLED BASE
(in millions of French francs)

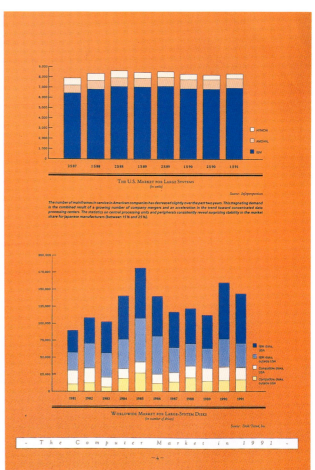

THE U.S. MARKET FOR LARGE SYSTEMS
(in units)

Source: Infoperspective

The number of mainframes in service in American companies has decreased slightly over the past two years. This stagnating demand is the combined result of a growing number of company mergers and an acceleration in the trend toward concentrated data processing centers. The statistics on central processing units and peripherals consistently reveal surprising stability in the market share for Japanese manufacturers (between 15% and 25%).

WORLDWIDE MARKET FOR LARGE-SYSTEM DISKS
(in number of drives)

Source: Disk/Trend, Inc.

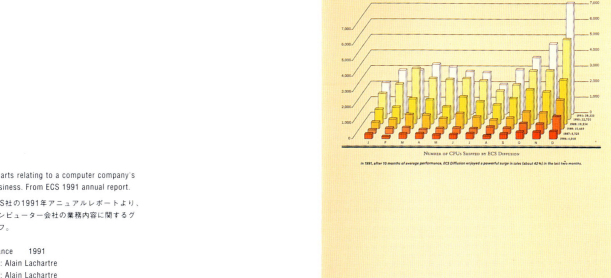

NUMBER OF CPUs SHIPPED BY ECS DIFFUSION

In 1991, after 10 months of average performance, ECS Diffusion enjoyed a powerful surge in sales (about 42%) in the last two months.

Charts relating to a computer company's business. From ECS 1991 annual report.

ECS社の1991年アニュアルレポートより、コンピューター会社の業務内容に関するグラフ。

France   1991
CD: Alain Lachartre
AD: Alain Lachartre
D: Jacques Aubert
I: Philippe Weisebeker
CL: ECS

Five-year charts of corporate results represented by photographs of buttons. From House of Fabrics 1993 annual report.

ハウス・オブ・ファブリックス社の1993年アニュアルレポートより、5年間の業績に関するデータをボタンをモチーフにして表したグラフ。

U.S.A.   1993
CD: Ron Jefferies
AD: Ron Jefferies/Scott Lambert
D: Scott Lambert
P: Craig Mohr
I: Scott Lambert
DF: The Jefferies Association
CL: House of Fabrics

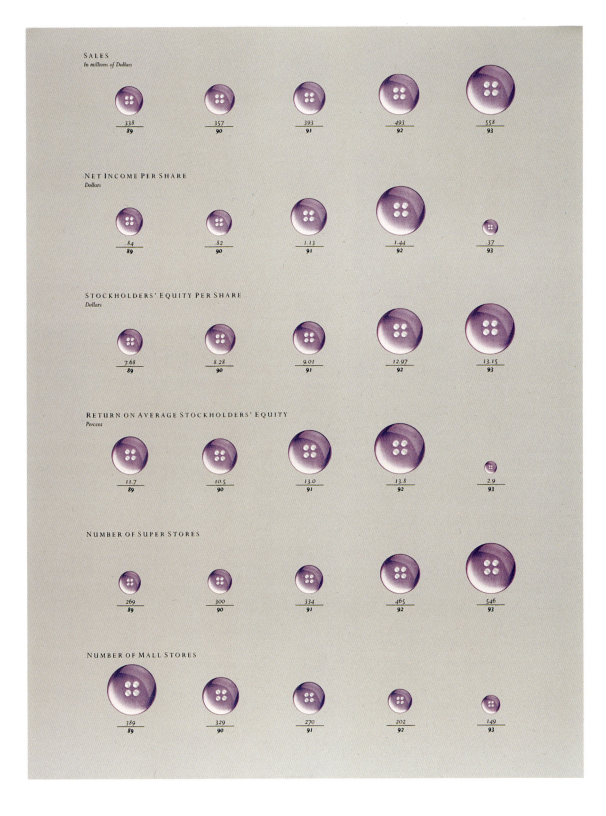

SALES
In millions of Dollars

338	357	393	493	558
89	90	91	92	93

NET INCOME PER SHARE
Dollars

.84	.82	1.13	1.44	.37
89	90	91	92	93

STOCKHOLDERS' EQUITY PER SHARE
Dollars

7.68	8.28	9.01	12.97	13.15
89	90	91	92	93

RETURN ON AVERAGE STOCKHOLDERS' EQUITY
Percent

11.7	10.5	13.0	13.8	2.9
89	90	91	92	93

NUMBER OF SUPER STORES

269	300	334	465	546
89	90	91	92	93

NUMBER OF MALL STORES

389	329	270	202	149
89	90	91	92	93

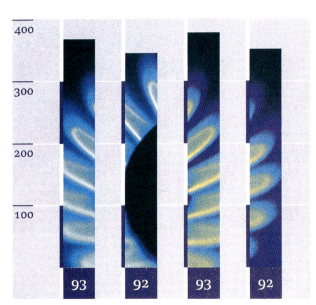

INKOOP GASUNIE
VERKOPEN

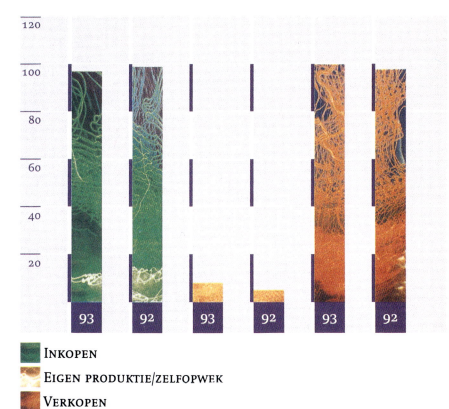

INKOPEN
EIGEN PRODUKTIE/ZELFOPWEK
VERKOPEN

1

60.3%
Customized

39.7%
Traditional
XOL

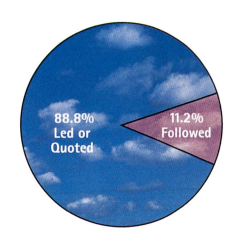

88.8%
Led or
Quoted

11.2%
Followed

54%
U.S.

46%
International

2

1

Bar graphs comparing a Dutch energy distributor's 1993 and 1992 results, for the purchase, production and sale of electricity, and the purchase and sale of natural gas. From NUON 1993 annual report.

NUON社の1993年アニュアルレポートより、オランダのエネルギー供給会社の電力の購入、発電、販売の実績、及び天然ガスの購入、販売の実績について1992年と1993年を比較した棒グラフ。

Netherlands   1994
CD: Gert Kootstra
AD: Gert Kootstra
D: Gert Kootstra
P: Benelux Press (stock photography)
DF: Tel Design
CL: NUON, Power for the North-Eastern Netherlands

2

Pie charts illustrating a reinsurance company's financial and underwriting strengths. From a Centre Cat Ltd. capabilities brochure.

センター・キャット社の宣伝用パンフレットより、保険会社の財務、及び引受能力を表す円グラフ。

U.S.A.   1994
CD: Andy Blankenburg
AD: Andy Blankenburg/Carol Layton
D: David Weinstock
DF: WYD Design Inc.
CL: Centre Cat Limited

Diagram illustrating proposed use of
pipeline capacity. From a UK-Continent
Gas Interconnector brochure.

UK コンチネントガス・インタコネクター社
のパンフレットより、パイプラインの有効
利用のためのダイアグラム。

U.K.   1993
CD: Geoff Aldridge
D: Duncan Wilson
I: Duncan Wilson
DF: Communication by Design Ltd,
London
CL: Interconnector Study Group

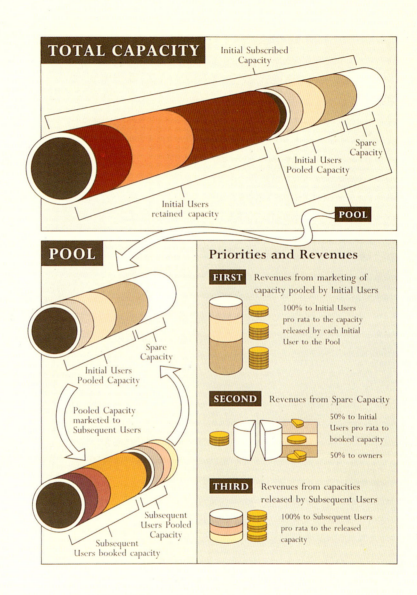

TOTAL CAPACITY

Initial Subscribed Capacity

Spare Capacity

Initial Users Pooled Capacity

Initial Users retained capacity

POOL

POOL

Spare Capacity

Initial Users Pooled Capacity

Pooled Capacity marketed to Subsequent Users

Subsequent Users Pooled Capacity

Subsequent Users booked capacity

Priorities and Revenues

FIRST Revenues from marketing of capacity pooled by Initial Users

100% to Initial Users pro rata to the capacity released by each Initial User to the Pool

SECOND Revenues from Spare Capacity

50% to Initial Users pro rata to booked capacity

50% to owners

THIRD Revenues from capacities released by Subsequent Users

100% to Subsequent Users pro rata to the released capacity

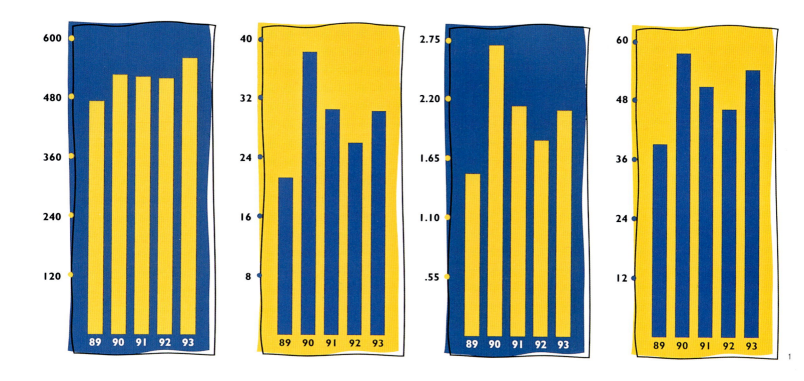

1
Bar charts of selected financial highlights.
From Club Med 1993 annual report.

クラブ・メッド社の1993年アニュアルレポ
ートより、強調して見せたい財務データを
表す棒グラフ。

U.S.A.　1994
CD: Steve Ferrari
D: Sue Balle
I: Scott Walters
DF: The Graphic Expression
CL: Club Med

2
Graphs of a shipping company's selected
corporate highlights. From OMI 1992 annual
report.

OMI社の1992年アニュアルレポートより、
海運会社の主な業績を表すグラフ。

U.S.A.　1993
CD: Steve Ferrari
D: Steven Flamm
I: Scott Walters
DF: The Graphic Expression
CL: OMI

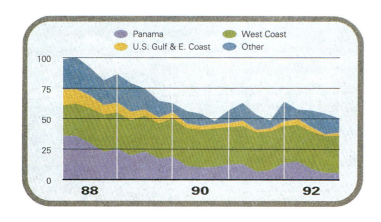

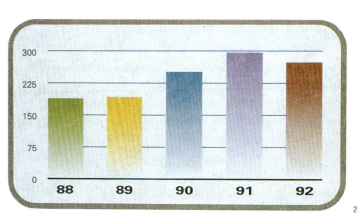

Graph showing computer and service expenditures in Europe between 1987 and 1994, excluding builders. From ECS 1989 annual report.

ECS社の1989年アニュアルレポートより、ヨーロッパの各種産業におけるコンピューターとサービスにかかった、1987年から1994年までの経費を表すグラフ。

France   1990
CD: Alain Lachartre
AD: Alain Lachartre
D: Philippe Caron/Cyril Cabry
I: Philippe Caron/Cyril Cabry
CL: ECS

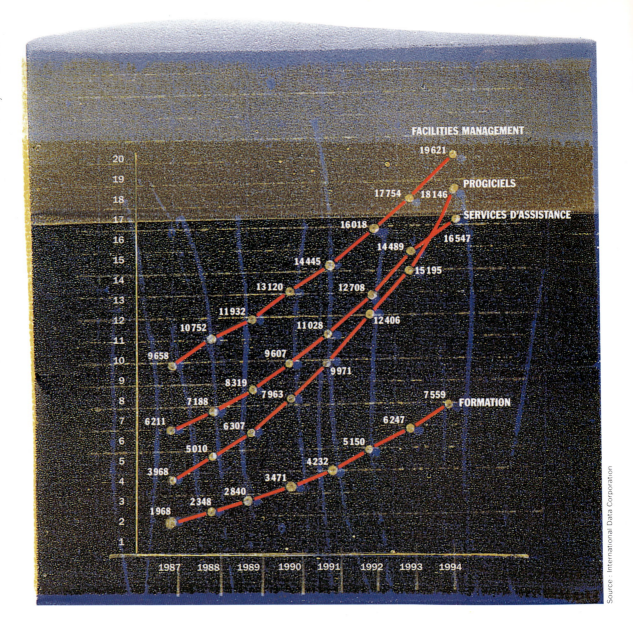

Source : International Data Corporation

Pie charts comparing the world market for information systems in 1987 and 1989. From ECS 1989 annual report.

ECS社の1989年アニュアルレポートより、情報システムの世界市場を1987年と1989年で比較したグラフ。

France   1990
CD: Alain Lachartre
AD: Alain Lachartre
D: Philippe Caron/Cyril Cabry
I: Philippe Caron/Cyril Cabry
CL: ECS

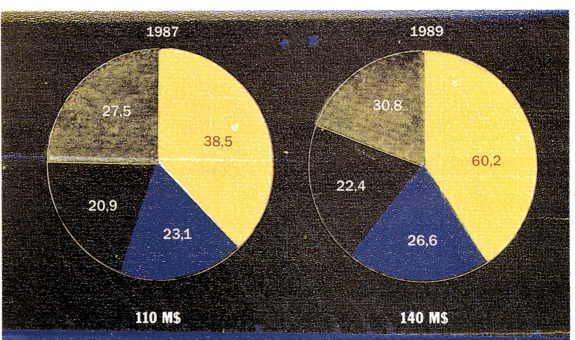

Source : International Data Corporation.

8.7

8.2

5.5

1991   1992   1993

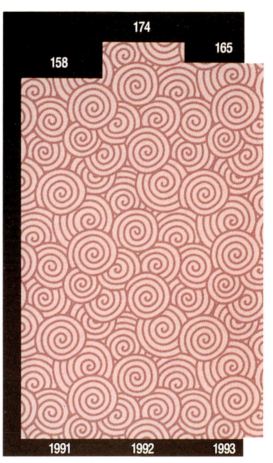

174

158

165

1991   1992   1993

Graphs showing net income and sales, from Clothestime 1994 annual report.

クロースタイム社の1994年アニュアルレポートより、純利益と売上高を表すグラフ。

U.S.A.   1994
CD: Carl Seltzer
AD: Carl Seltzer
D: Carl Seltzer/Luis Alvarado
DF: Carl Seltzer Design Office
CL: Clothestime

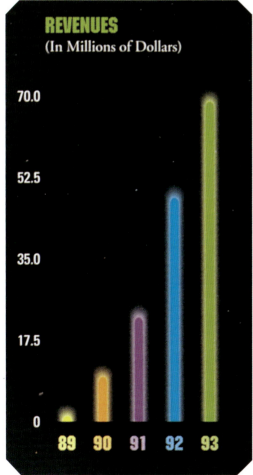

REVENUES
(In Millions of Dollars)

70.0

52.5

35.0

17.5

0

89   90   91   92   93

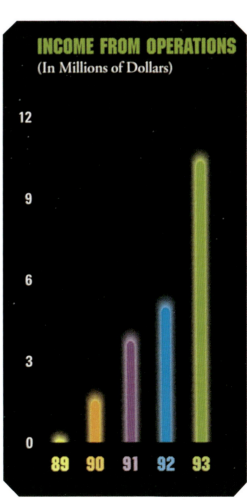

INCOME FROM OPERATIONS
(In Millions of Dollars)

12

9

6

3

0

89   90   91   92   93

Bar charts of selected financial results. From Sodak Gaming, Inc. 1993 annual report.

ソダック・ゲーミング社の1993年アニュアルレポートより、主な決算結果を表すグラフ。

U.S.A.   1994
CD: Steve Ferrari
D: Steven Flamm
I: Scott Walters
DF: The Graphic Expression
CL: Sodak Gaming, Inc.

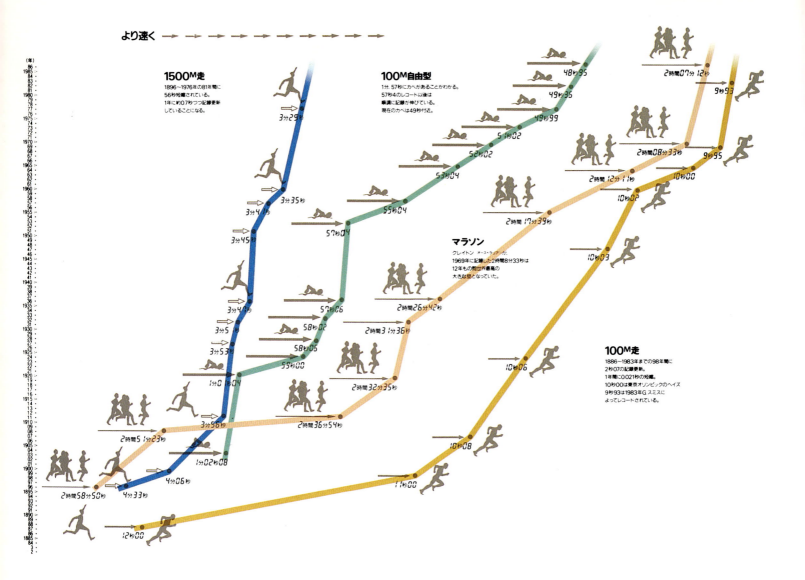

より速く →→→→→→→→→→

1500M走
1896〜1976年の81年間に
56秒短縮されている。
1年に約0.7秒つつ記録更新
していることになる。

100M自由型
1分、57秒にカベがあることがわかる。
57秒4のレコード以後は
順調に記録が伸びている。
現在のカベは49秒付近。

マラソン
クレイトン オーストラリア人が
1969年に記録した2時間8分33秒は
12年もの間世界最高の
大きな壁となっていた。

100M走
1886〜1983年までの98年間に
2秒07の記録更新。
1年に0.021秒の短縮。
10秒00は東京オリンピックのヘイズ
9秒93は1983年G.スミスに
よってレコードされている。

Graph illustrating new records in popular
sporting events over the last 100 years. From
Japan Coca-Cola Corporation's 'Sawayaka'
publicity feature.

日本コカコーラ社のＰＲ誌「爽」より、
100年間のスポーツ記録の推移を表したグ
ラフ。

Japan   1986
CD: Tetsuya Ohta
AD: Tetsuya Ohta
D: Tetsuya Ohta
CL: Japan Coca-Cola

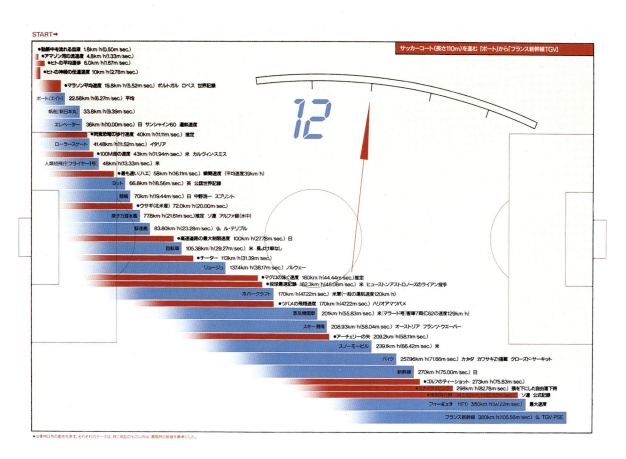

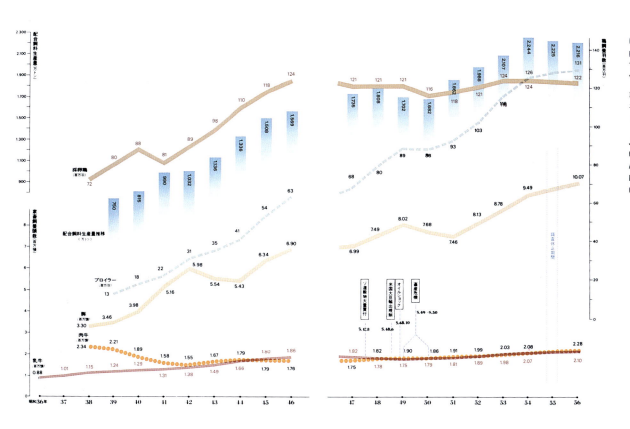

Graphs of financial data. From CorVel
Corporation 1992 annual report.

コーヴェル社の1992年アニュアルレポー
トより、財務データのグラフ。

U.S.A.   1992
AD: James Guerard
D: James Guerard
I: Cathie Bleck
DF: Runyan Hinsche Associates
CL: CorVel Corporation

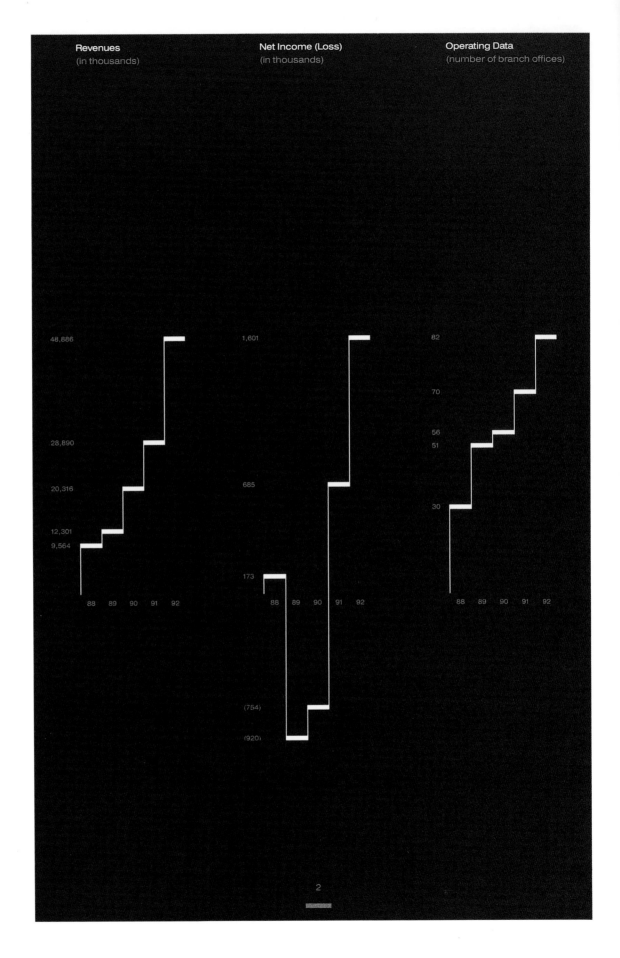

Bar chart showing growth in earnings from sales of power transistors between 1986 and 1993. From International Rectifier Corporation 1994 annual report.

インターナショナル・レクティフィア社の
1994年アニュアルレポートより、パワー・ト
ランジスターの販売による利益の伸びを表
す棒グラフ。

U.S.A.   1994
AD: Jim Berte
D: Maria Dellota/Jim Berte
DF: Runyan Hinsche Associates
CL: International Rectifier Corporation

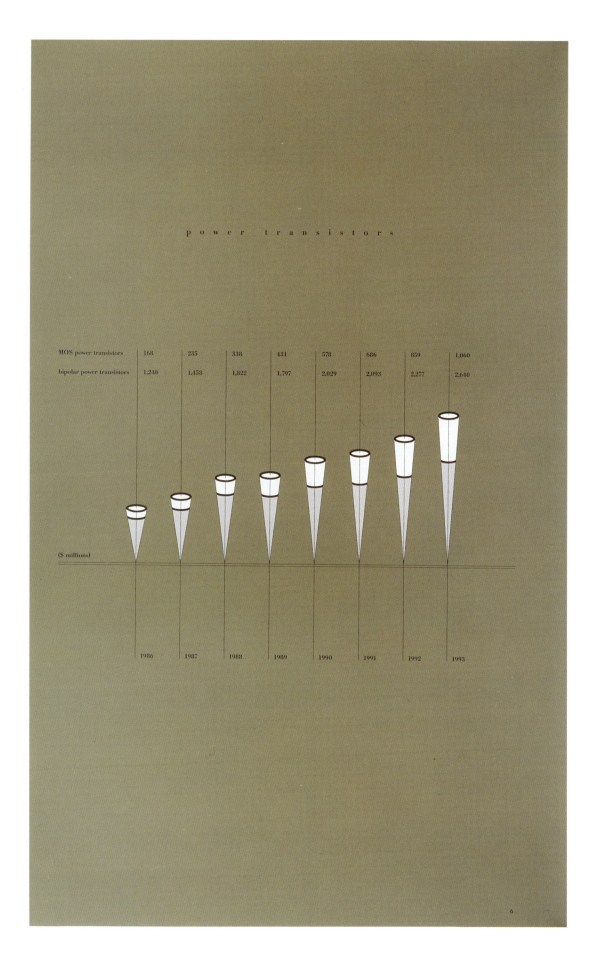

power transistors

	1986	1987	1988	1989	1990	1991	1992	1993
MOS power transistors	168	235	338	431	578	686	859	1,060
bipolar power transistors	1,210	1,458	1,822	1,797	2,029	2,093	2,277	2,640

($ millions)

Bar graphs showing futures and futures-options trading volume, from 1991 and 1992 annual reports of the Chicago Board of Trade.

シカゴ商品取引所の1991年、及び1992年アニュアルレポートより、先物と先物オプションの売買高を表す棒グラフ。

U.S.A.   1993
AD: Dana Arnett
D: Curtis Schreiber
P: François Robert
DF: VSA Partners, Inc.
CL: Michael Oakes
(Chicago Board of Trade)

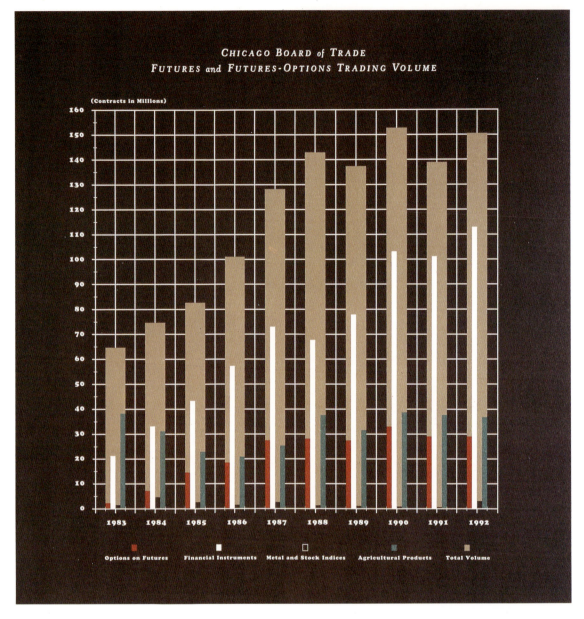

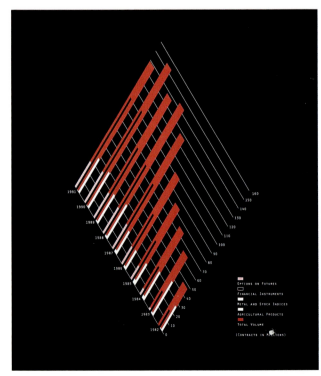

拡大する世界 [BC～1901] **探 検 と 航 海**

principia diagram

大航海時代を境に，ヨーロッパは次々に世界を 発見 してゆきます。造船技術や航海術の進歩にくわえて，多くの航海家や探検家の努力により，地理的な視野の拡大がもたらされたのはもとより，産業や科学などの分野にも新しい風が送り込まれることになりました。

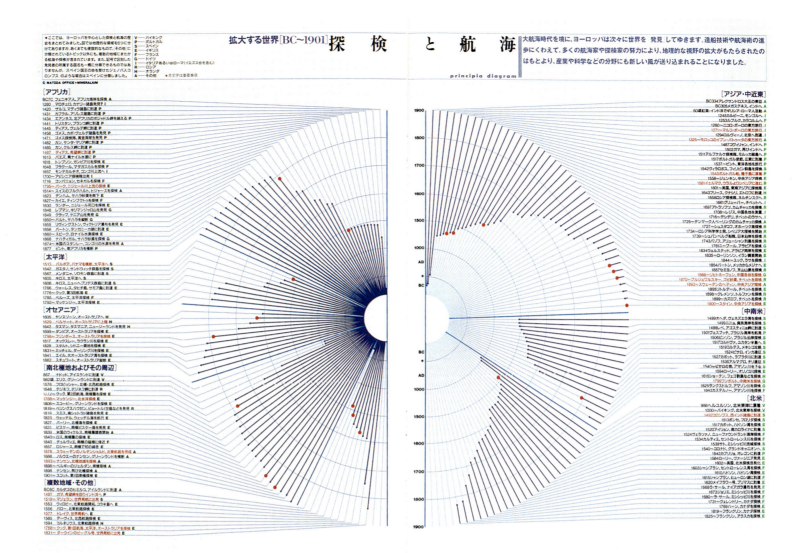

Diagram illustrating the history of exploration by land and sea. From "Principia", quarterly magazine of Ishikawajima-Harima Heavy Industries

石川島播磨重工業社発行の「季刊プリンキ ピア」より、探険と航海の歴史を表した図表。

Japan 1993
CD: Takashi Yonezawa
AD: Yukimasa Matsuda
D: Satoru Kawaharada
CL: IHI

Productivity

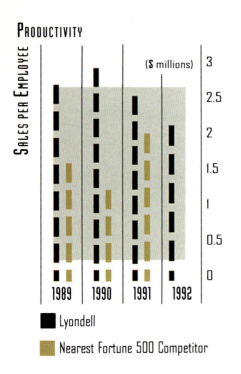

Sales per Employee

($ millions)

1989 1990 1991 1992

■ Lyondell

■ Nearest Fortune 500 Competitor

Quality Improvement Ideas

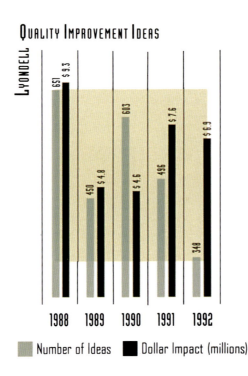

Lyondell

1988	651	$9.3
1989	450	$4.8
1990	603	$4.5
1991	496	$7.6
1992	348	$6.9

■ Number of Ideas ■ Dollar Impact (millions)

Progress Toward Workplace Diversity

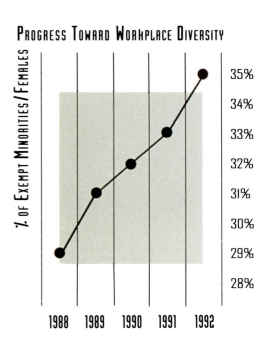

% of Exempt Minorities/Females

1988 1989 1990 1991 1992

Feedstock Flexibility

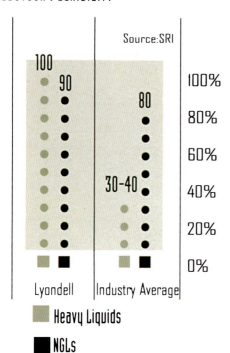

Olefins

Source: SRI

100 90 80 30-40

Lyondell   Industry Average

■ Heavy Liquids

■ NGLs

Ethylene Cost Structure

U.S. Gulf Coast

(¢ pound)
Source: 1990
Industry survey

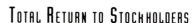

4 6 8 10 12

■ Lyondell

■ Individual Producers

Total Return to Stockholders

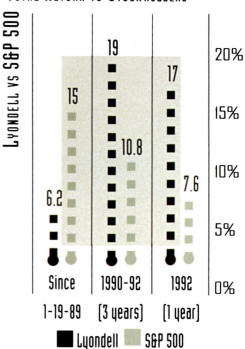

Lyondell vs S&P 500

| | 15 | 19 | 17 |
| | 6.2 | 10.8 | 7.6 |

Since   1990-92   1992
1-19-89   [3 years]   [1 year]

■ Lyondell   ■ S&P 500

Charts showing selected corporate data.
From Lyondell Petrochemical Company
1992 annual report.

ロインデル・ペトロケミカル社の1992年
アニュアルレポートより、強調して見せた
いデータのグラフ。

U.S.A.   1993
CD: Peat Jariya
AD: Peat Jariya
D: Peat Jariya/Scott Head
DF: Peat Jariya Design
CL: Lyondell Petrochemical Company

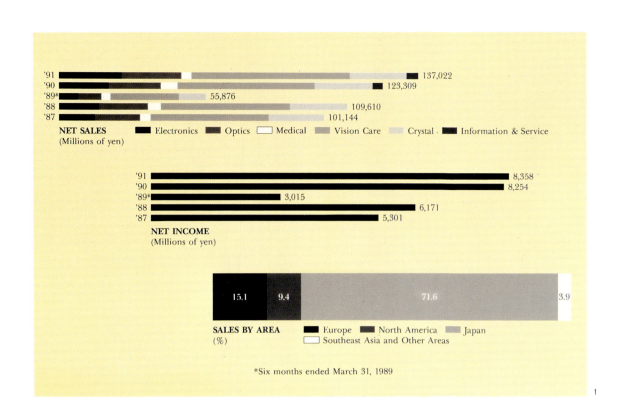

'91 137,022
'90 123,309
'89* 55,876
'88 109,610
'87 101,144

NET SALES ■ Electronics ■ Optics □ Medical ■ Vision Care □ Crystal ■ Information & Service
(Millions of yen)

'91 8,358
'90 8,254
'89* 3,015
'88 6,171
'87 5,301

NET INCOME
(Millions of yen)

| 15.1 | 9.4 | 71.6 | 3.9 |

SALES BY AREA ■ Europe ■ North America ■ Japan
(%) □ Southeast Asia and Other Areas

*Six months ended March 31, 1989

1

1
Graphs showing financial highlights, from Hoya Corporation's annual report.

HOYA社のアニュアルレポートより、売上と利益に関するグラフ。

Japan 1991
AD: Mari Sasaki
D: Mari Sasaki
DF: IBI Inc.
CL: Hoya Corporation

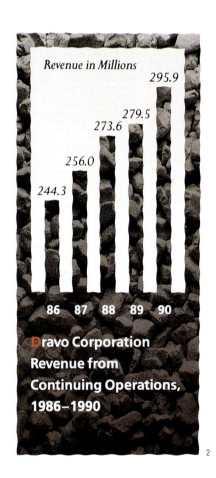

Revenue in Millions

295.9
279.5
273.6
256.0
244.3

86 87 88 89 90

Dravo Corporation
Revenue from
Continuing Operations,
1986–1990

2

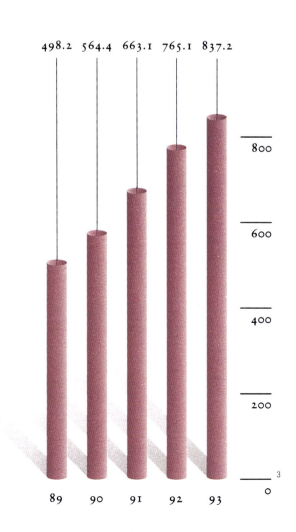

498.2 564.4 663.1 765.1 837.2

800

600

400

200

0

89 90 91 92 93

3

2
Bar chart illustrating financial results. From a Dravo Corporation publication.

ドラヴォ社の発行物より、同社の決算に関する棒グラフ。

U.S.A. 1991
AD: Ralph James Russini
D: Barbara Peak Long
P: Harry Giglio
DF: Adam Filippo & Associates
CL: Dravo Corporation

3
Five year financial summary bar chart of total sales, in millions of dollars. From Smart & Final 1993 annual report.

スマート&ファイナンシャル社の1993年アニュアルレポートより、5年間の売上高を百万ドル単位で表した棒グラフ。

U.S.A. 1993
CD: Ron Jefferies
AD: Ron Jefferies
D: Ron Jefferies/Troy McQuillen
P: Kim Tucker
I: Troy McQuillen
CL: Smart & Final

Bar graphs of financial highlights. From Summit Care Corporation 1992 annual report.

サミット・ケア社の1992年アニュアルレポートより、強調して見せたい5年間の財務データを表す棒グラフ。

U.S.A.   1992
CD: Ron Jefferies
AD: Ron Jefferies/Scott Lambert
D: Scott Lambert
I: Scott Lambert
DF: The Jefferies Association
CL: Summit Care Corporation

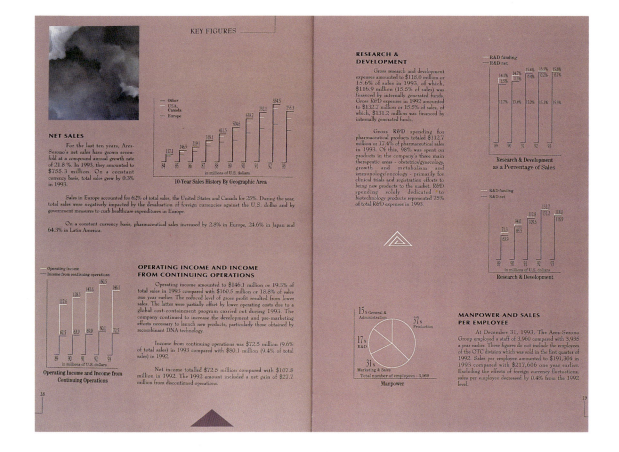

Charts of pharmaceutical firm's financial results. From Ares-Serono 1993 annual report.

アレス・セレノ社の1993年アニュアルレポートより、製薬会社の決算結果のグラフ。

Switzerland   1994
CD: Oscar Ribes
AD: Oscar Ribes
CL: Ares Serono

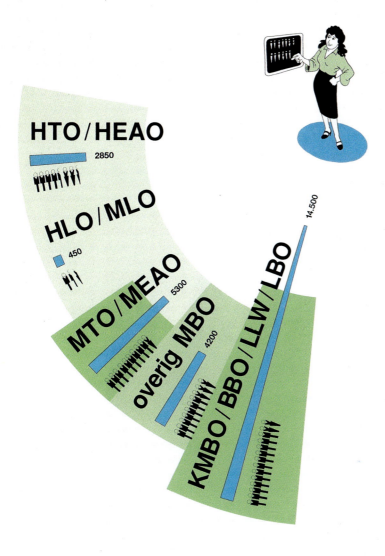

HTO/HEAO
2850

HLO/MLO
450

MTO/MEAO
5300

overig MBO
4200

KMBO/BBO/LLW/LBO
14.500

Charts indicating number of teachers at different education levels taking NaBoNT courses (above) and levels of interest and satisfaction indicated by participants (below). From interim report of NaBoNT, a Dutch government 5-year project seeking to boost teachers' knowledge of information technology.

教職員のIT（インフォメーション・テクノロジー）に対する知識を高めるための5カ国計画「NaBoNT」中間報告書より、教育課程別研修コース受講者数（上）、及び受講者の興味の度合いと満足度（下）を表すグラフ。

Netherlands   1990
CD: Paul Vermijs
AD: Paul Vermijs
D: Stephan Van Rijt
I: Erwin Suvaal
DF: Tel Design
CL: NaBoNT

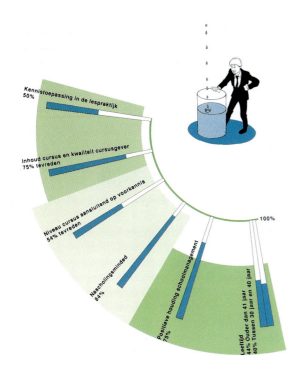

Kennistoepassing in de lespraktijk
50%

Inhoud cursus en kwaliteit cursusgever
75% tevreden

Niveau cursus aansluitend op voorkennis
54% tevreden

Nascholingsminded
84%

Positieve houding schoolmanagement
75%

Leeftijd
44% Ouder dan 41 jaar
40% Tussen 30 jaar en 40 jaar

100%

1, 2

Diagrams from 1991/92 annual report of
the Hospital for Sick Children, Ontario,
Canada. Charts (left) illustrate financial
statistics, and teddy bear graph (right)
shows types of treatment provided.

カナダ、オンタリオ州の小児科病院1991/92
年及び1993年のアニュアルレポートより、
財務統計に関する棒グラフ（左）と、テディ・
ベアをモチーフにして診療内容を表すグラフ
（右）。

Canada   1992
D: Donna Gedeon
I: Gary Mansbridge
DF: Eskind Waddell
CL: The Hospital for Sick Children

REVENUES

*Sick Kids relies on funding from the Ontario
provincial government to run the Hospital.
Revenue described as Patient Care and Other
comes fom foreign patients, other provincial
governments, and cafeteria and pharmacy sales.*

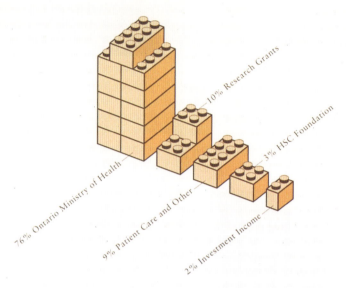

10% Research Grants

3% HSC Foundation

76% Ontario Ministry of Health

9% Patient Care and Other

2% Investment Income

USE OF FUNDS

*More than 80 percent of the Hospital revenue
is directed to patient care.*

1% Clinical Education

15% Research

84% Patient Care

EXPENSES

*At 71 percent of the entire operating budget,
salaries, wages and benefits combine to make
up the largest expense.*

4% Administration and General

10% Other Operating

63% Salaries

4% Amortization

11% Medical/Lab Drug Supplies

8% Benefits

THE PAT

*Not surpris
The Hospit
or surgical
ization, alm
the highly s
Paediatric
Intensive C*

1.1% Psychiatry

1.5% O

2

1

E SERVED

st children came to
Children for medical
. During their hospital-
rcent of them required
l services of either the
Care Unit or Neonatal

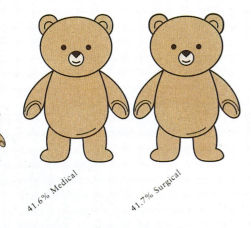

.1% Otolaryngology   41.6% Medical   41.7% Surgical

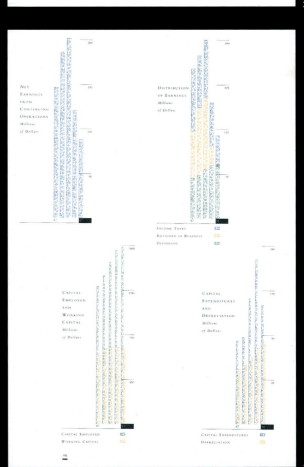

Sales
(millions)   89   90   91   92   93
           139.6 132.6 145.7 150.7 158.0

Net Income
(millions)   89   90   91   92   93
            9.5   7.3   12.9   4.8   6.7

Net Income
Per Share   89   90   91   92   93
(dollars)   1.42 1.11 1.93   .62 1.08

3

Net Earnings from Continuing Operations
Millions of Dollars

Distribution of Earnings
Millions of Dollars

Income Taxes
Retained in Business
Dividends

Capital Employed and Working Capital
Millions of Dollars

Capital Expenditures and Depreciation
Millions of Dollars

Capital Employed
Working Capital

Capital Expenditures
Depreciation

24

3
Bar charts illustrating financial results.
From Optical Radiation Corporation 1993
annual report.

オプティカル・ラジエーション社の1993
年アニュアルレポートより、決算について
表す棒グラフ。

U.S.A.   1993
AD: Jim Berte
D: Maria Dellota/Jim Berte
DF: Runyan Hinsche Associates
CL: Optical Radiation Corporation

4
Bar graphs illustrating financial statistics.
From the Moore Corporation Limited 1991
annual report.

ムーア社の1991年アニュアルレポートよ
り、財務統計に関する棒グラフ。

Canada   1992
D: Malcolm Waddell
I: Gary Mansbridge
DF: Eskind Waddell
CL: Moore Corporation Limited

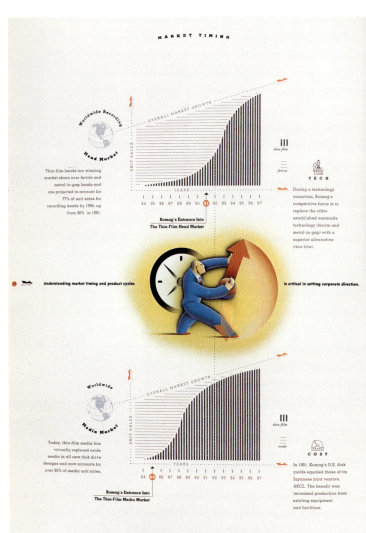
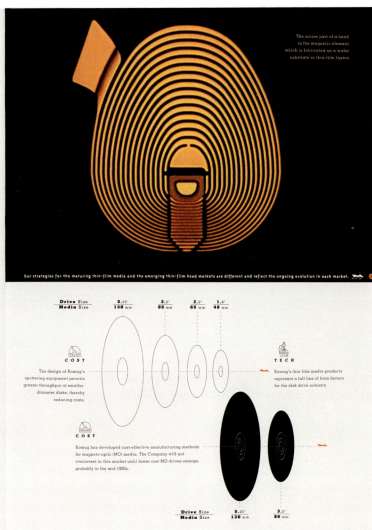

Graphs and diagrams illustrating the marketing strategy of a manufacturer of thin-film media. From Komag, Inc. 1991 annual report.

コマッグ社の1991年アニュアルレポートより、薄型フィルムメーカーの市場戦略を表すグラフ、及びダイアグラム。

U.S.A.　　1992
CD: Steve Tolleson
AD: Steve Tolleson
D: Steve Tolleson/Mark Winn
I: Jeff Kogel
DF: Tolleson Design
CL: Komag, Inc.

OUR NEW MALAYSIAN FACTORY PROVIDES US WITH THE OPPORTUNITY TO FURTHER REDUCE PRODUCTION COSTS. THIS STRATEGIC EXPANSION GIVES US AN ADDITIONAL ADVANTAGE OVER OUR JAPANESE COMPETITORS AND PROVIDES A LOWER COST ALTERNATIVE FOR OUR DISK DRIVE CUSTOMERS WITH VERTICAL MANUFACTURING STRATEGIES.

THIN-FILM HEADS PROVIDE A KEY ENABLING TECHNOLOGY FOR THE ADVANCEMENT OF DISK DRIVE RECORDING DENSITIES. AS THE ONLY INDEPENDENT VOLUME SUPPLIER OF BOTH THIN-FILM HEADS AND MEDIA, KOMAG IS IN A UNIQUE POSITION TO UNDERSTAND, CONTROL AND OPTIMIZE BOTH SIDES OF THE CRITICAL HEAD-DISK INTERFACE.

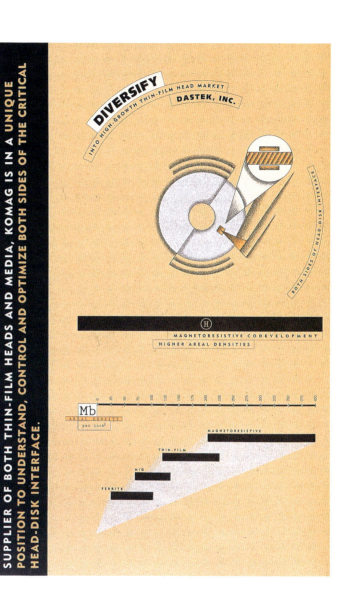

Graphs and diagrams illustrating the business strategy of a supplier of thin-film heads and media. From Komag, Inc. 1992 annual report.

コマッグ社の1992年アニュアルレポートより、薄型フィルムに関連する製品の供給会社の企業戦略を説明するグラフ、及びダイアグラム。

U.S.A.   1993
CD: Steve Tolleson
AD: Steve Tolleson
D: Steve Tolleson/Mark Winn
I: Black Dog
DF: Tolleson Design
CL: Komag, Inc.

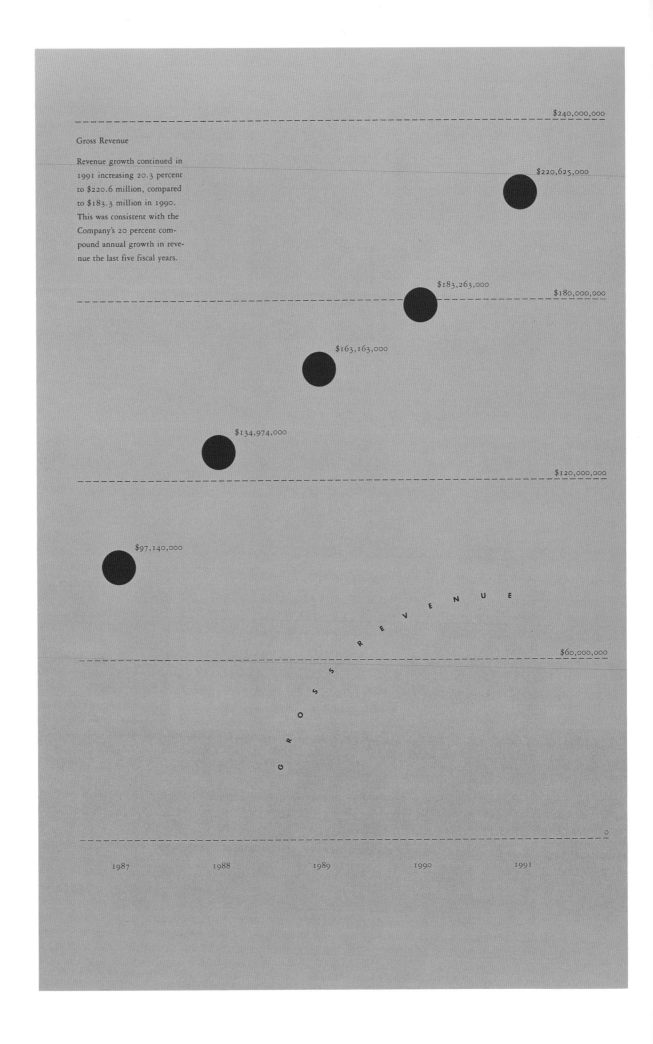

Gross Revenue

Revenue growth continued in
1991 increasing 20.3 percent
to $220.6 million, compared
to $183.3 million in 1990.
This was consistent with the
Company's 20 percent com-
pound annual growth in revenue the last five fiscal years.

$240,000,000

$220,625,000

$183,263,000

$180,000,000

$163,163,000

$134,974,000

$120,000,000

$97,140,000

$60,000,000

GROSS REVENUE

0

1987   1988   1989   1990   1991

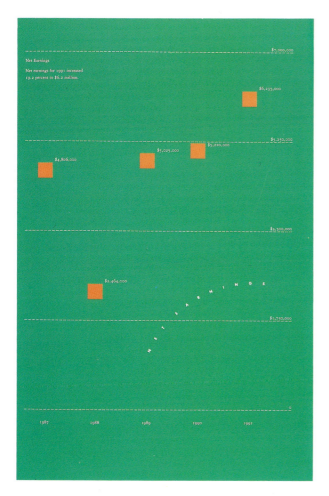

Net Earnings

Net earnings for 1991 increased
19.2 percent to $6.2 million.

$7,000,000

$6,235,000

$5,250,000

$5,220,000
$5,025,000
$4,806,000

$3,500,000

$2,464,000

$1,750,000

NET EARNINGS

0

1987   1988   1989   1990   1991

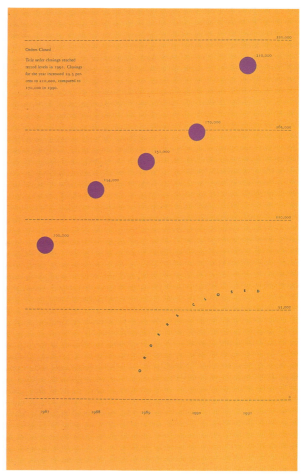

Orders Closed

Title order closings reached
record levels in 1991. Closings
for the year increased 23.5 percent to 210,000, compared to
170,000 in 1990.

220,000

210,000

170,000

165,000

151,000

134,000

110,000

100,000

55,000

ORDERS CLOSED

0

1987   1988   1989   1990   1991

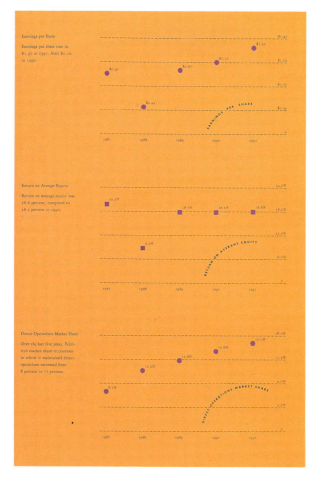

Earnings per Share

Earnings per share rose to
$1.30 in 1991, from $1.10
in 1990.

$1.40

$1.30

$1.10

$1.05

$0.92
$0.87

$0.70

$0.44

$0.35

EARNINGS PER SHARE

0

1987   1988   1989   1990   1991

Return on Average Equity

Return on average equity was
18.6 percent, compared to
18.5 percent in 1990.

22.0%

20.4%

18.5%   18.5%   18.6%

18.0%

12.0%

9.4%

6.0%

RETURN ON AVERAGE EQUITY

1987   1988   1989   1990   1991

Direct Operations Market Share

Over the last five years, Fidelity's market share in counties
in which it maintained direct
operations increased from
8 percent to 17 percent.

18.0%

17.0%

16.0%

13.5%

15.8%

13.6%

9.0%

8.0%

4.5%

DIRECT OPERATIONS MARKET SHARE

1987   1988   1989   1990   1991

Graphs showing growth in revenue,
earnings, and other financial-related
areas of a national title insurance
company. From Fidelity National
Financial, Inc. 1991 annual report.

フィデリティ・ナショナル・ファイナンシャ
ル社のアニュアルレポートより、同保険会
社の総収入、収益、その他の財務関連指標
の伸びを示すグラフ。

U.S.A.   1992
CD: Ron Jefferies
AD: Ron Jefferies/John Tom
D: John Tom
I: John Tom
DF: The Jefferies Association
CL: Fidelity National Financial, Inc.

Illustration representing useless information generated by the so-called 'information age'. From Champion International's 'Subjective Reasoning' promotional feature.

チャンピオンズ・インターナショナル社発行の「サブジェクティヴ・リーズニング」より、"情報化時代"が作り出してしまった無用の情報を描いたイラスト。

U.S.A. 1992
AD: Paula Scher/William Drenttel
D: Paula Scher
I: Paula Scher
DF: Pentagram Design
CL: Champion International Corporation

Number of people on the waiting list to see an execution in Florida: 100—Cost of building a new maximum security prison per cell is $50,000—Number of cats

The total amount convicted drug traffickers owe in criminal fines is $108,000,000—

under his desk at the White House 3 times—There is a 1 in 10 chance that a resident of Washington, D.C. is a lawyer—

the U.S. Army has shot in the head since 1983 to research battlefield injuries: 648—Pounds of fat that cosmetic surgeons remove from Americans each year: 200,000—Melting point of Dippity-Do: 122°F—

Average number of sperm per cubic millimeter of American male semen in 1990: 60,000,000—Dan Quayle has accidentally hit the Secret Service button

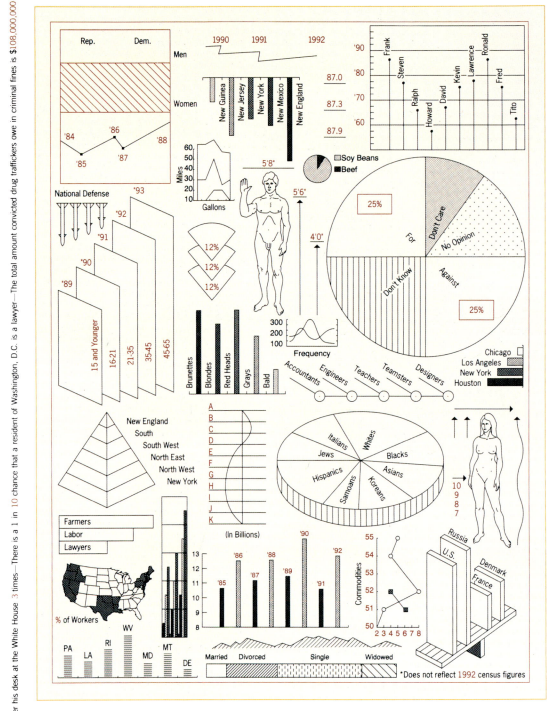

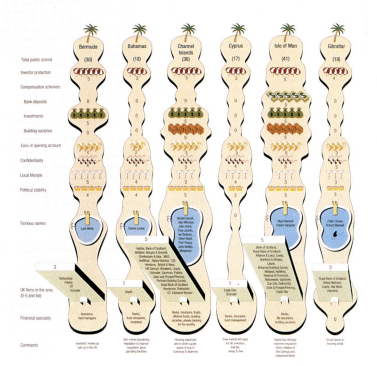

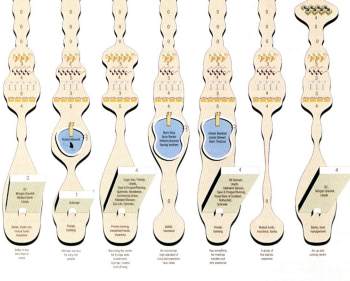

The infographic shows offshore banking tax havens with rows for: Total points scored, Investor protection, Compensation schemes: Bank deposits, Investments, Building societies, Ease of opening account, Confidentiality, Local lifestyle, Political stability, Famous names, UK firms in the area (0-5 and list), Financial speciality, Comments.

Columns: Bermuda (30), Bahamas (18), Channel Islands (36), Cyprus (17), Isle of Man (41), Gibraltar (19), Cayman Islands (22), Liechtenstein (19), Luxembourg (26), Monaco (16), Switzerland (23), Dutch Antilles (18), Dublin (26).

All this and havens too

Once only the wealthy could boast about having an offshore bank account, but now anyone can keep their cash in a tax haven. Research by MARGARET DIBBEN.

Stashing money offshore used to be the prerogative of the rich. Now, anyone with £1000 and a building society account can keep their savings in a sunny haven outside the UK.

The main advantage of an offshore account to UK-based investors is delaying the tax bills. Interest is paid gross, and tax is due only when you actually take the interest – moreover, you are taxed at the rate you are paying at the time you do take it. So high-rate taxpayers can wait until they are paying a lower rate – perhaps, for example, when they retire – and save themselves the difference, currently an extra 15%.

The other great attraction is that older offshore centres are known for their accomodating attitude to their clients' wealth, and the absolute privacy of their numbered accounts.

In the past, too many drugs barons and money launderers have taken advantage of this service, and nowadays, suspected criminals will be exposed. Still, privacy remains appealing to many investors, and a high score for confidentiality indicates a haven which retains a reputation for secrecy.

Investing offshore can be relatively easy; look for high scores in our gradings for the ease with which you can open an account. And you certainly don't need to visit the haven with a suitcase full of cash; we list firms which, at time of writing, can arrange for you to invest offshore through their UK offices.

The downside has always been the greater risks involved in some foreign investments. Ideally, you want a politically stable home for your funds; no overnight coups or nationalisation of bank assets. Again, look for a high score in the relevant grading.

And be wary of the other potential downside; many offshore havens offer little or no investor protection if anything should happen to your chosen bank, investment fund or building society. A high score in our grading means relatively good compensation schemes, but do examine them carefully before committing your funds.

The small investor never could evade tax and, even if you travel to your offshore haven and spend the money on local pleasures, the taxman will still expect his dues.

But as our guide shows, many havens do offer an attractive local lifestyle, and they have appealed to a number of famous names past and present, as residents, visitors or investors.

Whether you're seeking sun or secrecy, pleasures or profits, it seems there's more to be gained than just pennies from havens. ■

Illustration of offshore banking and tax havens. From Intercity magazine.

「インターシティ・マガジン」より、オフショ
ア金融とタックスヘブンに関するグラフ。

U.K.
AD: Rami Lippa
I: Michael Robinson
E: Neil Braidwood
CL: Redwood Publishing

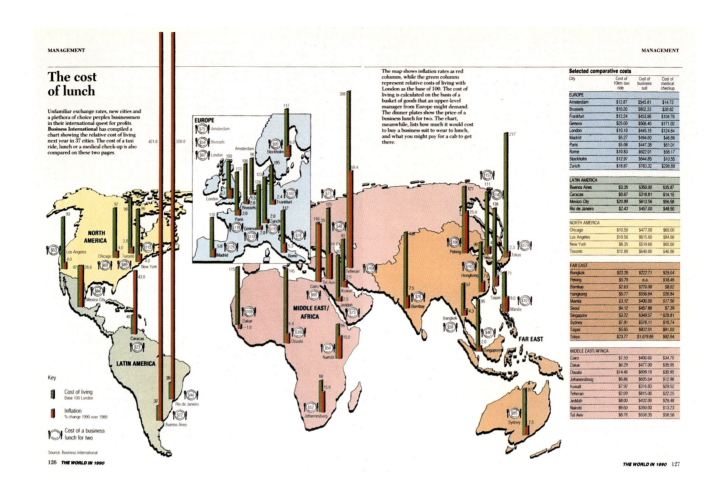

The cost of lunch

Unfamiliar exchange rates, new cities and a plethora of choice perplex businessmen in their international quest for profits. **Business International** has compiled a chart showing the relative cost of living next year in 37 cities. The cost of a taxi ride, lunch or a medical check-up is also compared on these two pages.

The map shows inflation rates as red columns, while the green columns represent relative costs of living with London as the base of 100. The cost of living is calculated on the basis of a basket of goods that an upper-level manager from Europe might demand. The dinner plates show the price of a business lunch for two. The chart, meanwhile, lists how much it would cost to buy a business suit to wear to lunch, and what you might pay for a cab to get there.

Key

- Cost of living — Base 100 London
- Inflation — % change 1990 over 1989
- Cost of a business lunch for two

Source: Business International

Selected comparative costs

City	Cost of 10km taxi ride	Cost of business suit	Cost of medical checkup
EUROPE			
Amsterdam	$12.87	$545.61	$14.73
Brussels	$10.20	$802.33	$38.82
Frankfurt	$12.24	$453.96	$104.76
Geneva	$25.00	$508.40	$171.02
London	$10.19	$445.18	$124.64
Madrid	$5.27	$494.60	$46.66
Paris	$5.06	$447.38	$61.01
Rome	$10.83	$922.01	$58.17
Stockholm	$12.97	$644.85	$10.55
Zurich	$18.67	$763.32	$298.89
LATIN AMERICA			
Buenos Aires	$3.35	$350.00	$35.97
Caracas	$0.87	$318.81	$14.15
Mexico City	$20.89	$612.56	$56.58
Rio de Janeiro	$2.43	$457.00	$48.50
NORTH AMERICA			
Chicago	$10.50	$477.00	$60.00
Los Angeles	$19.56	$615.60	$84.98
New York	$8.35	$519.60	$60.00
Toronto	$12.86	$640.00	$40.86
FAR EAST			
Bangkok	$23.20	$222.71	$29.04
Peking	$5.79	n.a.	$18.49
Bombay	$2.63	$270.00	$8.02
Hongkong	$5.77	$556.64	$26.84
Manila	$3.12	$406.66	$17.50
Seoul	$4.12	$457.88	$7.39
Singapore	$3.22	$349.57	$28.81
Sydney	$7.91	$578.11	$18.74
Taipei	$5.55	$802.51	$91.00
Tokyo	$23.77	$1,079.69	$82.64
MIDDLE EAST/AFRICA			
Cairo	$7.50	$400.00	$34.70
Dakar	$8.29	$477.00	$35.95
Douala	$14.40	$699.19	$39.95
Johannesburg	$6.86	$605.64	$12.98
Kuwait	$7.92	$316.83	$29.52
Teheran	$2.09	$815.00	$22.25
Jeddah	$8.00	$432.00	$29.48
Nairobi	$9.63	$350.00	$13.23
Tel Aviv	$8.76	$558.35	$58.56

is creating an estimated 1,000 new local jobs in Belfast. And the South Korean manufacturer, Daewoo, will bring 500 new jobs to Antrim.

Partnerships between the public and private sectors have achieved outstanding results. Instead of throwing money at old industries, government resources are being used to build the infrastructure and 'green' dereliction to give the depressed areas the chance to compete. The Valleys' Initiative in Wales will provide £500m in government money with the aim of unleashing a further £1 billion in private investment.

Something to celebrate

In the early 1980s the government established registers of public sector derelict land. By 1988, 11,000 acres had been put back to good use, but 84,000 acres remain idle.

Some 145 derelict acres of Ebbw Vale will blossom in the garden festival in 1992. Preparations for the Gateshead garden festival in 1990 are under way, with £33m of public sector support in the form of derelict-land grants. More initiatives like these will break the log-jam and let the market in.

A free market will naturally direct economic activity to those regions which offer the highest quality of life, the most competitive land prices and the cheapest supply of skilled labour. An acre of fully serviced land in Scunthorpe is ten times cheaper than its equivalent in the South-East. Scunthorpe has a pool of skilled labour and the city is as green as any, with 1,000 acres of parkland.

But the market cannot always operate freely: the dice of taxation are still loaded in favour of the concentration of wealth in the South-East, prejudicing the competitive ability of the regions from the start. The pension funds benefit from tax exemptions and attract savings away from the wealth-creating companies to the City institutions. The market for investment must be made more equitable and a start has been made.

The market has already begun to drive economic activity out to regional centres. The government must reinforce this momentum, by removing the obstacles that keep the market out and by providing the infrastructure to allow it to flow. Within a decade the regions could, once again, have restored a better balance with London and the South-East. Good.

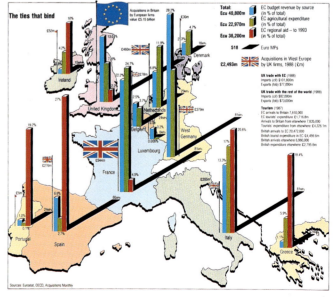

The ties that bind

Sources: Eurostat, OECD, Acquisitions Monthly

Diagrams from The Economist's 'The World in 1990'. Bars and other symbols illustrate the cost of living and inflation rates around the world (above), and financial and other data for individual EC countries (below).

「ザ・エコノミスト」誌の特集"ザ・ワールド・イン1990"より、世界各地の生活費や物価上昇率（上）、及びEC諸国のそれぞれの財政やその他のデータ（下）を地図上に棒グラフと記号で表したダイアグラム。

U.K.   1990
AD: Dennis Bailey/Mike Kenny
I: Michael Robinson
E: Dudley Fishburn
CL: The Economist

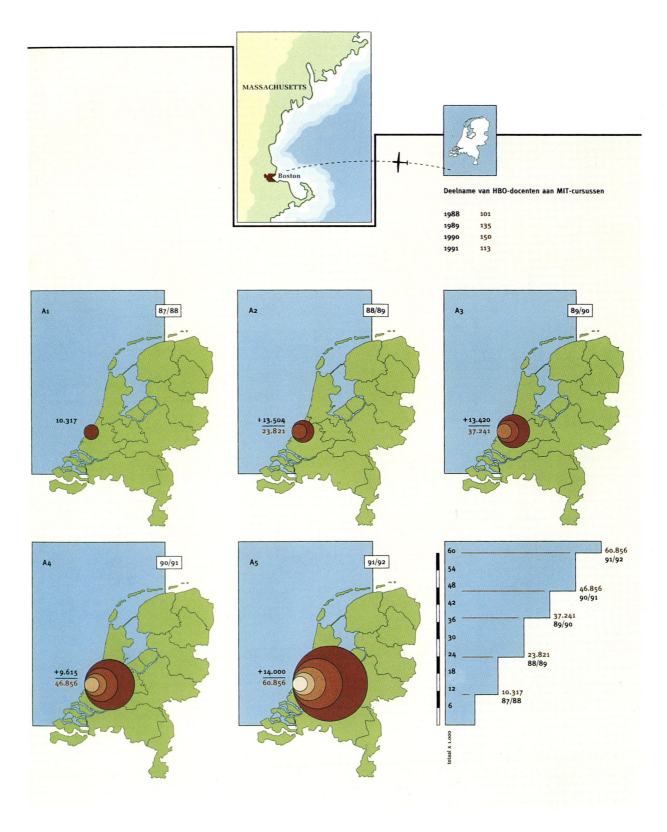

MASSACHUSETTS

Boston

Deelname van HBO-docenten aan MIT-cursussen

1988	101
1989	135
1990	150
1991	113

A1   87/88

10.317

A2   88/89

+13.504
23.821

A3   89/90

+13.420
37.241

A4   90/91

+9.615
46.856

A5   91/92

+14.000
60.856

60   60.856 91/92
54
48   46.856 90/91
42
36   37.241 89/90
30
24   23.821 88/89
18
12   10.317 87/88
6

totaal x 1.000

Diagrams from the final report of NaBoNT, a Dutch government 5-year project seeking to boost teachers' knowledge of information technology. They show the growth in the number of teachers taking NaBoNT courses (below), and annual attendance of NaBoNT participants on MIT courses in Boston, USA (above).

教職員のIT（インフォメーション・テクノロジー）に対する知識を高めるための5カ年計画「NaBoNT」最終報告書より、教職者の研修コース受講者数の増加を示すダイアグラム（下）、及びNaBoNT参加者でアメリカ、ボストンのMITコースの年間受講者数を表すダイアグラム（上）。

Netherlands   1992
CD: Paul Vermijs
AD: Jaco Emmen
D: Jaco Emmen
I: Jaco Emmen
DF: Tel Design
CL: NaBoNT

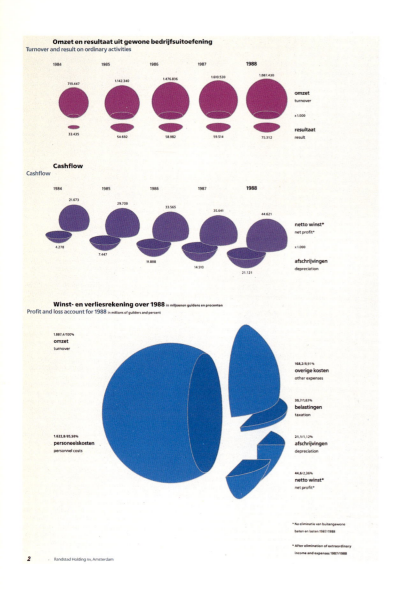

Omzet en resultaat uit gewone bedrijfsuitoefening
Turnover and result on ordinary activities

1984	1985	1986	1987	**1988**	
719.447	1.142.340	1.476.836	1.610.530	1.887.430	**omzet** turnover x 1.000
33.435	54.692	58.982	59.514	75.312	**resultaat** result

Cashflow
Cashflow

1984	1985	1986	1987	**1988**	
21.673	29.700	33.565	35.641	44.621	**netto winst*** net profit* x 1.000
4.278	7.447	11.888	14.510	21.121	**afschrijvingen** depreciation

Winst- en verliesrekening over 1988 in miljoenen guldens en procenten
Profit and loss account for 1988 in millions of guilders and percent

1.887,4/100%
omzet
turnover

168,2/8,91%
overige kosten
other expenses

30,7/1,63%
belastingen
taxation

1.622,8/85,98%
personeelskosten
personnel costs

21,1/1,12%
afschrijvingen
depreciation

44,6/2,36%
netto winst*
net profit*

* Na eliminatie van buitengewone
baten en lasten 1987/1988

* After elimination of extraordinary
income and expenses 1987/1988

2   Randstad Holding nv, Amsterdam

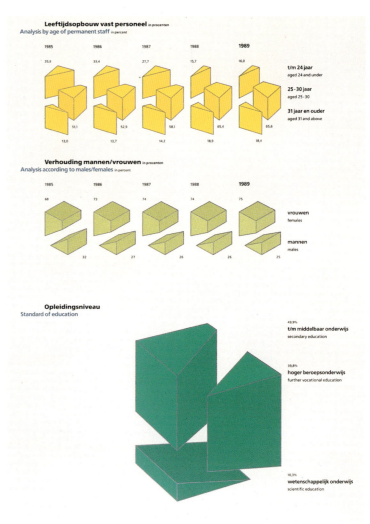

Leeftijdsopbouw vast personeel in procenten
Analysis by age of permanent staff in percent

1985	1986	1987	1988	**1989**	
35,9	33,4	27,7	15,7	16,0	**t/m 24 jaar** aged 24 and under
					25 - 30 jaar aged 25 - 30
51,1	52,9	58,1	65,4	65,6	**31 jaar en ouder** aged 31 and above
13,0	13,7	14,2	18,9	18,4	

Verhouding mannen/vrouwen in procenten
Analysis according to males/females in percent

1985	1986	1987	1988	**1989**	
68	73	74	74	75	**vrouwen** females
32	27	26	26	25	**mannen** males

Opleidingsniveau
Standard of education

49,9%
t/m middelbaar onderwijs
secondary education

39,8%
hoger beroepsonderwijs
further vocational education

10,3%
wetenschappelijk onderwijs
scientific education

20   Randstad Holding nv, Amsterdam

Charts from Ranstad Holding nv annual
reports. The left hand figures show
financial results from the 1988 report;
the right hand figures illustrate data on
company personnel from the 1989
report.

左：1988年のランスタッド・ホールディング社
のアニュアルレポートより、決算内容を表す
グラフ。右：1989年の同レポートより、同社
の職員に関するデータのグラフ。

Netherlands   1989-1990
D: Wim Verboven
CL: Randstad Uitzendbureau

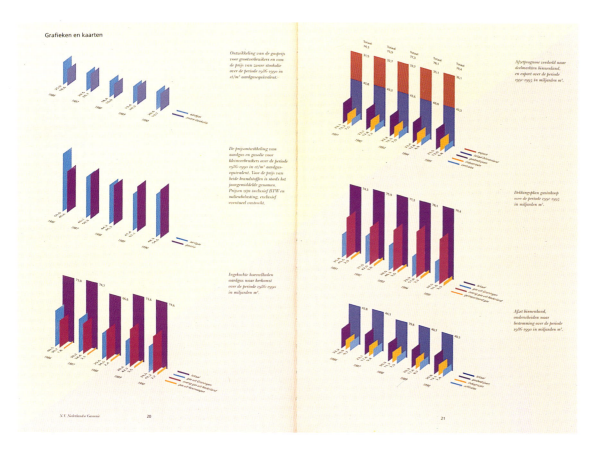

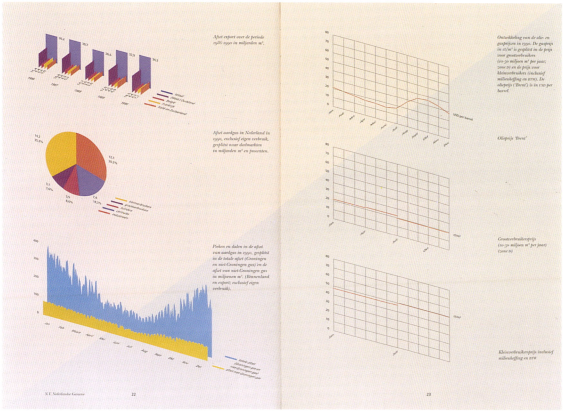

Charts illustrating a range of corporate statistics and other information for a Dutch natural gas distributor. Gasunie (Dutch Gas) 1991 annual report.

オランダのガス会社 Gasunie 社の1991年アニュアルレポートより、天然ガスの供給に関する企業統計他、様々なデータを示すグラフ。

Netherlands   1991
CD: Ronald van Lit
AD: Andrew Fallon
D: Ronald van Lit
DF: Tel Design
CL: Gasunie (Dutch Gas)

Elektriciteitsprijs, omzet en investeringen
Electricity price, turnover and investments

Elektriciteitsprijs
Gemiddelde elektriciteitsprijs in centen per kWh
(excl. BTW) voor klein- en grootverbruikers.
Per jaar zijn links de kleinverbruikers en rechts de
grootverbruikers weergegeven.

Electricity price
Average electricity price in Dutch cents/kWh
(excl. of VAT) for small-scale and bulk consumers.
For each year small-scale consumers are
indicated on the left-hand side and bulk
consumers on the right.

brandstofvergoeding
fuel components

overige tariefbestanddelen
other components

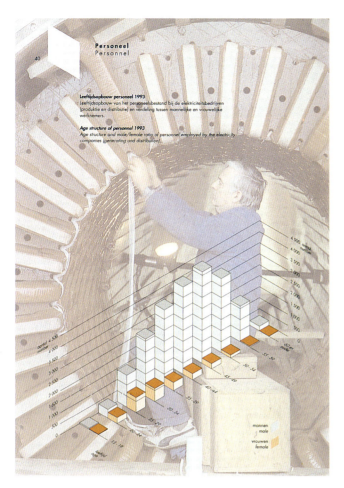

Personeel
Personnel

Leeftijdsopbouw personeel 1993
Leeftijdsopbouw van het personeelsbestand bij de elektriciteitsbedrijven (produktie en distributie) en verdeling tussen mannelijke en vrouwelijke werknemers.

Age structure of personnel 1993
Age structure and male/female ratio of personnel employed by the electricity companies (generating and distribution).

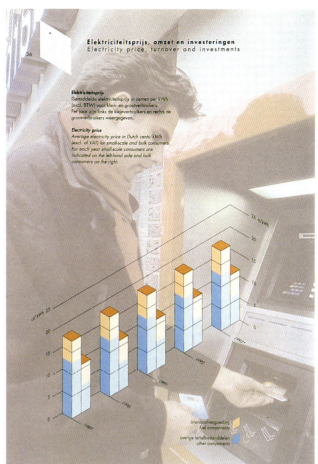

Elektriciteitsprijs, omzet en investeringen
Electricity price, turnover and investments

Elektriciteitsprijs
Gemiddelde elektriciteitsprijs in centen per kWh (excl. BTW) voor klein- en grootverbruikers. Per jaar zijn links de kleinverbruikers en rechts de grootverbruikers weergegeven.

Electricity price
Average electricity price in Dutch cents/kWh (excl. of VAT) for small-scale and bulk consumers. For each year small-scale consumers are indicated on the left-hand side and bulk consumers on the right.

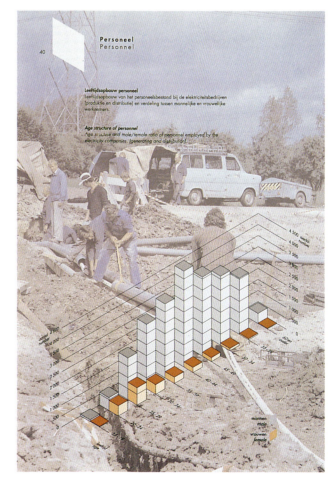

Personeel
Personnel

Leeftijdsopbouw personeel
Leeftijdsopbouw van het personeelsbestand bij de elektriciteitsbedrijven (produktie en distributie) en verdeling tussen mannelijke en vrouwelijke werknemers.

Age structure of personnel
Age structure and male/female ratio of personnel employed by the electricity companies. (generating and distribution).

Bar graphs from 1990 and 1993 reports of the Dutch Electricity Generating Board, showing changes in electricity prices, and the age structure of personnel.

オランダ発電局の1990年と1993年の報告書
より、電気料金の変化、及び職員の年齢構
成を表した棒グラフ。

Netherlands   1990-1993
D: Gerard Wagemans
CL: Dutch Electricity Generating Board

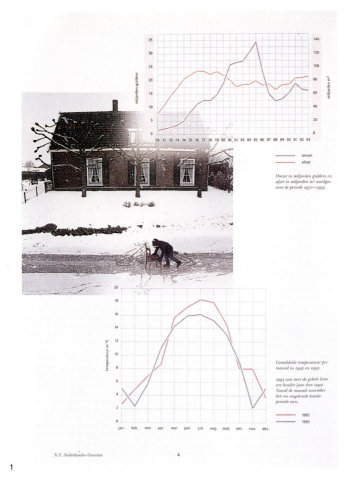

N.V. Nederlandse Gasunie

Omzet in miljarden guldens en
afzet in miljarden m³ aardgas
over de periode 1970–1993.

Gemiddelde temperatuur per
maand in 1992 en 1993.
1993 was over de gehele linie
een kouder jaar dan 1992.
Vooral de maand november
liet een opvallende koude-
periode zien.

1992
1993

1

N.V. Nederlandse Gasunie

Afzet aardgas in Nederland in 1993,
exclusief eigen verbruik, gesplitst naar
deelmarkten in miljarden m³ en procenten.

¹) Inclusief kleinverbruik.

Gasunie's research-inspanningen richten zich zowel op de ontwikkeling
van efficiënte en comfortabele gastoepassingen voor de openbare
gasvoorziening als op industriële toepassingen.
Foto boven: in het Proedinscollege in Groningen is een nieuwe,
kostenbesparende methode voor ruimteverwarming in gebouwen toegepast.
Foto onder: een hoge-temperatuurtoepassing bij de fabricage van lampen.
De research voor industriële toepassingen draagt een sterk accent op de
vermindering van NO₂-emissies.

2

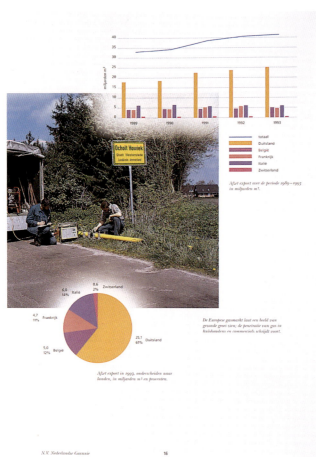

N.V. Nederlandse Gasunie

Afzet export over de periode 1989–1993
in miljarden m³.

totaal
Duitsland
België
Frankrijk
Italië
Zwitserland

De Europese gasmarkt laat een beeld van
grote groei zien; de penetratie van gas in
huishoudens en commercieels schrijdt voort.

Afzet export in 1993, onderscheiden naar
landen, in miljarden m³ en procenten.

3

1, 2, 3
Graphs from the 1993 annual report of
Gasunie, a Dutch natural gas distributor.
Upper left: Natural gas sales and average
monthly temperatures in 1992 and 1993.
Upper right: Breakdown of 1993 sales by
type of market. Lower left: Natural gas
exports, by county of destination.

オランダのガス供給会社Gasunieの1993年
アニュアルレポートより、1992年と1993年の
天然ガスの販売実績と月別平均気温を表すグ
ラフ（左）、及び業界別に1993年の販売内訳
（右）、仕向国別に天然ガスの輸出状況を表す
円グラフ（下）。

Netherlands   1994
CD: Andrew Fallon
AD: Ronald van Lit
D: Andrew Fallon
DF: Tel Design
CL: Gasunie (Dutch Gas)

4, 5, 6, 7
Bar charts showing an air courier's net
earnings and active customer base, from
Airborne Express annual reports. Upper
charts from 1992 report, lower charts
from 1993 report.

航空輸送会社の純利益と得意先の拠点を表す
棒グラフ。上のグラフはエアボーン・エキス
プレス社の1992年アニュアルレポート、下
のグラフは1993年同レポートからの出典。

U.S.A.   1993-1994
AD: John Hornall
D: John Hornall/Julia LaPine/
Heidi Hatlestad
P: Robin Bartholick/Jeff Zaruba/
Dan Freeman
DF: Hornall Anderson Design Works
CL: Airborne Express

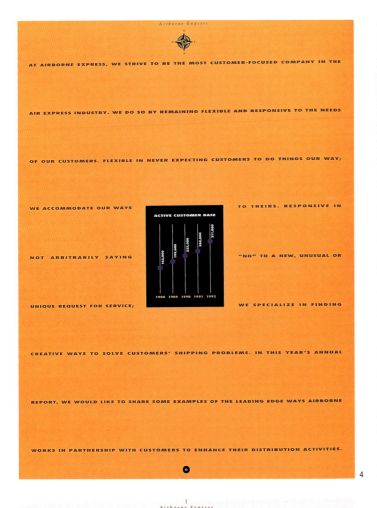

AT AIRBORNE EXPRESS, WE STRIVE TO BE THE MOST CUSTOMER-FOCUSED COMPANY IN THE

AIR EXPRESS INDUSTRY. WE DO SO BY REMAINING FLEXIBLE AND RESPONSIVE TO THE NEEDS

OF OUR CUSTOMERS. FLEXIBLE IN NEVER EXPECTING CUSTOMERS TO DO THINGS OUR WAY;

WE ACCOMMODATE OUR WAYS   TO THEIRS. RESPONSIVE IN

NOT ARBITRARILY SAYING   "NO" TO A NEW, UNUSUAL OR

UNIQUE REQUEST FOR SERVICE;   WE SPECIALIZE IN FINDING

CREATIVE WAYS TO SOLVE CUSTOMERS' SHIPPING PROBLEMS. IN THIS YEAR'S ANNUAL

REPORT, WE WOULD LIKE TO SHARE SOME EXAMPLES OF THE LEADING EDGE WAYS AIRBORNE

WORKS IN PARTNERSHIP WITH CUSTOMERS TO ENHANCE THEIR DISTRIBUTION ACTIVITIES.

4

made the critical strategic decision, not only to rely on Airborne Express for customer delivery, but also to close down its Seattle area warehouse, and turnover to Airborne its entire distribution function. The company maintains its headquarters staff, marketing and sales operations in the Seattle area, but its entire inventory, warehouse and distribution management is handled by Airborne Express from the Airborne Stock Exchange in Wilmington. ○ Among the many advantages Multiple Zones has realized from this move is the ability to process customer orders as late as 11:00 pm Pacific time (2:00 am Eastern), for overnight delivery anywhere in the United States via Airborne Express. In this highly competitive industry, being able to process orders late into the evening is an important competitive advantage. ○ Under the new system, Multiple Zones' salespeople take orders from their customers throughout the day and late into the evening, transmitting the orders electronically to the Stock Exchange in Wilmington. Airborne personnel then fill the orders and ship directly to Multiple Zones' customers. ○ Based on shipping data provided by a sophisticated inventory management system, Multiple Zones purchases replenishment inventory from its vendors for direct shipment to the Airborne Stock Exchange. Copies of the purchase orders are sent to the Stock Exchange so that the accuracy of shipments can be verified upon arrival. ○ Shipments from vendors in this industry typically have a high error rate – on average about 20% – which has necessitated establishing an elaborate quality process to catch such a high number of errors. Given the thousands of items received each day, a major responsibility of Airborne on behalf of Multiple Zones is controlling the error rate and reconciling actual shipments with purchase orders to ensure that customer orders are processed correctly. ○ Multiple Zones never handles the products it sells. They go directly from the manufacturer, to the Stock Exchange, and then to Multiple Zones' customers. ○ Multiple Zones generates, fills and ships thousands of orders per night without having a single employee on site at the Airborne Stock Exchange. All of the work is done by a dedicated staff of Airborne employees who are responsible for fulfilling the distribution needs of Multiple Zones. ○ Airborne operates a similar total distribution program for Mac's Place, another major company in this industry. Two other leading companies – MicroWarehouse and PC Connection – operate their own warehouse facilities; but they do so from centralized facilities at the Airborne Commerce Park, located just a few hundred feet away from the Airborne Stock Exchange. And each of the four companies uses Airborne Express as its air express carrier for delivering products to customers. All four companies have benefitted enormously from staging their distribution operations from centralized facilities at the Airborne Commerce Park adjacent to the Airborne Express airport and central sort facility. ○ Airborne has been able to create a flexible, custom solution to meet each of these companies' distribution goals, up to and including providing the entire distribution network.

5

On the face of it, Airborne Express has a simple mission: Pick up a package at Point A and move it to Point B – quickly and reliably. But move two packages and the job becomes more complicated. Move 700,000 packages overnight through a central hub and ten regional hubs and it becomes a task of giant proportions – a miraculous daily ballet. At each stage, Airborne must balance cost vs. service, price vs. volume, schedule vs. accuracy. Even our aircraft must balance the physics of flight: lift vs. weight, thrust vs. drag. As a Company, Airborne maintains its balance by tough cost controls and continuously improving productivity. Being the low cost producer is our competitive advantage. On the following pages, we will show you some of the ways we achieve this balance.

6

The Airborne Express fleet reflects the Company's philosophy – keeping costs low. ABX Air, Inc., the wholly-owned airline subsidiary that supports Airborne Express' nationwide shipping business, underwent a number of changes and improvements in 1993, resulting in increased productivity. Among the changes was a dramatic reduction in the time required to perform a major maintenance activity, an internal program that cuts across departmental lines to reduce the airline's costs, and a new flight planning system that improves aircraft efficiency. ■ ABX, through its integrated air and ground system, transports in excess of three million pounds of documents and express packages each night – some 700,000 pieces. The airline reflects the Airborne Express operating philosophy: perform high-quality work, deliver the best customer service, and do so in the most efficient and economical way. Some examples:

■ In 1993, ABX's maintenance facility in Wilmington, Ohio – the airline's headquarters – was able to reduce the time necessary to perform a regularly scheduled, major maintenance process from 24 work days to 13. And by beating its own records, the same facility was able to cut the time needed to convert a passenger aircraft into an Airborne freighter from 82 days to 51. Safety, of course, remains Airborne's overriding concern.

■ The newly formed Process Evaluation and Design group helped increase package sorting productivity at our Wilmington

operation and enhanced our ability to identify and move freight through our integrated air and ground system.

■ With our Flow Control Program, we were able to cut fuel costs by precise scheduling of aircraft departures across the nation. This allowed more accuracy in the arrivals of some 85 aircraft, and it resulted in an average of five minutes less flying time for each aircraft, reducing the amount of fuel burned. In addition, an integrated flight planning and crew scheduling system increased productivity by reducing paperwork and creating more efficient crew schedules.

■ More than 150 aircraft carry freight across the United States for Airborne. About one-third are charter aircraft that carry packages from smaller communities to larger cities, where shipments are placed into the nearly 90 aircraft owned or operated by Airborne. The fleet, in top mechanical condition, consists of McDonnell Douglas DC-8 and DC-9 jets, along with several YS-11 turboprops. ■ In modifying the McDonnell Douglas aircraft from passenger to cargo use, the main deck is strengthened and a cargo floor installed so that lightweight, durable containers – designed and patented by Airborne – can be locked in place during flight. Noise suppressors for the jet engines, called "Hush Kits," are being installed that will meet the 1999 Federal Stage 3 noise requirement. The cost of buying and modifying these McDonnell Douglas aircraft is significantly less than the price of new aircraft with a similar cargo capacity. Both get

7

Charts illustrating corporate results.
From Centre Reinsurance (Bermuda) Ltd.
1989 annual report.

センター・リインシュアランス・バミューダ
社の1989年アニュアルレポートより、決
算の内容を表すチャート。

U.S.A.　1990
CD: Frank Oswald
AD: Frank Oswald
D: Randall Smith
DF: WYD Design Inc.
CL: Centre Reinsurance (Bermuda) Limited

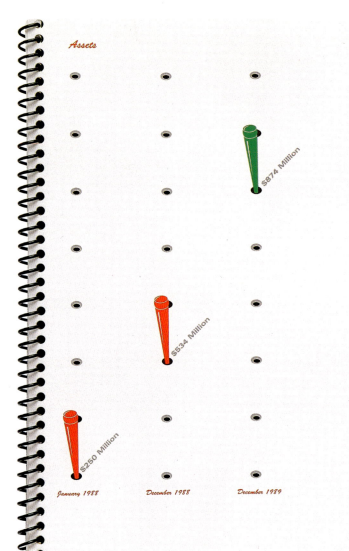

Assets

$874 Million

$534 Million

$250 Million

January 1988   December 1988   December 1989

Centre Reinsurance

Formed as a private company in 1988, Centre Reinsurance is already one of the largest professional reinsurance companies in the world. Our charter is to bring new ideas to reinsurance that respond to the needs of our clients, enhance their financial positions, and improve the overall management and profitability of their businesses.

1989 Operating Report: Financial Review

We are pleased to report the results of our first two years of operations. As the only sizeable reinsurer writing exclusively finite risk business, our financial statements are unique, and do not always easily lend themselves to traditional analysis. We've prepared this brief financial review to help our clients better understand our business and its performance.

First, it is important to establish that we are in the REINSURANCE business. Unlike some "financial" reinsurers, Centre Re is not in the business of banking dressed up to look like insurance. Our finite risk contracts clearly assume both underwriting and timing risks. Though "risk transfer" remains a hot topic in accounting circles, we are confident that, by any definition, our business is risk-exposed reinsurance, and we will continue to operate within the regulatory and tax rules governing the industry.

Some of those regulations, however, often contribute to misunderstandings about our financial statements. Looking first at our income statement, for example, one might wonder how good the finite risk reinsurance business is if Centre Re, the market leader, wrote only $68 million

of premiums in 1989. The answer is simple: Revenues recorded on our income statement reflect only a portion of the reinsurance business we transact.

Our REINSURANCE VOLUME chart on page 12 helps illustrate this point. As shown, Centre Re transacts two kinds of business — prospective and retrospective. Prospective reinsurance is written to assume future losses; retrospective reinsurance assumes losses that have already occurred (whether those losses have been reported or not). United States generally accepted accounting principles (U.S. GAAP) require us to record only PROSPECTIVE business on our income statement as premium; RETROSPECTIVE business can only be recorded on our balance sheet, bypassing our income statement.

When you add this retrospective business to the "premiums" written on prospective reinsurance, Centre Re actually transacted $268 million in total reinsurance business in 1989 compared to $313 million in 1988. Because we tend to conclude a relatively small number of large transactions, it will not be unusual to see year-to-year fluctuations in the amount of business that we transact.

The second item of note on our income statement is a negative $15 million of acquisition cost expense in 1989, compared to acquisition cost expense of $47.1 million in 1988. One might assume that we either discovered remarkable budgetary controls or are practicing alchemy. The correct interpretation again relates to the unique nature of our business — because our programs tend to be large, any one transaction can have a significant impact on our financial statements. In 1988, for instance, we booked a large transaction with a sizeable provisional ceding commission with a sliding scale adjustment — in other words, larger losses mean a smaller ceding commission for our client. During 1989, the ceding company reported a large increase in incurred losses, which caused a corresponding decrease in ceding commission — also referred to as acquisition cost on our income statement. This transaction by itself was enough to offset all other acquisition costs incurred during 1989. This acquisition cost income did not artificially inflate net income. The reduction in acquisition costs was offset by an increase in losses incurred.

Financial statement management is an important element in the purchase of reinsurance. The companies who cede business to us utilize our surplus; Centre Re absorbs these financial statement fluctuations while the ceding companies' reported results remain stable.

Our balance sheet remains the truest reflection of the volume and quality of our reinsurance business. From initial capitalization of $250 million two years ago, total assets grew to $534 million at December 31, 1988 and $874 million at December 31, 1989, a 64% increase from 1988 to 1989. Reinsurance liabilities, a measure of the contractholder funds entrusted to us by ceding companies, exceeded $608 million at December 31, 1989, a 110% increase over 1988.

Investment Strategy
Risk is a significant component of reinsurance underwriting, not our investment strategy. As a matter of policy, we avoid taking currency risk and seek to minimize interest rate risk through the construction of a varying number of highly complex duration-matched asset portfolios.

Use of duration matching techniques does not eliminate the risk in a reinsur-

Assets in millions

$874
$534
1988   1989

Net Income in millions

$33.1
$12.5
1988   1989

Letter To Shareholders

Dear Shareholder

As the charts on the opposite page indicate, 1993 was a very successful year for Premiere Page. Even though the year was full of change — such as the initial public offering, new market entries, new store openings and high growth — Premiere's management team was able to generate record growth in revenue, customers and EBITDA (Earnings before Interest, Taxes, Depreciation and Amortization). For 1993, revenue grew 35%, to $20,927,000; pagers in service grew to 122,996, up from 89,396 in 1992; voice mail in service more than doubled in 1993, to 26,868 from 12,348 in 1992; and EBITDA grew to $9,118,000, a 34% increase over 1992.

Our strict adherence to well-defined policies, procedures and processes generated high growth while controlling operating expenses, thus yielding high operating margins. A good example is our low cost to acquire new customers. Our sales people are highly productive, averaging 125 activations per representative per month, as well as providing service to our customers. This is beneficial to your company because high margins provide much of the capital the Company needs to expand into new markets and further penetrate existing markets.

In our larger markets, our retail strategy has given us the competitive advantage to access the growing consumer market in paging products. Our strategy of serving the untapped consumer market with multiple, convenient locations in high-visibility, high-traffic shopping areas, has produced very encouraging results. As our new and existing customers have experienced the convenient locations, extended weekday and weekend hours and redesigned transactions that make obtaining service and paying bills faster and easier, the feedback has been extremely positive.

So have the results: with the opening of new stores in the second half of 1993, sales from walk-in customers increased 38% over the first half of the year. In addition, walk-in sales for the first quarter of 1994 increased 88% over the fourth quarter of 1993. This further supports our strategy of growing through new retail store openings.

Premiere Page opened six new stores in 1993 in the following markets: two in Birmingham and one each in Florence and Montgomery — all in Alabama — and one each in St. Louis and Bloomington, Illinois.

In the first quarter of 1994, we opened three new stores: our second in St. Louis, a third in Birmingham and our first in Nashville. The two new market entries, St. Louis and Nashville, are already meeting expectations. The Company plans to open four more stores in 1994, including another St. Louis location.

Nashville was the first new market entry under our excellent, high-capacity, wide-area 900mhz network.

The initial public offering of our stock in December 1993, provided $27 million in funds, which we used to reduce debt and supply working capital for the Company's core market growth and new market entries. Premiere's deleveraged balance sheet puts the Company on sound footing for the future.

Premiere Page measures itself in many ways, but the most important are our focus on high-quality products and service at highly competitive rates; our dedication to grow the business at above-average industry rates while constantly looking for new ways to improve our cost structure; and by building shareholder value.

With our recent transition to a public company, this annual report provides the first opportunity to report to shareholders, and I'm pleased to be providing good news. I'm also happy to report that revenues for the first quarter ending March 31, 1994 increased 40% over the comparable quarter in 1993. This demonstrates that Premiere Page is on a consistent, solid growth path. I look forward to keeping you informed of our progress.

Sincerely,

James A. Queen
CEO and
Chairman of the Board

1990 1991 1992 1993
Paging Units

1990 1991 1992 1993
Total Revenue

Corporate statistics from Premiere Page 1993 annual report.

プリミエ・ページ社の1993年アニュアル
レポートより、企業統計に関するグラフ。

U.S.A.   1994
CD: John Muller
AD: John Muller/
Scott Chapman
D: John Muller
P: Dan White
DF: Muller+Company
CL: Premiere Page

Premiere Page

Premiere Page, headquartered in the Kansas City suburb of Leawood, Kansas, is a regional provider of wide-area paging services and products, including voicemail and other ancillary products.

Premiere operates in two primary regions: the Midwest and Southeastern United States. Premiere maintains a leadership position in its core markets in Alabama and Illinois. More recently, the Company opened new marketing and retail outlets in St. Louis, Missouri, and Nashville, Tennessee.

The Company's strategy is to provide high-quality products and services at the best prices in the marketplace. Employing innovative marketing and operational strategies, the Company has been able to outpace the average growth performance of the paging industry in paging units in service, revenue and Earnings Before Interest, Taxes, Depreciation and Amortization (EBITDA). EBITDA is a key performance measure in the paging industry.

The Company has three primary goals for expansion: geographic expansion, growth through market leadership in its core markets and through acquisitions. Premiere is currently expanding its operations into contiguous and other markets through new market start-ups.

Premiere's management takes great pride in its low-cost operations, vigilantly seeking new ways to improve efficiency and capacity to achieve high operating margins; this in a high-growth environment that provides its customers with high-quality products and services at very competitive rates. Currently, the Company is engaged in constructing a super-wide area, satellite-controlled 900mhz wireless network that will create a regional paging system, allowing the Company to open new markets in Tennessee, Kentucky, Mississippi, Iowa, Northern Florida and Missouri. These new market openings will fuel significant growth for the Company over the next few years.

The Company was founded in 1988 by James A. Queen, its Chairman and Chief Executive Officer, and Rodney A. Weary, a director of the Company. Premiere Page was formed via the acquisition of several local and regional paging companies in Illinois and Alabama.

At the end of 1993, the Company had 174 employees in its field operations and 16 employees at its headquarters.

Premiere Page has continued a four-year trend of growth. During that time, revenue grew at an annual rate of 31.8%. In 1993, revenue increased by 35.1%. The Company currently has one of the highest EBITDA margins of all public paging companies, at 43.6% for 1993. Last year, pager units in service increased by 38% to 122,996, while the number of subscribers for voicemail services increased 118% to 26,868. With the pager industry expected to grow at an annual rate of 15% over the next five years, Premiere Page should be able to maintain its rapid growth strategy.

Financial Highlights

	Year Ended December 31,			
	1990	1991	1992	1993
	(In thousands, except per share data)			
Total revenue ($000's)	$ 9,130	$ 13,008	$ 15,485	$ 20,927
Net loss ($000's)	$ (7,268)	$ (10,049)	$ (8,608)	$ (7,466)
Net loss per share	$ (2.40)	$ (2.81)	$ (2.45)	$ (2.08)
EBITDA (1)	$ 3,500	$ 5,539	$ 6,800	$ 9,118
Ratio of EBITDA to interest expense	.94x	1.17x	1.68x	2.37x
Ratio of long-term debt to EBITDA	11.61x	7.82x	6.45x	2.71x
Pagers in service (end of year)	61,500	70,865	89,396	122,996
Voicemail subscribers (end of year)	1,780	3,765	12,348	26,868

(1) EBITDA consists of income before interest, taxes, depreciation and amortization. EBITDA is a financial measure commonly used in the Company's industry and should not be construed as an alternative to operating income (as determined in accordance with generally accepted accounting principles) as an indicator of operating performance or as an alternative to cash flow from operating activities as a measure of liquidity. EBITDA is also a primary financial measure by which the Company's covenants are calculated under its senior debt agreement.

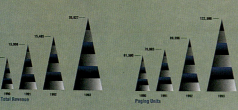

70,927
15,485
13,008
9,130
1990 1991 1992 1993
Total Revenue

122,996
89,396
70,865
61,500
1990 1991 1992 1993
Paging Units

9,118
6,800
5,539
3,500
1990 1991 1992 1993
EBITDA

43.8%   **43.6%**
38.3%
27.2%   **26.8%**
25.8%
1990 1991 1992 1993
EBITDA Margin   ■ Premiere Page ▲ Industry

Charts illustrating levels of use of various Community Psychiatric Center services. From Community Psychiatric Center 1993 annual report.

コミュニティ・サイキアトリック・センターの1993年アニュアルレポートより、同精神病治療センターで受けられる様々なサービスの利用状況を表すグラフ。

U.S.A. 1993
AD: Jim Berte
D: Maria Dellota/Jim Berte
DF: Runyan Hinsche Associates
CL: Community Psychiatric Center

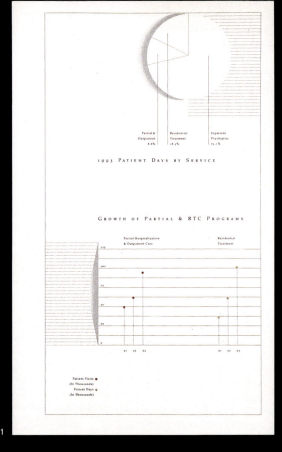

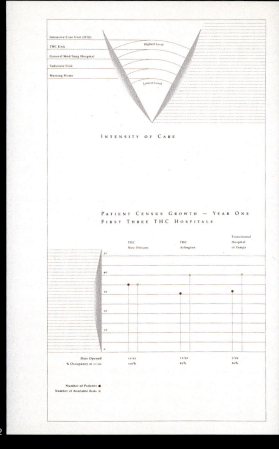

3, 4
Bar and pie graphs of financial results. From International Rectifier Corporation 1993 annual report.

インターナショナル・レクティフィア社の1993年アニュアルレポートより、決算に関する棒グラフと円グラフ。

U.S.A. 1993
AD: Jim Berte
D: Maria Dellota/Jim Berte
DF: Runyan Hinsche Associates
CL: International Rectifier Corporation

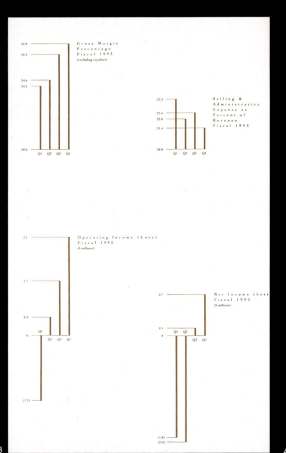

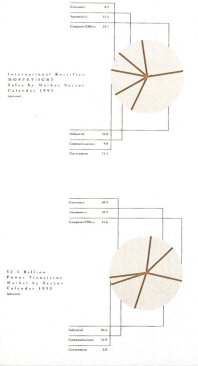

KEY INDICATORS

TOTAL ASSETS

Assets climbed to more

than $800 million, further

strengthening the Company.

(millions of dollars)

CAPITAL & SURPLUS

A record capital & surplus level of

more than $147 million helped

ensure protection for members.

(millions of dollars)

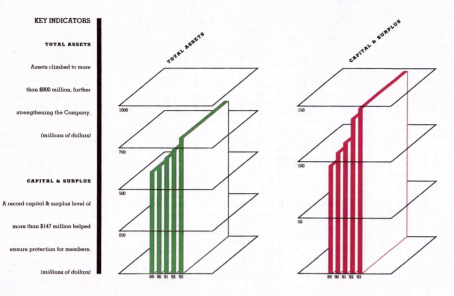

Bar graphs illustrating key indicators.
Fr**o**m Medical Inter-Insurance Exchange
1993 annual report.

メディカル・インターインシュランス・エ
クスチェンジ社の1993年アニュアルレポ
ートより、同社の主な指標を表す棒グラフ。

U.S.A.　　1994
AD: Roger Cook/Don Shanosky
D: Cathryn Cook
I: Cook and Shanosky Associates, Inc.
DF: Cook and Shanosky Associates, Inc.
CL: Medical Inter-Insurance Exchange

Key Indicators

Total Assets

Assets topped the $700 million

range, further strengthening the

financial stability of the Company.

(millions of dollars)

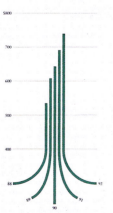

Surplus

Record surplus level of $138 million

to ensure financial solvency and

protection for its members.

(millions of dollars)

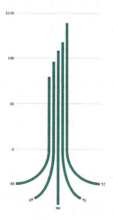

Bar graphs illustrating key indicators.
From Medical Inter-Insurance Exchange
1992 annual report.

メディカル・インターインシュランス・エ
クスチェンジ社の1992年アニュアルレポー
トより、同社の主な指標を表す棒グラフ。

U.S.A.　　1993
AD: Roger Cook/Don Shanosky
D: Cathryn Cook
I: Cathryn Cook
DF: Cook and Shanosky Associates, Inc.
CL: Medical Inter-Insurance Exchange

Graphs showing financial highlights.
From ECS 1989 annual report.

ECS社1989年アニュアルレポートより、強
調したい財務内容を表すグラフ。

France   1990
CD: Alain Lachartre
AD: Alain Lachartre
D: Philippe Caron/Cyril Cabry
I: Philippe Caron/Cyril Cabry
CL: ECS

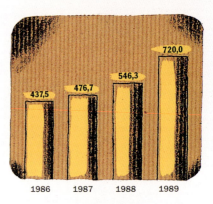

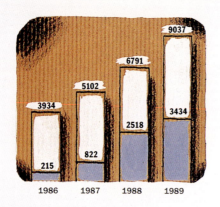

CHIFFRE D'AFFAIRES CONSOLIDÉ
(en millions de francs)
CHIFFRE D'AFFAIRES INTERNATIONAL (HORS FRANCE)
(en millions de francs)

MARGE BRUTE CORRIGÉE
(en millions de francs)

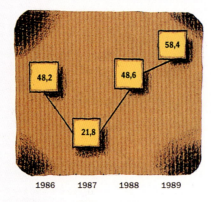

RÉSULTAT NET
(en millions de francs)

**CHIFFRE D'AFFAIRES DE DISTRIBUTION
DE MICRO-ORDINATEURS**
(en millions de francs)

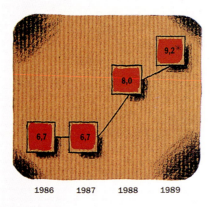

DIVIDENDE PAR ACTION EN FRANCS
＊*dividende proposé à l'Assemblée*

TOTAL BILAN CONSOLIDÉ
(en millions de francs)

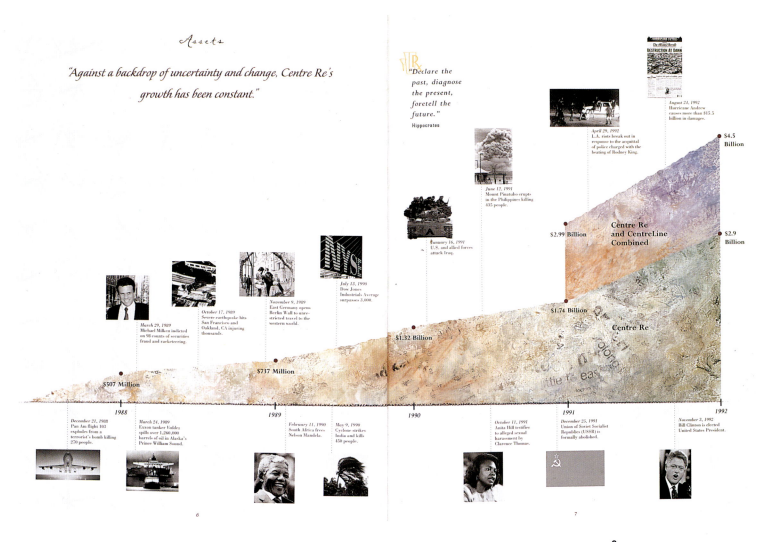

Assets

"Against a backdrop of uncertainty and change, Centre Re's growth has been constant."

₩R

"Declare the past, diagnose the present, foretell the future."

Hippocrates

August 24, 1992 Hurricane Andrew causes more than $15.5 billion in damages.

$4.5 Billion

April 29, 1992 L.A. riots break out in response to the acquittal of police charged with the beating of Rodney King.

June 12, 1991 Mount Pinatubo erupts in the Philippines killing 435 people.

$2.99 Billion

Centre Re and CentreLine Combined

$2.9 Billion

January 16, 1991 U.S. and allied forces attack Iraq.

$1.74 Billion

Centre Re

July 13, 1990 Dow Jones Industrials Average surpasses 3,000.

March 29, 1989 Michael Milken indicted on 98 counts of securities fraud and racketeering.

October 17, 1989 Severe earthquake hits San Francisco and Oakland, CA injuring thousands.

November 9, 1989 East Germany opens Berlin Wall to unrestricted travel to the western world.

$1.32 Billion

$737 Million

$507 Million

1988

1989

1990

1991

1992

December 21, 1988 Pan Am flight 103 explodes from a terrorist's bomb killing 270 people.

March 24, 1989 Exxon tanker Valdez spills over 1,260,000 barrels of oil in Alaska's Prince William Sound.

February 11, 1990 South Africa frees Nelson Mandela.

May 9, 1990 Cyclone strikes India and kills 450 people.

October 11, 1991 Anita Hill testifies to alleged sexual harassment by Clarence Thomas.

December 25, 1991 Union of Soviet Socialist Republics (USSR) is formally abolished.

November 3, 1992 Bill Clinton is elected United States President.

6

7

Production - the rewarding harvest

UK PRODUCTION

Since 1987, the Company's production has nearly quadrupled. This reflects both the growth of its E&P business, and a strategy of making better use of existing assets. In the same period, oil production has risen from three per cent of total production to over 25 per cent.

MUCH OF the Company's increased production has come from South Morecambe, still E&P's major single asset. Offshore compressors installed in 1992 have improved recoverable reserves and increased the field's peak production capacity by 50%.

Technology has also improved the performance of the Rough storage field, off the Humberside coast. This unique offshore facility utilises a partly depleted gas field as a seasonal store to ensure security of supply to the UK during the cold winter months. The Company's first use of horizontal drilling contributed to improving production capacity by 200 million cubic feet (5.7 million cubic metres) per day in 1992.

New compression module being lifted into place at the South Morecambe field.

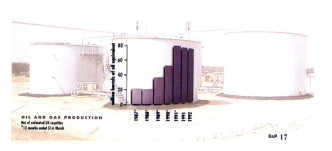

OIL AND GAS PRODUCTION
Net of estimated UK royalties
*12 months ended 31st March

E&P 17

Chart illustrating a reinsurance company's strong growth amid an environment of turmoil and change. From Centre Reinsurance 1992 annual report.

センター・リインシュランス社の1992年アニュアルレポートより、社会状況の混乱と変化の中で同保険会社が急成長している様子を表したグラフ。

U.S.A.   1993
CD: Frank Oswald
AD: Frank Oswald/David Dunkelberger
D: David Dunkelberger
DF: WYD Design Inc.
CL: Centre Reinsurance (Bermuda) Limited

Bar chart showing oil and gas production overlaid on a photographic background. From a British Gas E & P brochure.

ブリティッシュガスE&P社のパンフレットより、写真を背景に石油やガスの生産高を表した棒グラフ。

U.K.   1993
CD: Geoff Aldridge
D: Louise Haigh
I: Jon Tubman
DF: Communication by Design Ltd, London
CL: British Gas E & P

Graph showing changes in the numbers
and types of new medicines being tested
from 1989 through 1993. From U.S.
Pharmacist magazine.

「USファーマシストマガジン」より、1989
年から1993年にかけて試験が行なわれた
新薬の数と種類の推移を表すグラフ。

U.S.A.   1994
CD: Carey Crawford
I: Eliot Bergman
CL: Jobson Publishing

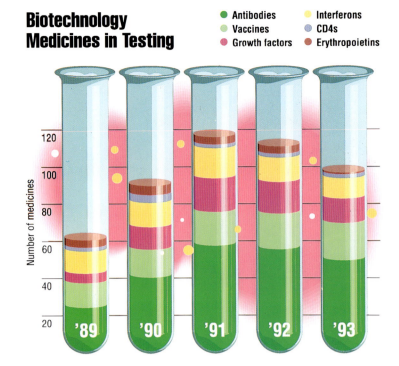

Biotechnology Medicines in Testing

- ● Antibodies
- ● Vaccines
- ● Growth factors
- ● Interferons
- ● CD4s
- ● Erythropoietins

Number of medicines

120
100
80
60
40
20

'89 '90 '91 '92 '93

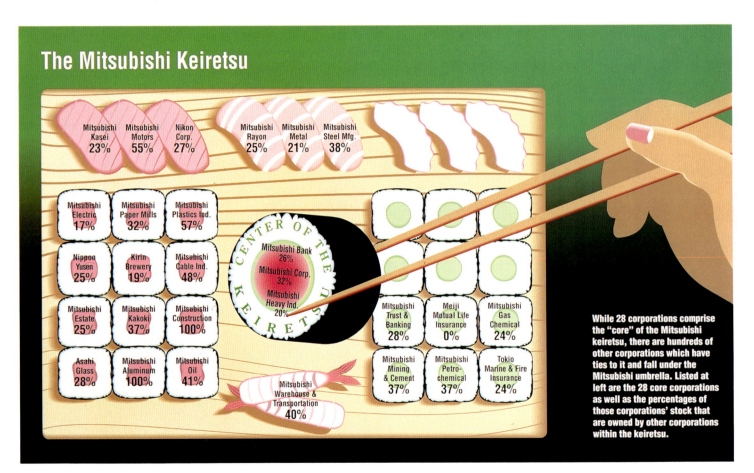

The Mitsubishi Keiretsu

Mitsubishi Kasei 23%
Mitsubishi Motors 55%
Nikon Corp. 27%

Mitsubishi Rayon 25%
Mitsubishi Metal 21%
Mitsubishi Steel Mfg. 38%

Mitsubishi Electric 17%
Mitsubishi Paper Mills 32%
Mitsubishi Plastics Ind. 57%

Nippon Yusen 25%
Kirin Brewery 19%
Mitsubishi Cable Ind. 48%

Mitsubishi Estate 25%
Mitsubishi Kakoki 37%
Mitsubishi Construction 100%

Asahi Glass 28%
Mitsubishi Aluminum 100%
Mitsubishi Oil 41%

CENTER OF THE KEIRETSU
Mitsubishi Bank 26%
Mitsubishi Corp. 32%
Mitsubishi Heavy Ind. 20%

Mitsubishi Warehouse & Transportation 40%

Mitsubishi Trust & Banking 28%
Meiji Mutual Life Insurance 0%
Mitsubishi Gas Chemical 24%

Mitsubishi Mining & Cement 37%
Mitsubishi Petro-chemical 37%
Tokio Marine & Fire Insurance 24%

While 28 corporations comprise
the "core" of the Mitsubishi
keiretsu, there are hundreds of
other corporations which have
ties to it and fall under the
Mitsubishi umbrella. Listed at
left are the 28 core corporations
as well as the percentages of
those corporations' stock that
are owned by other corporations
within the keiretsu.

Illustration of the Mitsubishi keiretsu
group, from Industry Week magazine.

「インダストリー・ウィーク・マガジン」よ
り、三菱グループの系列関係を表したダイ
アグラム。

U.S.A.   1992
CD: Nicolas Dankovich
I: Eliot Bergman
CL: Penton Publishing

Illustration of changes in eating habits.
From Cook's magazine.

「クックスマガジン」より、食習慣の変化を
表したイラスト。

U.S.A   1991
AD: C. Formisano
D: Mike Quon
I: Mike Quon
DF: Mike Quon Design Office, Inc.
CL: Cook's Magazine

Illustration of growth in meat consumption.
From Cook's magazine.

「クックスマガジン」より、肉の消費量の増
加を示すイラスト。

U.S.A   1991
CD: C. Formisano
AD: C. Formisano
D: Mike Quon
I: Mike Quon
DF: Mike Quon Design Office, Inc.
CL: Cook's Magazine

Illustration of changes in dessert orders.
From Cook's magazine.

「クックスマガジン」より、デザートの注文
内容の変化を表したイラスト。

U.S.A
AD: C. Formisano
D: Mike Quon
I: Mike Quon
DF: Mike Quon Design Office, Inc.
CL: Cook's Magazine

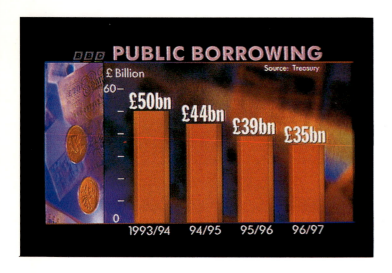

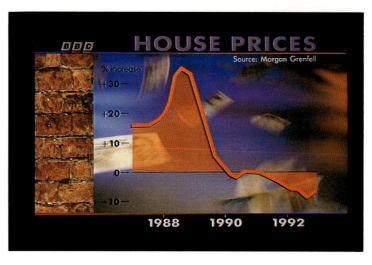

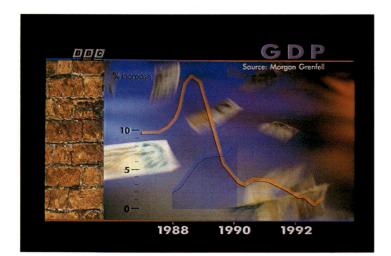

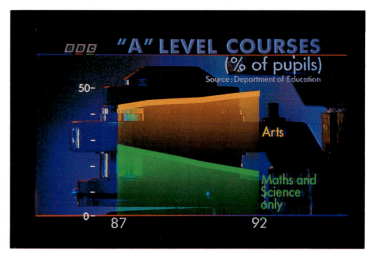

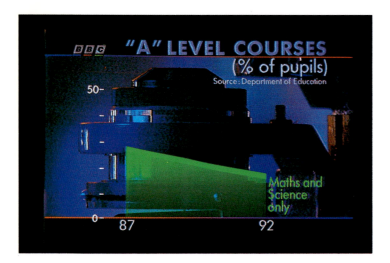

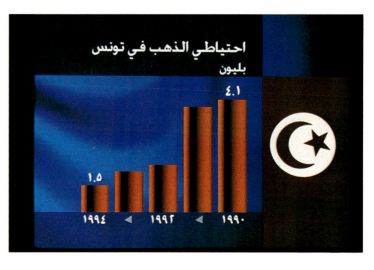

Graphs to illustrate BBC TV news and
documentary programmes.

BBCのニュースやドキュメンタリーの解説
用に制作されたグラフ。

U.K.   1994
D: BBC News, Graphic Design
CL: BBC News & Current Affairs/
BBC World Service Arabic TV News

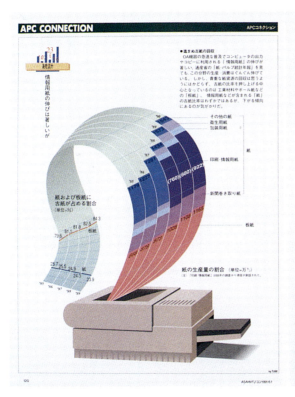

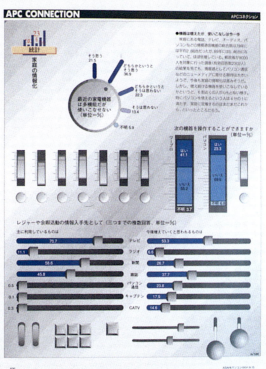

Graphs showing data on consumption of paper for office equipment and recycling of paper. From Asahi Shimbun's magazine 'ASAHI Personal Computing'.

朝日新聞社の「アサヒパソコン」誌より、OA機器用紙の消費と古紙の回収に関するグラフ。

Japan   1991
AD: Hiroyuki Kimura
D: Hiroyuki Kimura/Yoko Yabuta
CL: Asahi Shimbun

Graph illustrating article on domestic and imported wines. From Asahi Shimbun's AERA magazine.

朝日新聞社の「アエラ」誌より、ワイン市場における国産品と輸入品を比較する記事に使用されたグラフ。

Japan   1993
AD: Hiroyuki Kimura
D: Hiroyuki Kimura/Sachiko Hagiwara
CL: Asahi Shimbun

1

Graph showing growth in the cellular telephone market. From Pacific magazine.

「パシフィック・マガジン」より、移動電話市場の伸びを表すグラフ。

U.S.A.　1990
AD: Pentagram
D: Pentagram
I: Nigel Holmes
DF: Pentagram
CL: Pacific Telesis

2

Graph comparing the sales of three books. From Time magazine.

「タイム・マガジン」より、3冊の本の売上高を比較するグラフ。

U.S.A.　1991
AD: Nigel Holmes
D: Nigel Holmes
I: Nigel Holmes
CL: Time Magazine

3

Five-year growth charts of a restaurant development corporation showing system-wide revenues and number of restaurants. From a Brinker International annual report.

ブリンカー・インターナショナル社のアニュアルレポートより、レストラン事業会社5年間の発展の様子を、組織全体の収入やレストランの店舗数の推移で表したグラフ。

U.S.A.　1993
AD: Joe Rattan
D: Joe Rattan/Greg Morgan
I: Mary Langridge
DF: Joseph Rattan Design
CL: Brinker Internaitonal

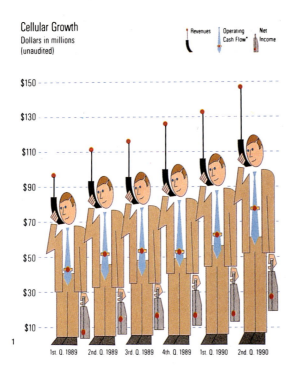

Cellular Growth
Dollars in millions
(unaudited)

Revenues　Operating Cash Flow*　Net Income

1st. Q. 1989　2nd. Q. 1989　3rd. Q. 1989　4th. Q. 1989　1st. Q. 1990　2nd. Q. 1990

1

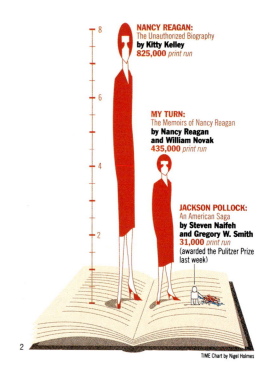

NANCY REAGAN:
The Unauthorized Biography
by Kitty Kelley
825,000 *print run*

MY TURN:
The Memoirs of Nancy Reagan
**by Nancy Reagan
and William Novak**
435,000 *print run*

JACKSON POLLOCK:
An American Saga
**by Steven Naifeh
and Gregory W. Smith**
31,000 *print run*
(awarded the Pulitzer Prize last week)

TIME Chart by Nigel Holmes

2

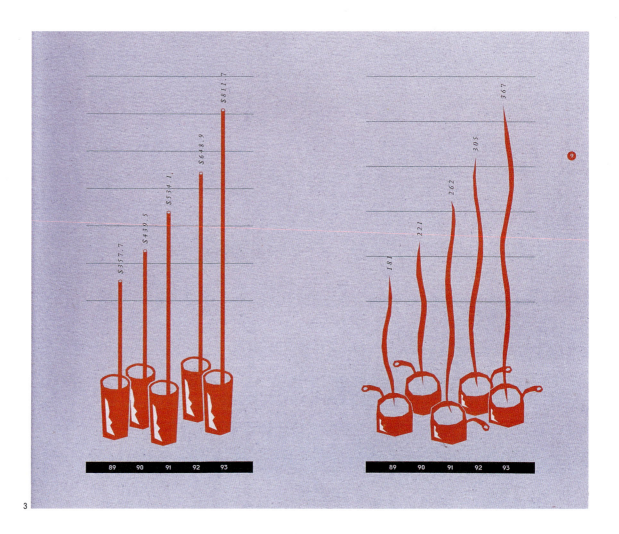

3

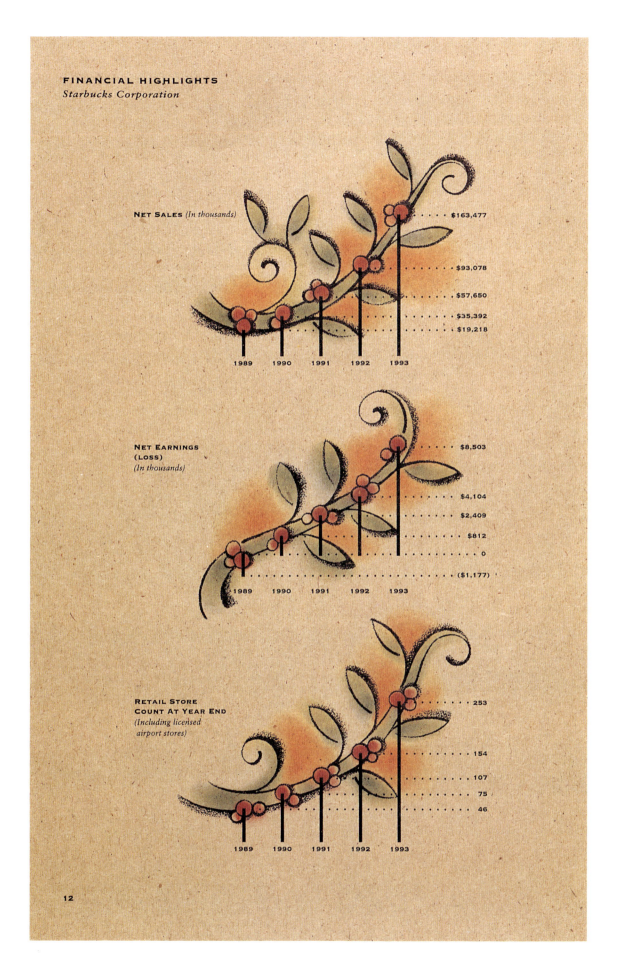

FINANCIAL HIGHLIGHTS
Starbucks Corporation

NET SALES *(In thousands)*

$163,477
$93,078
$57,650
$35,392
$19,218

1989 1990 1991 1992 1993

NET EARNINGS (LOSS) *(In thousands)*

$8,503
$4,104
$2,409
$812
0
($1,177)

1989 1990 1991 1992 1993

RETAIL STORE COUNT AT YEAR END *(Including licensed airport stores)*

253
154
107
75
46

1989 1990 1991 1992 1993

12

Coffee seedling illustration of financial highlights of a coffee processing company. From Starbucks 1993 annual report.

スターバックス社の1993年アニュアルレポートより、同社の主な財務内容を、コーヒーの苗木をモチーフにして表したグラフ。

U.S.A. 1994
AD: Jack Anderson
D: Jack Anderson/Julie Tanagi-Lock/
Bruce Branson-Meyer/
Mary Chin Hutchison
I: Julia LaPine
DF: Hornall Anderson Design Works
CL: Starbucks Coffee Company

Chart illustrating the cost of home improvements and percentage that can be recouped. From Correspondent magazine.

「コレスポンデント・マガジン」より、住宅の改築費と、その住宅の売却時に、改築にかかった費用の何割が戻って来るのかを表した棒グラフ。

U.S.A.　1994
AD: Louis Colescott
D: Nigel Holmes
I: Nigel Holmes
CL: Downey Weeks Toomey

Adding Value To Your Home

If you're daydreaming of a larger family room, another bath or a more functional kitchen, it may be time to remodel your home.

But how do you turn your house into a dream home and not a money pit?

"Homeowners should consider putting on an addition—whether it's a new kitchen, screened porch or a family room—when they see that their neighbors' homes or newer homes are having these additions or improvements," says Miami real estate analyst Michael Y. Cannon, president of Appraisal and Real Estate Economics Associates.

Rather than "keeping up with the Joneses," improving your home is a good way to protect your investment. Yet you need to remodel appropriately for the neighborhood. Instead of adding a Tara-like columned facade to a modest one-story ranch, enlarging a bathroom or building on a pretty deck would probably make more sense.

Kitchen Remodeling Tips

■ Plan a recycling area in your kitchen. More than one-third of all kitchen remodelings include space for recycling.

■ Don't spend too much on customized cabinetry. Simple roll-out drawers are better. You can get to what's in back and there's no dead space.

■ Trim costs by keeping existing appliances if they are in good condition.

Source: National Kitchen & Bath Association.

Bath Remodeling Tips

■ Pay attention to storage when remodeling a bath. Most older baths don't have enough.

■ Tile bathroom walls to the ceiling so you never have to paint or wallpaper above the tile.

■ Most older baths need more light. If privacy is a concern, try glass block panels which are semi-opaque and diminish the need for light-inhibiting curtains.

Source: National Kitchen & Bath Association.

To get fresh ideas as well as to learn which features attract buyers, homeowners should check out new homes. "But," warns Cannon, "avoid features so customized to personal taste that they may not be marketable."

How long should you plan to remain in your home to get a monetary return on a remodeling project? Cannon says the average home ownership is 10 to 12 years, but "people shouldn't consider their home merely as an investment. They should enjoy it."

Nationally, kitchens and baths are the most frequently remodeled rooms and bring the greatest return on the investment if homeowners use a qualified designer and quality products, says Paul Kohmescher, executive director of the National Kitchen & Bath Association (NKBA).

However, Kohmescher advises against overimproving a kitchen or bath. The most expensive refrigerator or the biggest hot tub may be a waste of money if you don't plan to stay in your home very long.

One great investment is adding a bath to a one or one-and-a-half bathroom house, realtors say.

Remodeling a kitchen—including new cabinets, appliances, tile, electrical and plumbing—is expensive. Most kitchen experts say that a modest kitchen remodeling project averages around $20,000. However, even a minor kitchen make over can lift a homeowner's spirits and offers a large potential payoff if a home is sold.

It's also wise to be conservative when choosing colors and materials for a new kitchen or bath. Ellen Cheever, a nationally known kitchen designer and author based in Wilmington, Delaware, says that white cabinets in the kitchen and white tile and fixtures in the bath are safe choices and the most popular nationwide.

"The place to be adventuresome is along the back splash, wall treatments or area rugs, those items that are changeable," says Cheever.

Don't confine your remodeling ideas simply to the interior of your home. Minor investments in landscaping can quickly improve your home's appearance.

But what if the kids are begging for a swimming pool. Is it a good investment?

"A pool is almost a liability rather than an asset because of the maintenance involved," says Debra Reed, president of Reed Pools in Oakland Park, Florida.

Whatever you decide to do to your home, remember to make it pleasing to the eye and the pocketbook. ◆

HOME IMPROVEMENTS
The cost of some popular additions, and the percent you can expect to recoup when you sell your house.

New siding — TOTAL COST $8,592 — WHAT YOU WILL RECOUP 67% ($5,715)
New windows — $7,344 — 71% ($5,199)
Sun space addition — TOTAL COST $21,968 — 71% ($15,616)
Deck addition — $6,312 — 77% ($4,863)
Attic bedroom — $21,309 — 84% ($18,002)
Master suite — $19,210 — 85% ($16,400)
Family room addition — $28,736 — 86% ($24,666)

Source: Remodeling Magazine (percentages rounded)
Illustration: Nigel Holmes

The staff of the Metropolitan Police Service. From a Metropolitan Police Service brochure.

ロンドン警察のパンフレットより、同警察の人員構成に関するグラフ。

U.K.　1993
CD: Geoff Aldridge
D: Sally Mcintosh
DF: Communication by Design Ltd.
CL: Metropolitan Police Service

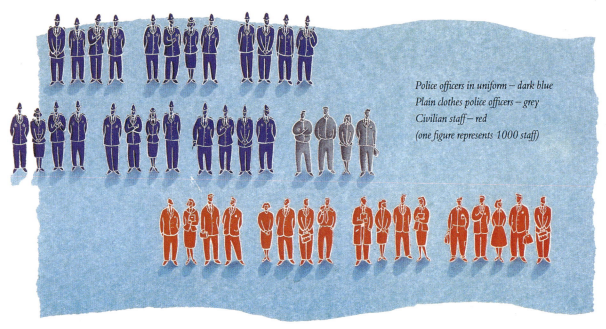

Police officers in uniform – dark blue
Plain clothes police officers – grey
Civilian staff – red
(one figure represents 1000 staff)

衣食住のバランスを保とう
24%対46%
住関心 東京：パリ

あなたは住まいの何にこだわりますか
100対67
動線 対 美（東京）

住まいとのふれあいが、住まいの愛着を育てます
20人に1人
自分の部屋の掃除をする日本の小学生

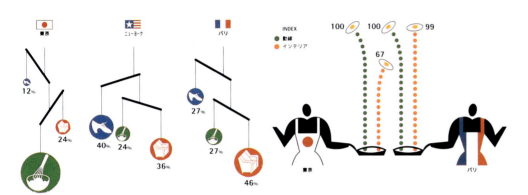

衣食住の関心度
食関心は高いけれど、住関心は低い東京人
資料：都市生活研究所

台所に対するこだわり指数
機能だけにこだわる日本、美にもこだわるパリ
資料：都市生活研究所

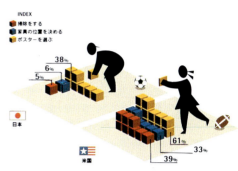

子ども部屋の管理を行う小学生
住まいとの触れ合いが少ない、日本の子ども
資料：大阪市立大学 北浦かほる

住まいの健康が、あなたの健康です
2050匹
じゅうたん1m²あたり

あなたのためにも、高齢者にやさしい住まいを考えてください
13%から56%へ
視力の老化を感じる 30代以下→40代

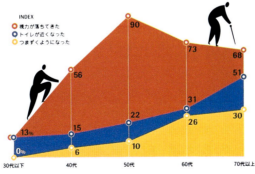

住まいにいるダニの数
身の廻りにダニはこれだけ住んでいます
資料：吉川翠「ダニ・カビ・結露」

老化を感じる人の割合
老化は意外と早くやってきます
資料：都市生活研究所

Graphs comparing attitudes of people in selected countries on Issues related to home life. From a publication about Japanese people's lifestyle published by Urban Life Research Institute of Tokyo Gas Co , Ltd.

東京ガス社都市生活研究所発行の「日本人の住まい方データ集」より、各国民の住居に関する意識についてのグラフ。

Japan   1994
AD: Kenzo Nakagawa
D: Hiroyasu Nobuyama/
Satoshi Morikami/Norika Nakayama
DF: NDC Graphics Inc.
CL: Urban Life Research Institute,
Tokyo Gas Co., Ltd.

Graphs showing attitudes towards home
interior decoration, from Living Design
Center Corporation publicity material.

リビングデザインセンター社のダイレクト
メールより、家庭内の室内装飾に関する意
識を表すグラフ。

Japan   1994
AD: Kenzo Nakagawa
D: Satoshi Morikami/Norika Nakayama
P: Norio Innami
DF: NDC Graphics Inc.
CL: Living Design Center Corporation

74.9%

絵画を飾っている家庭

43.5%

28.4%

飾りつけに夫が全く参加しない家庭

来客時に飾りものを換える家庭

TOTAL ASSETS
(billions of dollars)

20
16
12
8
4

89 90 91 92 **93**

NET INCOME
(millions of dollars)

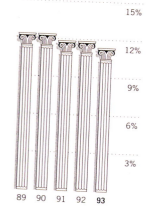

150
120
90
60
30

89 90 91 92 **93**

RETURN ON COMMON EQUITY
(percent)

15%
12%
9%
6%
3%

89 90 91 92 **93**

GROWTH IN SHAREHOLDERS' EQUITY
(millions of dollars)

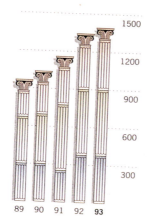

1500
1200
900
600
300

89 90 91 92 **93**

▪ Retained Earnings
▫ Common Shares
▪ Preferred Shares

1

Protection of kyoto arts

日本国宝の宝庫、京都。

227
219
197
365

1
Bar graphs illustrating financial data. From London Insurance Group 1993 annual report.

ロンドン・インシュランスグループの1993年アニュアルレポートより、財務に関するデータを表す棒グラフ。

Canada   1993
AD: Roslyn Eskind/Donna Gedeon
D: Donna Gedeon
I: Maggi Cash
DF: Eskind Waddell
CL: London Insurance Group

2
Graph using Buddhist images to illustrate data on protection of works of art in Kyoto.

仏像をモチーフにした、京都の芸術保護に関するグラフ。

Japan   1994
CD: Yurio Seki
AD: Yurio Seki
D: Yurio Seki
I: Yurio Seki

2

Table showing regional di
Dutch government agency
technical projects. From
annual report.

センター社の1993年アニ
より、オランダ政府機関の
ト予算の地域配分を表した

Netherlands 1994
CD: Andrew Fallon
AD: Andrew Fallon
D: Andrew Fallon
I: Andrew Fallon
DF: Tel Design
CL: Senter

Table of quick-reference product
information, attached to K2 snowboards
as a sticker.

K2スノーボードに貼付されるシールに印
刷された、製品についての早見表。

U.S.A. 1994
CD: Brent Turner
AD: Vittorio Costarella
D: Vittorio Costarella
I: Vittorio Costarella
DF: Modern Dog
CL: K2 Snowboards

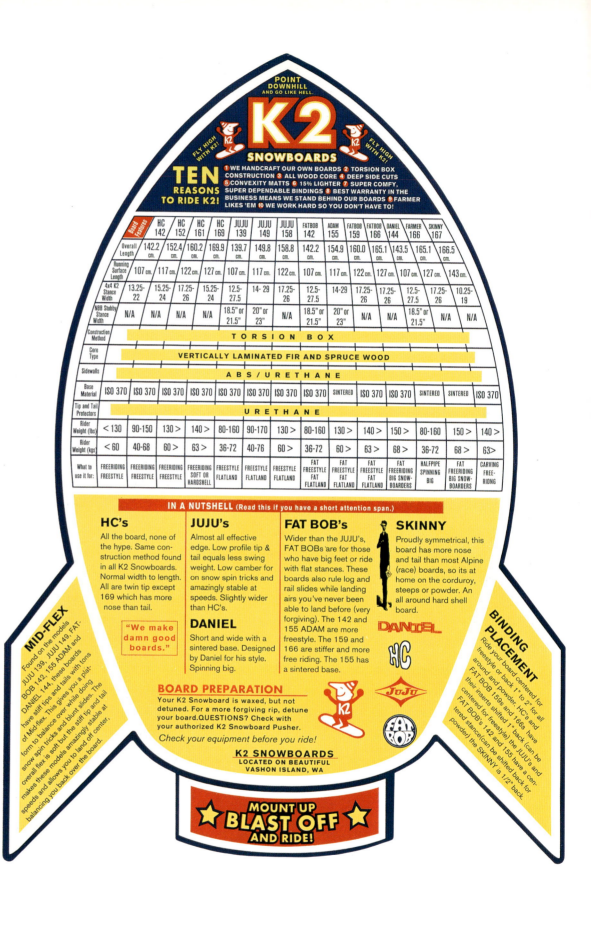

TOTAL ASSETS
(billions of dollars)

NET INCOME
(millions of dollars)

RETURN ON
COMMON EQUITY
(percent)

GROWTH IN
SHAREHOLDERS' EQUITY
(millions of dollars)

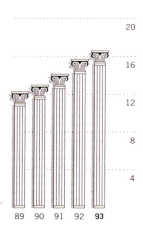

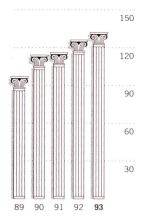

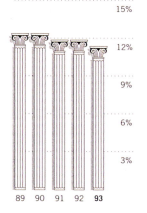

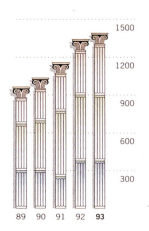

20		
16		
12		
8		
4		

89 90 91 92 **93**

150
120
90
60
30

89 90 91 92 **93**

15%
12%
9%
6%
3%

89 90 91 92 **93**

1500
1200
900
600
300

89 90 91 92 **93**

■ Retained Earnings
■ Common Shares
■ Preferred Shares

1

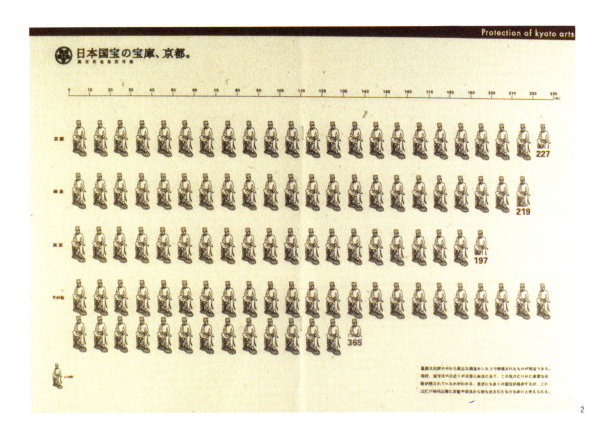

Protection of kyoto arts

日本国宝の宝庫、京都。

227
219
197
365

1

Bar graphs illustrating financial data.
From London Insurance Group 1993
annual report.

ロンドン・インシュランスグループの1993
年アニュアルレポートより、財務に関する
データを表す棒グラフ。

Canada   1993
AD: Roslyn Eskind/Donna Gedeon
D: Donna Gedeon
I: Maggi Cash
DF: Eskind Waddell
CL: London Insurance Group

2

Graph using Buddhist images to illustrate
data on protection of works of art in Kyoto.

仏像をモチーフにした、京都の芸術保護に
関するグラフ。

Japan   1994
CD: Yurio Seki
AD: Yurio Seki
D: Yurio Seki
I: Yurio Seki

2

Table showing regional distribution of a Dutch government agency's budget for technical projects. From Senter 1993 annual report.

センター社の1993年アニュアルレポートより、オランダ政府機関の工業プロジェクト予算の地域配分を表した一覧表。

Netherlands 1994
CD: Andrew Fallon
AD: Andrew Fallon
D: Andrew Fallon
I: Andrew Fallon
DF: Tel Design
CL: Senter

2.6.4 Regionale verdeling van de TOK- en PBTS-budgetten

Provincie	Technische ontwikkelingskrediet		Programmatische bedrijfsgerichte technologiestimulering	
	Aantal toegezegde kredieten	Toegezegd kredietbedrag in miljoenen guldens	Aantal toegezegde subsidies	Toegezegd subsidiebedrag in miljoenen guldens
Groningen	0	–	5	0,86
Friesland	1	1,2	10	2,11
Drenthe	3	2,2	1	0,07
Overijssel	6	14,0	26	6,93
Gelderland	11	10,0	47	16,48
Utrecht	9	2,5	23	5,37
Noord-Holland	5	29,7	42	12,8
Zuid-Holland	22	46,8	59	21,27
Zeeland	1	0,1	4	3,69
Noord-Brabant	10	5,0	59	20,39
Limburg	4	21,0	32	17,63
Flevoland	2	1,2	0	–
Totaal	74	133,7	308	107,6

Een indicatie van de regionale spreiding van innovatie in het Nederlandse bedrijfsleven, vormt de verdeling van toekenningen over de provincies in TOK- en PBTS-verband. In het jaarverslag over 1994 zal een meer uitgebreide analyse op dit punt worden opgenomen. Daarbij zullen ook de dan beschikbare resultaten van de wet bevordering speur- en ontwikkelingswerk (WBSO) worden meegenomen.

27

Table showing possible applications for company products. From International Rectifier Corporation 1993 annual report.

インターナショナル・レクティフィア社の1993年アニュアルレポートより、同社製品の応用方法を表した表。

U.S.A.   1993
AD: Jim Berte
D: Maria Dellota/Jim Berte
DF: Runyan Hinsche Associates
CL: International Rectifier Corporation

IR Product Opportunities

Energy-Sensitive Applications

	IGBTs	IGBT Modules	MOSFETs	MOSFET Modules	Power ICs	HEXFREDs	Rectifiers	SCRs	Micro-Elec. Relays
Variable-speed HVAC	●				●	●			
Efficient refrigerators	●				●	●			
Electronic fluorescent lighting			●		●				
Electronic ignition	●		●		●				
Fuel injection			●		●				
Electric vehicles (EVs)	●	●		●		●			
Public transportation EV		●				●	●	●	
EV recharging stations	●	●			●	●	●		
Utility load mgmt systems	●							●	
Utility power-condition equipment		●				●		●	
Sensors			●		●				●
Hand tools	●		●		●	●			
Industrial motor controls	●	●	●		●		●	●	
Uninterruptible power supplies	●	●	●	●	●	●	●	●	

Table of the 10 top-ranking computer systems installed in the US as of 1 January,1990 (by value). From ECS 1989 annual report.

ECS社の1989年アニュアルレポートより、1990年1月1日現在、アメリカに設置されたコンピューターシステムの売上高ベストテンに関する表。

France 1990
CD: Alain Lachartre
AD: Alain Lachartre
D: Philippe Caron/Cyril Cabry
I: Philippe Caron/Cyril Cabry
CL: ECS

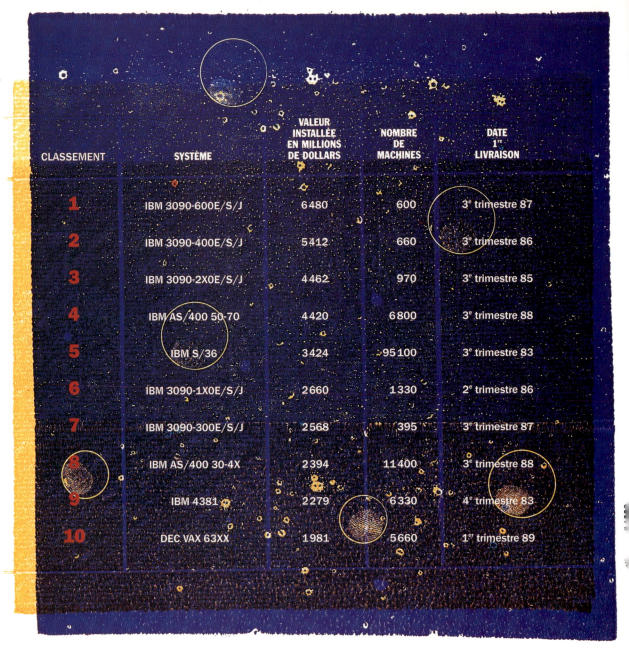

CLASSEMENT	SYSTÈME	VALEUR INSTALLÉE EN MILLIONS DE DOLLARS	NOMBRE DE MACHINES	DATE 1re LIVRAISON
1	IBM 3090-600E/S/J	6480	600	3e trimestre 87
2	IBM 3090-400E/S/J	5412	660	3e trimestre 86
3	IBM 3090-2X0E/S/J	4462	970	3e trimestre 85
4	IBM AS/400 50-70	4420	6800	3e trimestre 88
5	IBM S/36	3424	95100	3e trimestre 83
6	IBM 3090-1X0E/S/J	2660	1330	2e trimestre 86
7	IBM 3090-300E/S/J	2568	395	3e trimestre 87
8	IBM AS/400 30-4X	2394	11400	3e trimestre 88
9	IBM 4381	2279	6330	4e trimestre 83
10	DEC VAX 63XX	1981	5660	1er trimestre 89

Table showing major markets for industrial gases. From Air Products and Chemicals, Inc. 1991 annual report.

エア・プロダクツ＆ケミカル社の1991年アニュアルレポートより、産業用ガスの主な市場を表した表。

U.S.A. 1991
CD: Steve Ferrari
D: Janet Scanlon
I: Janet Scanlon
DF: The Graphic Expression
CL: Air Products and Chemicals, Inc.

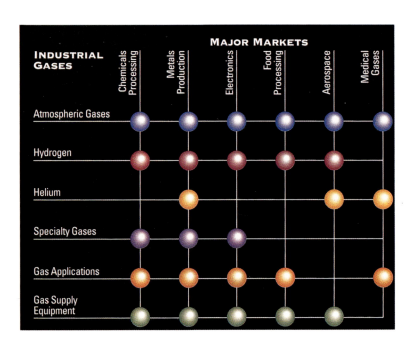

C hart illustrating consumption of small items (postage stamps, cups of coffee) over a five-year Dutch government project. From NaBoNT final report.

NaBontの最終報告書より、5年間にわるオランダ政府プロジェクトの期間中、小物（郵便切手、コーヒーなど）がどれだけ消費されたかを表す表。

Netherlands   1992
CD: Paul Vermijs
AD: Jaco Emmen
D: Jaco Emmen
I: Jaco Emmen
DF: Tel Design
CL: NaBoNT

TIJD TUSSEN AANMELDING DOCENT EN BETALING AAN DE SCHOOL	UITGEGEVEN NaBoNT PREMIUMS	UREN POSTBEHANDELING
AANMELDING - BETALING GEM. 8 WEKEN	SPELDEN 39	0,5 DAG PER DAG (1 PERSOON)
AANVRAAG BETALING - BETALING DOOR NaBoNT GEM. 4 WEKEN	BROCHES 26	=638 DAGEN
	WIJN 151	≈2,9 MENSJAAR
	ONDERZETTERS 537	
	WUPPIES 3.000	**AANTAL FORMULIEREN**
	BONBONS (PER 4) 2.025	**PER NAGESCHOOLDE DOCENT**
		(VAN AANMELDING TOT
		BETALING AAN SCHOOL)
		≈6 FORMULIEREN

KLEINVERBRUIK
Projektburo NaBoNT

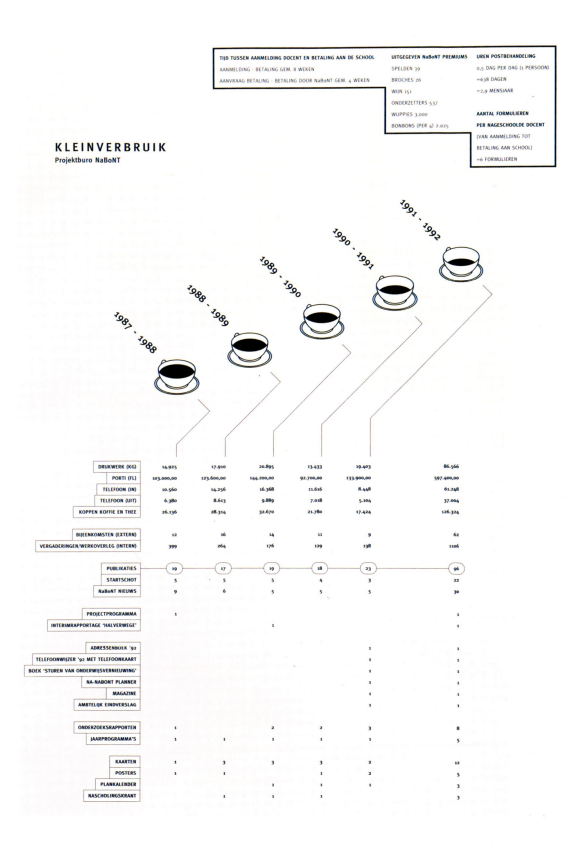

	1987 - 1988	1988 - 1989	1989 - 1990	1990 - 1991	1991 - 1992	
DRUKWERK (KG)	14.925	17.910	20.895	13.433	19.403	86.566
PORTI (FL)	103.000,00	123.600,00	144.200,00	92.700,00	133.900,00	597.400,00
TELEFOON (IN)	10.560	14.256	16.368	11.616	8.448	61.248
TELEFOON (UIT)	6.380	8.613	9.889	7.018	5.104	37.004
KOPPEN KOFFIE EN THEE	26.136	28.314	32.670	21.780	17.424	126.324
BIJEENKOMSTEN (EXTERN)	12	16	14	11	9	62
VERGADERINGEN/WERKOVERLEG (INTERN)	399	264	176	129	138	1106
PUBLIKATIES	19	17	19	18	23	96
STARTSCHOT	5	5	5	4	3	22
NaBoNT NIEUWS	9	6	5	5	5	30
PROJECTPROGRAMMA	1					1
INTERIMRAPPORTAGE 'HALVERWEGE'			1			1
ADRESSENBOEK '92					1	1
TELEFOONWIJZER '92 MET TELEFOONKAART					1	1
BOEK 'STUREN VAN ONDERWIJSVERNIEUWING'					1	1
NA-NABONT PLANNER					1	1
MAGAZINE					1	1
AMBTELIJK EINDVERSLAG					1	1
ONDERZOEKSRAPPORTEN	1		2	2	3	8
JAARPROGRAMMA'S	1	1	1	1	1	5
KAARTEN	1	3	3	3	2	12
POSTERS	1	1		1	2	5
PLANKALENDER			1	1	1	3
NASCHOLINGSKRANT		1	1	1		3

Table of quick-reference product information, attached to K2 snowboards as a sticker.

K2スノーボードに貼付されるシールに印刷された、製品についての早見表。

U.S.A.   1994
CD: Brent Turner
AD: Vittorio Costarella
D: Vittorio Costarella
I: Vittorio Costarella
DF: Modern Dog
CL: K2 Snowboards

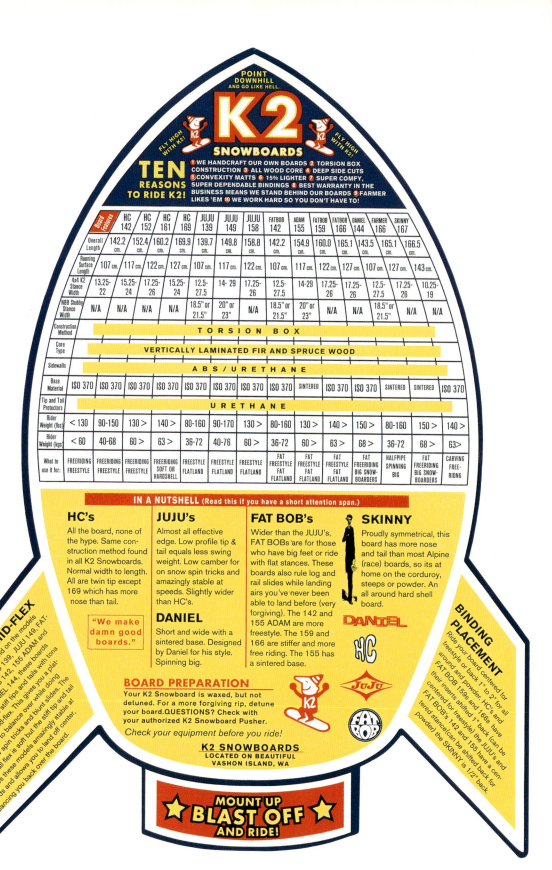

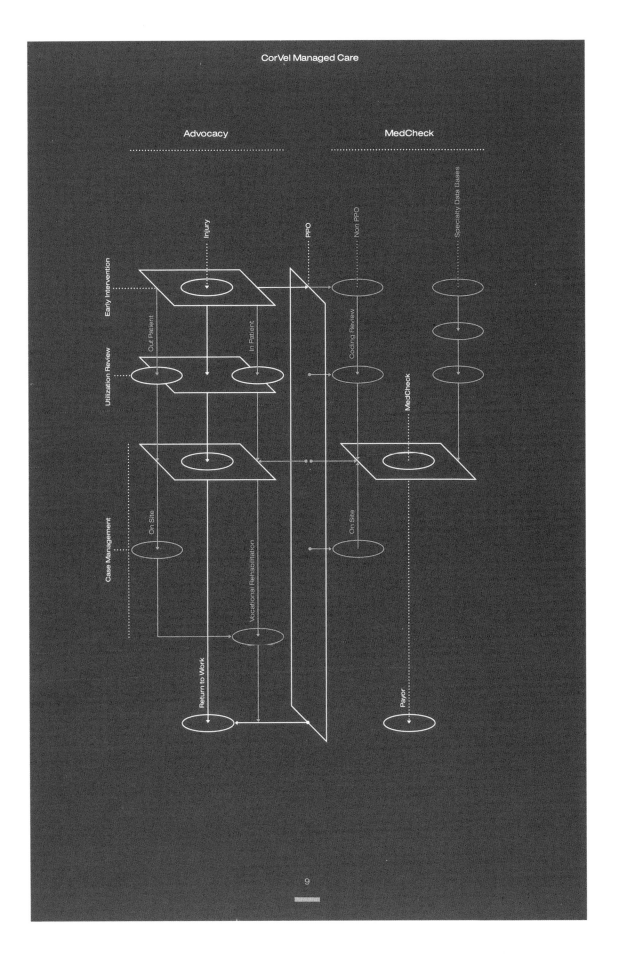

CorVel Managed Care

Advocacy　　　　　　　　MedCheck

9

Flow chart detailing CorVel Managed
Care. From CorVel Corporation 1992
annual report.

コーヴェル社の1992年アニュアルレポー
トより、同社の健康管理システムサービス
を詳しく説明するフローチャート。

U.S.A.　　1992
AD: James Guerard
D: James Guerard
I: Cathie Bleck
DF: Runyan Hinsche Associates
CL: CorVel Corporation

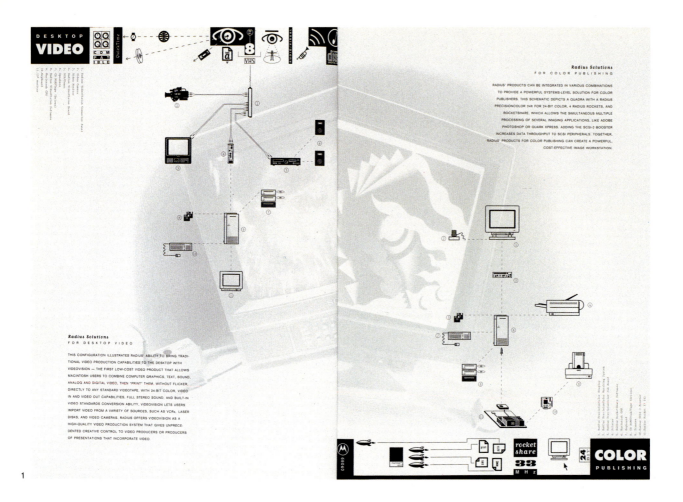

Radius Solutions
FOR COLOR PUBLISHING

RADIUS' PRODUCTS CAN BE INTEGRATED IN VARIOUS COMBINATIONS
TO PROVIDE A POWERFUL SYSTEMS-LEVEL SOLUTION FOR COLOR
PUBLISHERS. THIS SCHEMATIC DEPICTS QUADRA WITH A RADIUS
PRECISIONCOLOR 24X FOR 24-BIT COLOR, 4 RADIUS ROCKETS, AND
ROCKETSHARE, WHICH ALLOWS THE SIMULTANEOUS MULTIPLE
PROCESSING OF SEVERAL IMAGING APPLICATIONS, LIKE ADOBE
PHOTOSHOP OR QUARK XPRESS. ADDING THE SCSI-2 BOOSTER
INCREASES DATA THROUGHPUT TO SCSI PERIPHERALS. TOGETHER,
RADIUS' PRODUCTS FOR COLOR PUBLISHING CAN CREATE A POWERFUL,
COST-EFFECTIVE IMAGE WORKSTATION.

Radius Solutions
FOR DESKTOP VIDEO

THIS CONFIGURATION ILLUSTRATES RADIUS' ABILITY TO BRING TRADI-
TIONAL VIDEO PRODUCTION CAPABILITIES TO THE DESKTOP WITH
VIDEOVISION — THE FIRST LOW-COST VIDEO PRODUCT THAT ALLOWS
MACINTOSH USERS TO COMBINE COMPUTER GRAPHICS, TEXT, SOUND,
ANALOG AND DIGITAL VIDEO, THEN "PRINT" THEM, WITHOUT FLICKER,
DIRECTLY TO ANY STANDARD VIDEOTAPE. WITH 24-BIT COLOR, VIDEO
IN AND VIDEO OUT CAPABILITIES, FULL STEREO SOUND, AND BUILT-IN
VIDEO STANDARDS CONVERSION ABILITY, VIDEOVISION LETS USERS
IMPORT VIDEO FROM A VARIETY OF SOURCES, SUCH AS VCRs, LASER
DISKS, AND VIDEO CAMERAS. RADIUS OFFERS VIDEOVISION AS A
HIGH-QUALITY VIDEO PRODUCTION SYSTEM THAT GIVES UNPRECE-
DENTED CREATIVE CONTROL TO VIDEO PRODUCERS OR PRODUCERS
OF PRESENTATIONS THAT INCORPORATE VIDEO.

1

BALANCED GROWTH

Komag pursues growth through
the balanced management of
three key elements.

Superior Technology:
serving large and growing
markets that demand techni-
cally advanced products.

Cost-effective Capacity:
manufacturing high-quality
products in large volumes
at competitive costs.

Strong Financial Resources:
supporting corporate growth.

2

1
Diagrams of a graphic systems company's
configurations for desktop video and color
publishing. From Radius Inc. 1992 annual
report.

レイディアス社の1992年アニュアルレ
ポートより、グラフィック・システム会社
が開発したデスクトップ・ビデオとカラー
印刷のシステムを説明した機能図。

U.S.A.   1993
CD: Steve Tolleson
AD: Steve Tolleson
D: Steve Tolleson/Mark Winn
I: Tolleson Design
DF: Tolleson Design
CL: Radius Inc.

2
Diagram showing significant corporate
events contributing to balanced growth.
From Komag, Inc. 1991 annual report.

コマッグ社の1991年アニュアルレポートよ
り、均整のとれた企業発展のために同社にと
って重要な要素を表したダイアグラム。

U.S.A.   1992
CD: Steve Tolleson
AD: Steve Tolleson
D: Steve Tolleson/Mark Winn
I: Jeff Kogel
DF: Tolleson Design
CL: Komag, Inc.

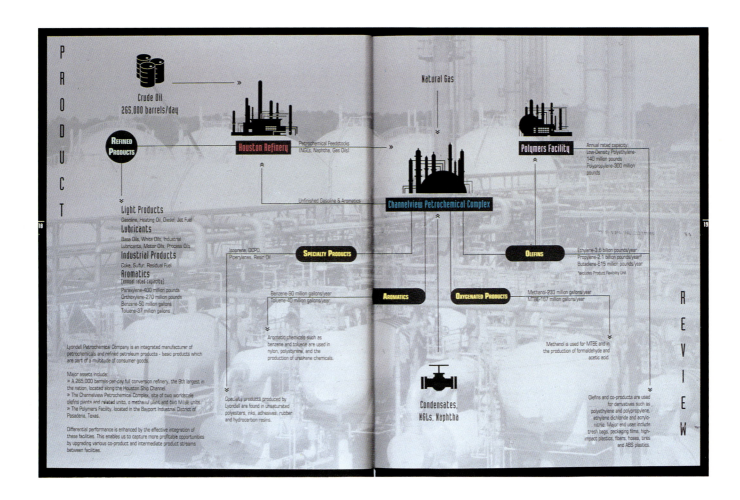

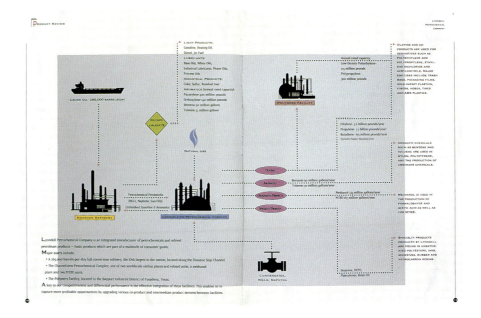

Product review flow charts from Lyondell Petrochemical Company's annual reports for 1992 (above) and 1991 (below).

ロインデル・ペトロケミカル社の製品検査の方法を表したフローチャート。上: 同社の1992年アニュアルレポートより。下: 1991年同レポートより。

U.S.A. 1992
CD: Peat Jariya
AD: Peat Jariya
D: Peat Jariya/Scott Head
DF: Peat Jariya Design
CL: Lyondell Petrochemical Company

Chronological chart showing rental equipment inventory and major corporate events. From Electro Rent Corporation 1994 annual report.

エレクトロ・レント社の1994年アニュアルレポートより、レンタル用品の商品目録と主な企業イベントを年代順に表わした年表。

U.S.A.   1994
AD: Jim Berte
D: Maria Dellota/Jim Berte
DF: Runyan Hinsche Associates
CL: Electro Rent Corporation

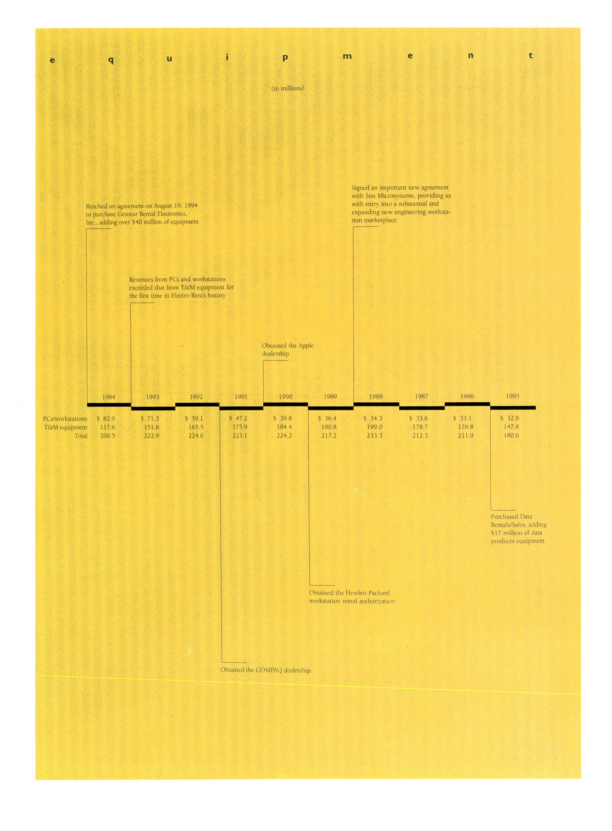

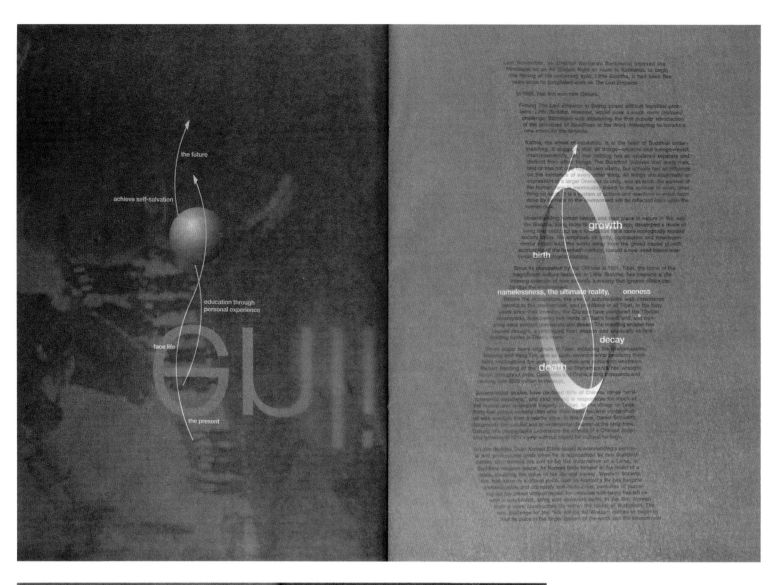

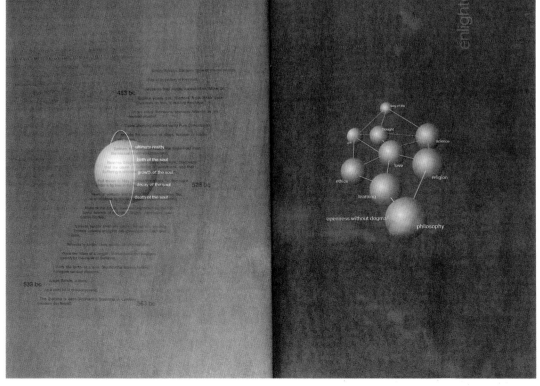

Topic illustrations for a MÂP magazine feature related to Buddhism.

「マップ・マガジン」の仏教特集のための主題図。

U.S.A.　1993
CD: Robert Bergman-Ungar
AD: Robert Bergman-Ungar
D: Robert Bergman-Ungar
DF: Art W/O Borders
CL: MÂP Publications

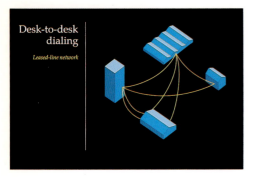

Desk-to-desk
dialing

Leased-line network

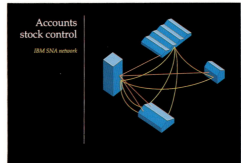

Accounts
stock control

IBM SNA network

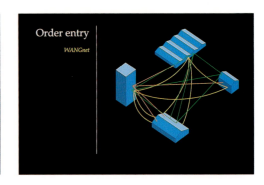

Order entry

WANGnet

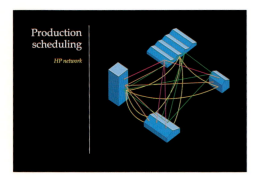

Production
scheduling

HP network

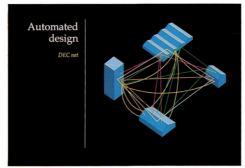

Automated
design

DEC net

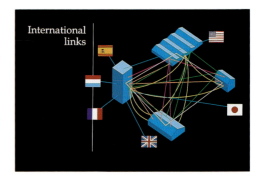

International
links

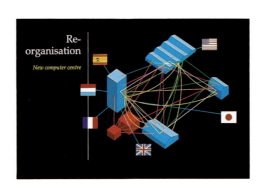

Re-
organisation

New computer centre

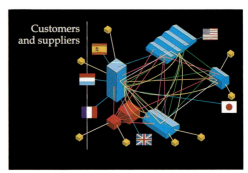

Customers
and suppliers

Sequence of visuals to illustrate the lack of I.T.synergy and integration due to specialist but uncoordinated implementation of systems over time. From an Andersen Consulting publication.

アンダーセン・コンサルティング社の発行
物より、専門性には富んでいるが、整合性
のない機器類を少しづつ導入したために、
IT（インフォメーション・テクノロジー）の共
通化と調整が図れないことを視覚化して説
明した関係図。

U.K.   1993
CD: John Rushworth, Pentagram
AD: John Rushworth, Pentagram
D: Alistair Kennedy,
The Presentation Company
I: Alistair Kennedy,
The Presentation Company
DF: The Presentation Company
CL: Andersen Consulting

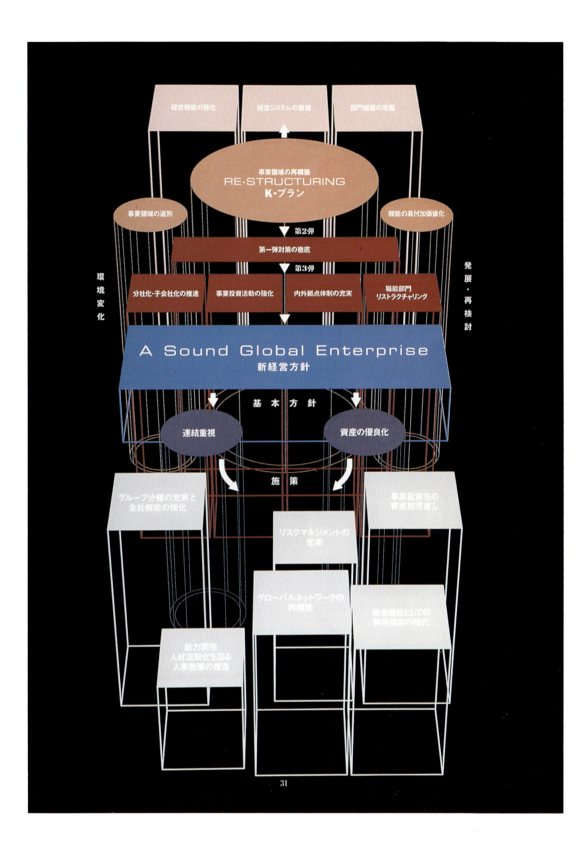

Flow chart illustrating management strategy, from Mitsubishi Corporation corporate profile.

三菱商事社の会社案内より、同社の経営戦略を表したフローチャート。

Japan   1994
D: Gento Matsumoto
DF: Saru Brunei Co., Ltd.
CL: Mitsubishi Corporation

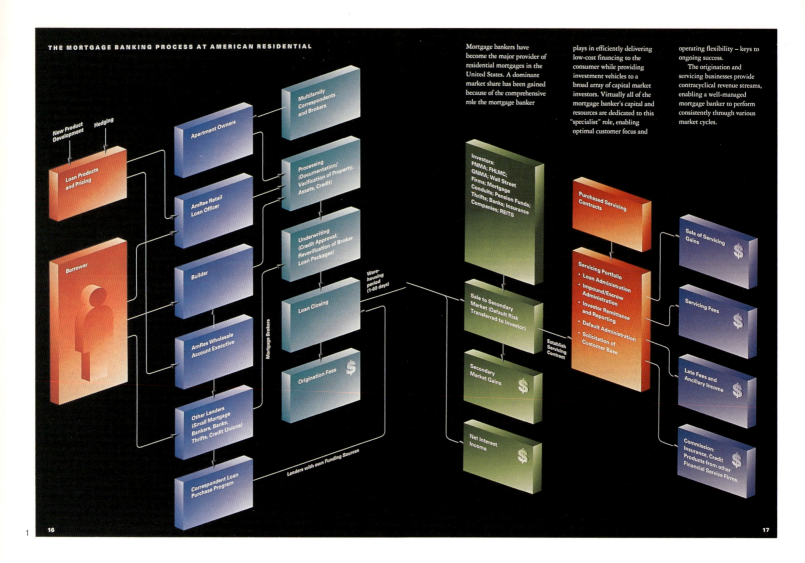

THE MORTGAGE BANKING PROCESS AT AMERICAN RESIDENTIAL

Mortgage bankers have become the major provider of residential mortgages in the United States. A dominant market share has been gained because of the comprehensive role the mortgage banker plays in efficiently delivering low-cost financing to the consumer while providing investment vehicles to a broad array of capital market investors. Virtually all of the mortgage banker's capital and resources are dedicated to this "specialist" role, enabling optimal customer focus and operating flexibility – keys to ongoing success.

The origination and servicing businesses provide contracyclical revenue streams, enabling a well-managed mortgage banker to perform consistently through various market cycles.

1 16

17

1

Flow chart illustrating the mortgage banking business. From American Residential Holding Corporation 1993 annual report.

アメリカン・レジデンシャル・ホールディング社の1993年アニュアルレポートより、モーゲージ金融業についてのフローチャート。

U.S.A.   1993
CD: Carl Seltzer
AD: Carl Seltzer
D: Carl Seltzer/Luis Alvarado
DF: Carl Seltzer Design Office
CL: American Residential Holding Corp.

2

Flow chart of printig procedures, comparing former methods with new methods using DTP or CEPS. From a Fukuhaku Sogo Printing Company brochure.

福博綜合印刷会社の会社案内より、印刷作業の流れにおける、従来の方法とDTPとCEPSでおこなう新しい方法とを比較したフローチャート。

Japan   1994
CD: Koichi Demura
AD: Nobuo Nakagaki
D: Nobuo Nakagaki/Kaoru Mitsuhashi
CL: Fukuhaku Sogo Printing Co., Ltd.

2

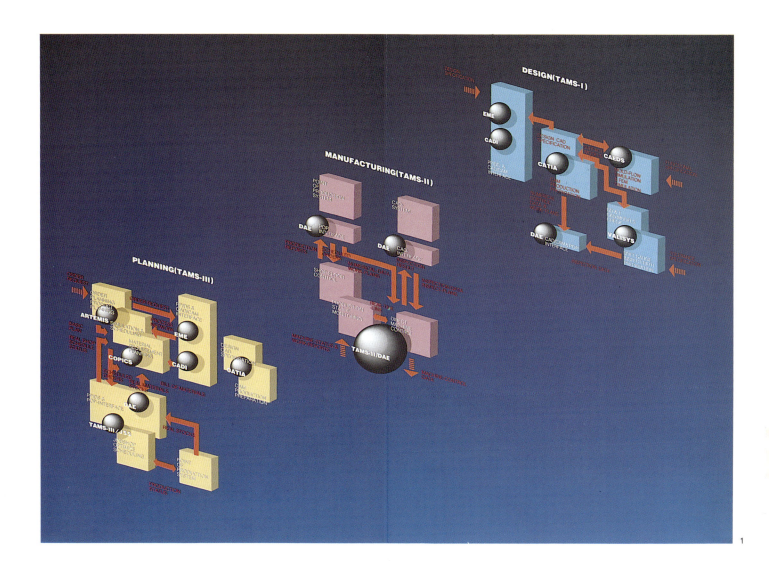

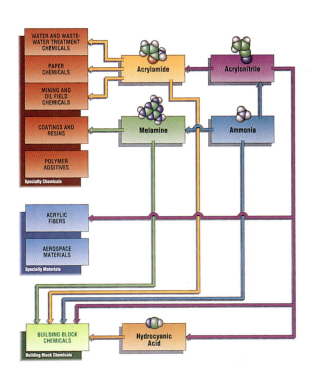

1
Flow chart illustraing activities of a company providing computer-related services. From a TAM corpoation brochure.

TAM社の業務案内より、同コンピュータ関連会社のサービス内容を説明するフローチャート。

Japan   1990
CD: Koichi Shinozaki
AD: Naoki Sato
D: Hiroto Kobayashi
DF: Shoeisha Design Lab
CL: TAM Corporation

2
Flow chart showing the uses of a chemical manufacturer's products. From Cytec Industries Inc.1994 annual report.

サイテック・インダストリー社の1994年アニュアルレポートより、化学工業製品の用途を表したフローチャート。

U.S.A.   1993
CD: Gil Roessner
D: Leslie Dawson
I: Scott MacNeill-MacNeill & Macintosh
DF: Roessner & Co.
CL: Cytec Chemicals

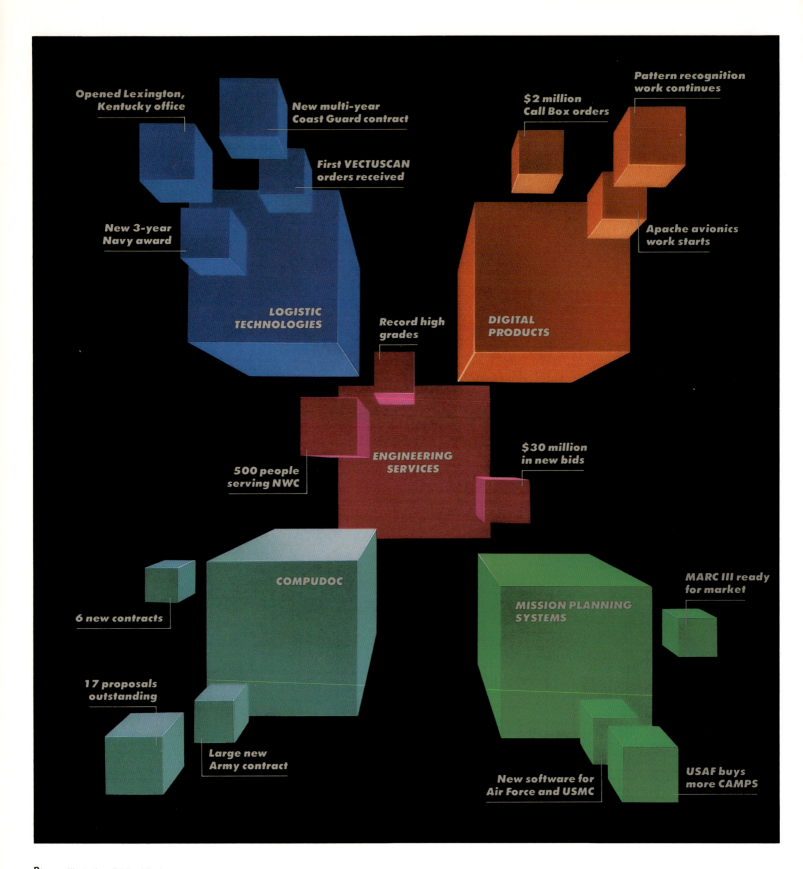

Opened Lexington,
Kentucky office

New multi-year
Coast Guard contract

First VECTUSCAN
orders received

New 3-year
Navy award

LOGISTIC
TECHNOLOGIES

$2 million
Call Box orders

Pattern recognition
work continues

Apache avionics
work starts

DIGITAL
PRODUCTS

Record high
grades

ENGINEERING
SERVICES

500 people
serving NWC

$30 million
in new bids

COMPUDOC

6 new contracts

MISSION PLANNING
SYSTEMS

MARC III ready
for market

17 proposals
outstanding

Large new
Army contract

New software for
Air Force and USMC

USAF buys
more CAMPS

Diagram illustrating divisional business
highlights. From Comarco 1986 annual
report.

コマルコ社の1986年アニュアルレポートよ
り、部門ごとの主な業務内容を表したダイア
グラム。

U.S.A.   1986
CD: Carl Seltzer
AD: Carl Seltzer
D: Carl Seltzer
DF: Carl Seltzer Design Office
CL: Comarco

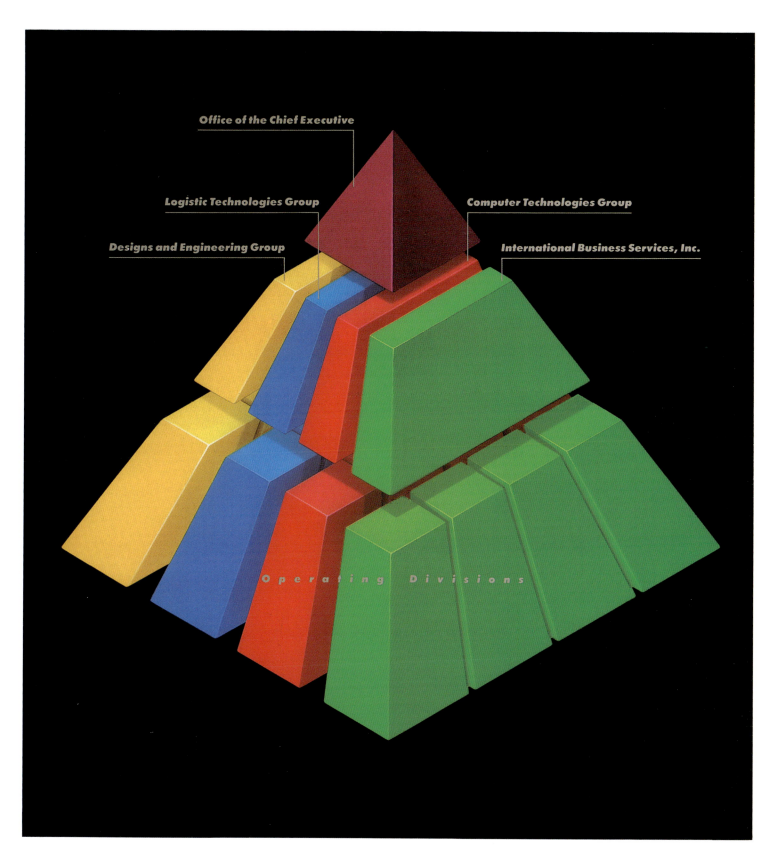

Office of the Chief Executive

Logistic Technologies Group

Computer Technologies Group

Designs and Engineering Group

International Business Services, Inc.

Operating Divisions

Diagram illustrating operating divisions, from Comarco 1986 annual report.

コマルコ社の1986年アニュアルレポート より、経営部門の組織図。

U.S.A.　1986
CD: Carl Seltzer
AD: Carl Seltzer
D: Carl Seltzer
DF: Carl Seltzer Design Office
CL: Comarco

Randstad Holding nv

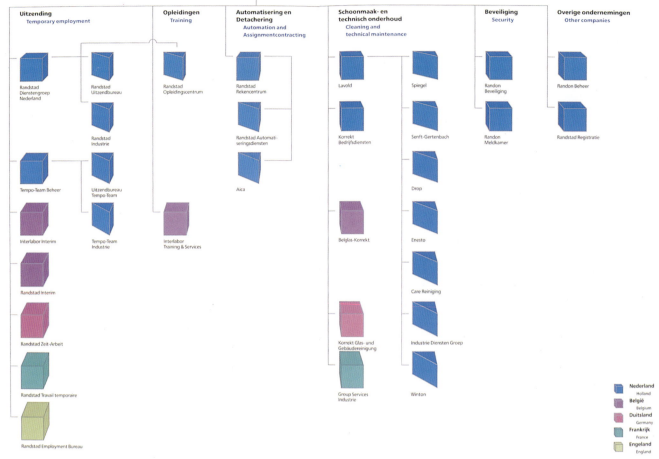

Uitzending
Temporary employment

Opleidingen
Training

Automatisering en Detachering
Automation and Assignmentcontracting

Schoonmaak- en technisch onderhoud
Cleaning and technical maintenance

Beveiliging
Security

Overige ondernemingen
Other companies

Randstad Dienstengroep Nederland

Randstad Uitzendbureau

Randstad Industrie

Tempo-Team Beheer

Uitzendbureau Tempo-Team

Interlabor Interim

Tempo-Team Industrie

Randstad Interim

Randstad Zeit-Arbeit

Randstad Travail temporaire

Randstad Employment Bureau

Randstad Opleidingscentrum

Interlabor Training & Services

Randstad Rekencentrum

Randstad Automatiseringsdiensten

Aica

Lavold

Korrekt Bedrijfsdiensten

Belglas-Korrekt

Korrekt Glas- und Gebäudereinigung

Group Services Industrie

Spiegel

Senft-Gertenbach

Drop

Enesto

Care Reiniging

Industrie Diensten Groep

Winton

Randon Beveiliging

Randon Meldkamer

Randon Beheer

Randstad Registratie

Nederland Holland
België Belgium
Duitsland Germany
Frankrijk France
Engeland England

14   Randstad Holding nv, Amsterdam

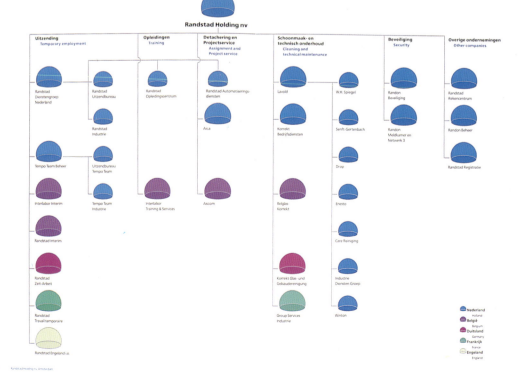

Randstad Holding nv

Uitzending
Temporary employment

Opleidingen
Training

Detachering en Projectservice
Assignment and Project service

Schoonmaak- en technisch onderhoud
Cleaning and technical maintenance

Beveiliging
Security

Overige ondernemingen
Other companies

Randstad Dienstengroep Nederland

Randstad Uitzendbureau

Randstad Industrie

Tempo Team Beheer

Uitzendbureau Tempo Team

Interlabor Interim

Tempo Team Industrie

Randstad Interim

Randstad Zeit-Arbeit

Randstad Travail temporaire

Randstad Engeland i.o.

Randstad Opleidingscentrum

Interlabor Training & Services

Randstad Automatiserings-diensten

Aica

Ascom

Lavold

Korrekt Bedrijfsdiensten

Belglas-Korrekt

Korrekt Glas- und Gebäudereinigung

Group Services Industrie

W.H. Spiegel

Senft-Gertenbach

Drop

Enesto

Care Reiniging

Industrie Diensten Groep

Winton

Randon Beveiliging

Randon Meldkamer en Netwerk 3

Randstad Rekencentrum

Randon Beheer

Randstad Registratie

Nederland Holland
België Belgium
Duitsland Germany
Frankrijk France
Engeland England

10   Randstad Holding nv, Amsterdam

Corporate family organization charts from Ranstad Holding nv annual reports for 1989 (above) and 1988 (below).

ランドスタッド・ホールディング社のアニュアルレポートより、同企業グループの組織図。

Netherlands   1989-1990
D: Wim Verboven
CL: Randstad Uitzendbureau

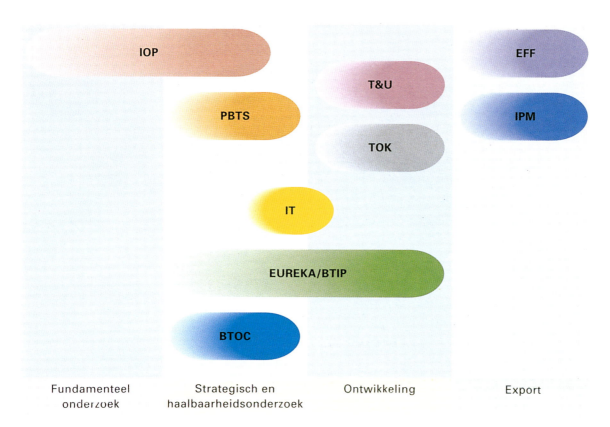

Fundamenteel onderzoek   Strategisch en haalbaarheidsonderzoek   Ontwikkeling   Export

Flow chart showing financial instruments relative to development phases (above), and organization chart (below), of a Dutch government agency for development of technology, energy and environmental policies. From Senter 1993 annual report.

工業、エネルギー、環境に関する政策を推進するオランダの政府機関「センター」の1993年アニュアルレポートより、政策の進行の度合いに応じた財政手段を表すフローチャート（上）と同機関の組織図（下）。

Netherlands   1994
CD: Andrew Fallon
AD: Andrew Fallon
D: Andrew Fallon
I: Andrew Fallon
DF: Tel Design
CL: Senter

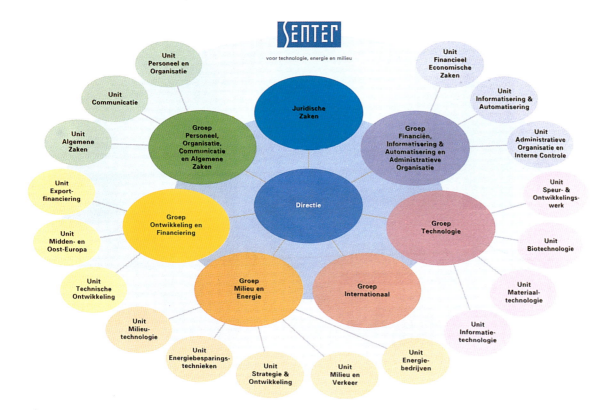

Humorous diagram illustrating features of economic cycles. From Champion international's 1992 'Subjective Reasoning' promotional feature.

チャンピオン・インターナショナル社発行の「1992年サブジェクティヴ・リーズニング」の特集記事より、景気循環の特徴を表したユーモラスな関係図。

U.S.A.　1992
AD: Paula Scher/William Drenttel
D: Paula Scher
I: Paula Scher
DF: Pentagram Design
CL: Champion International

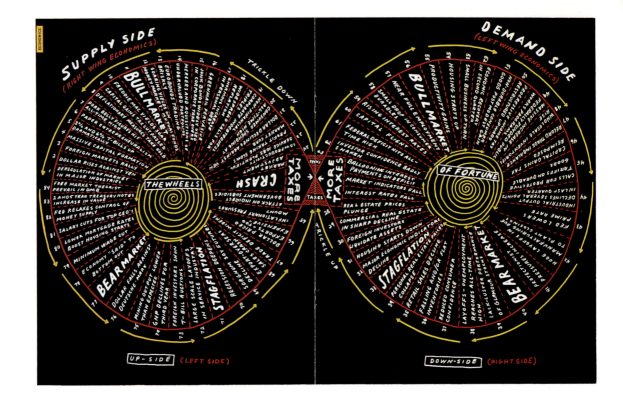

Relationship diagram showing the arrangement of genes in human DNA and known locations of mutations causing diseases. From Time magazine.

「タイムマガシン」より、人間のDNAに組み込まれている遺伝子の配列と、病気を引き起こす変異分子のうち、今までにその位置が解明されているものの相関関係を表した関係図。

U.S.A.　1994
AD: Nigel Holmes
D: Nigel Holmes
I: Nigel Holmes
CL: Time Magazine

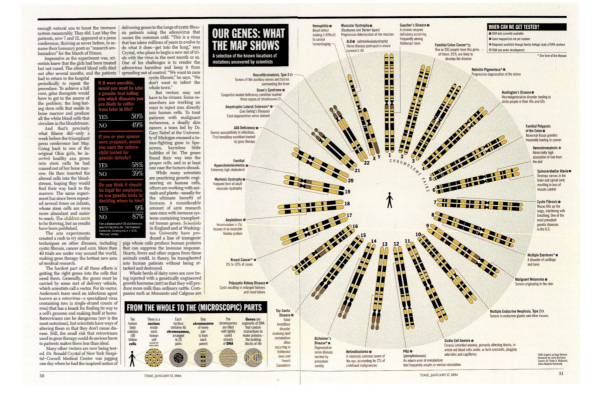

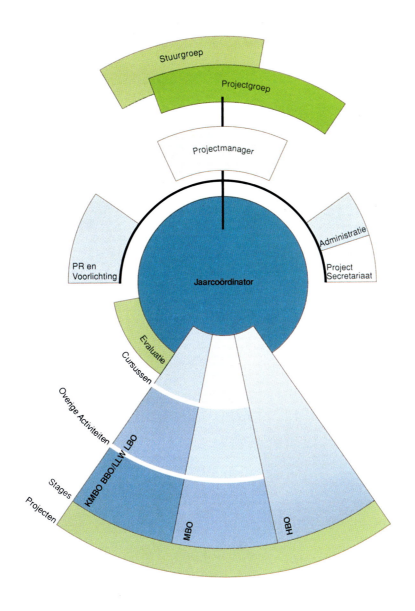

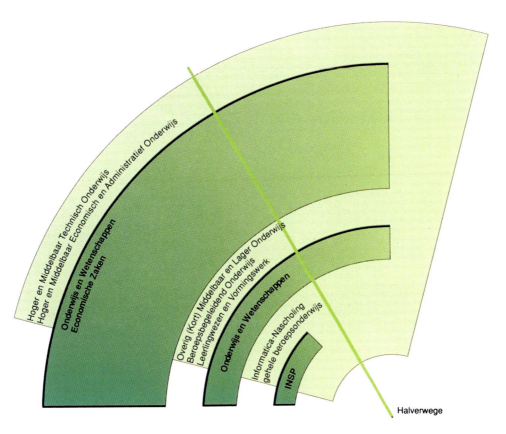

Charts from a NaBoNT interim report, showing organization structure in relation to activity structure (above) for this Dutch government 5-year project, and the relative sizes of component projects and their status at the halfway stage (below).

オランダ政府の5カ年計画中間報告書より、計画内容と組織構成の相関関係（上）、及び各プロジェクトの相対的な規模とそれらの途中段階での状況（下）を表すダイアグラム。

Netherlands   1990
CD: Paul Vermijs
AD: Paul Vermijs
D: Stephan van Rijt
I: Stephan van Rijt
DF: Tel Design
CL: NaBoNT

Mainframe Server   *Fat Client*

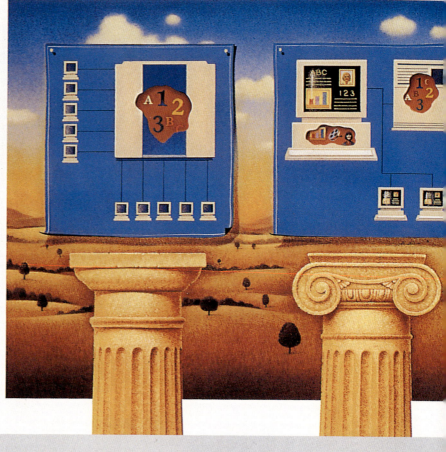

The information highway requires an information architecture that can handle all forms of information: tables, text, images, high-fidelity audio, and full-motion video. ■ The architecture also must be able to handle distribution on an enormous scale. It must guarantee privacy and be completely reliable. It must work with existing and new devices. And the architecture must be able to adapt as the information highway grows. ■ Except for mainframe-based servers, all proposed architectures follow the *client/server* model: *clients* are devices and software that request information; *servers* are the large computers and software that manage libraries of information. ■ Traditional models for organizing and distributing information on computers worked well for specific limited purposes. But in the fast lane of the information highway, those older models must yield to a flexible new architecture capable of adapting to future requirements.

| **1906**
Motion Picture Sound
Eugene Augustin Lauste | **1911**
Multiplying and
Dividing Calculating Machine
Jay R. Monroe | **1917**
VHF Transatlantic Radio
Guglielmo Marconi | **1920**
First Commercial AM Radio
Broadcast in U.S.
KDKA, Pittsburgh | **1921**
Facsimile Technology
(Wirephoto)
Western Union | **1926**
Television
*John Baird, C.F. Jenkins,
and D. Mihaly* | **1929**
Coaxial Cable
*Bell Telephone
Laboratories* |

19 SPEED

T
It unites five
devices —
Building and
in several ind
and software
tronics manu
the informa
detours by n

Functional diagrams illustrating the features and applications of the information highway. From an Oracle Corporation 1994 informative brochure.

オラクル社の1994年広報用パンフレットより、インフォメーション・ハイウェイの特徴と可能性を表した機能図。

U.S.A.   1994
CD: Robert Kastigar
AD: Earl Gee
D: Earl Gee/Fani Chung
I: David Wilcox/Philippe Weisbecker
DF: Earl Gee Design
CL: Oracle Corporation

1808
Mechanical Loom
Joseph-Marie Jacqu

FAT CLIENT Since the early 1980s, users have loaded their personal computers with more and more software and data. PCs often are connected to file servers that store information. With each loaded PC costing thousands of dollars, the fat client model has a high cost per machine. Example: A PC or Macintosh.

THIN CLIENT The thin client model stores and processes more data on the server, but keeps the user interface and application functions on the client device. Example: A television with a set-top box, Apple's Newton Personal Digital Assistant, or a low-end PC.

MAINFRAME SERVER Mainframe systems store lots of data, but they're expensive, slow, and difficult to use. Because all the processing happens on one large computer, they can't move large amounts of multimedia information to large numbers of users. Example: The IBM ES/9000, Amdahl's 5995-1400, or any plug-compatible mainframe.

MEDIA SERVER The media server harnesses the power of the fastest computers ever built — *massively parallel* computers. Media servers support diverse clients so that users don't have to discard existing systems. They provide storage, network interfaces, and memory — plus support for all forms of multimedia information. Because they use thousands of low-cost microprocessors, media servers offer astonishing performance at low cost. Example: An nCUBE Model 20 or IBM SP/2.

1933	1938	1944	1946	1947	1956	1957
FM Radio	Xerography	Automatic Sequence Controlled Calculator	Electronic Vacuum Tube Computer (ENIAC)	Transistor	Videotape Recorder	Sputnik Satellite
Edwin H. Armstrong	*Chester Carlson*	*Howard Aiken*	*John W. Mauchly and J. Presper Eckert*	*John Bardeen, Walter Brattain, and William Shockley*	*Ampex*	*USSR*

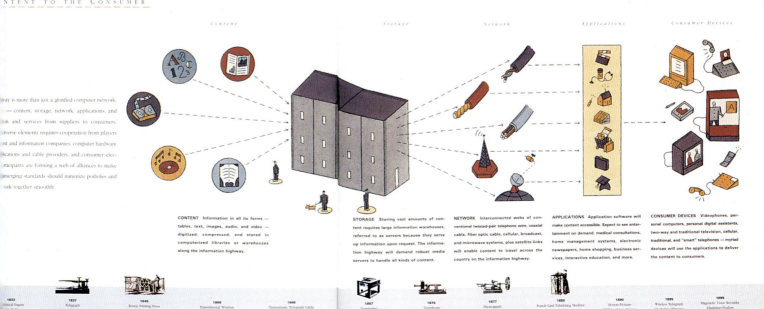

Content   *Storage*   *Network*   *Applications*   *Consumer Devices*

...way is more than just a glorified computer network.
— content, storage, network, applications, and
...on and services from suppliers to consumers.
...iverse elements requires cooperation from players
...nt and information companies, computer hardware
...cations and cable providers, and consumer elec-
...rticipants are forming a web of alliances to make
...emerging standards should minimize potholes and
...ork together smoothly.

CONTENT Information in all its forms — tables, text, images, audio, and video — digitized, compressed, and stored in computerized *libraries* or *warehouses* along the information highway.

STORAGE Storing vast amounts of content requires large information warehouses, referred to as servers because they serve up information upon request. The information highway will demand robust media servers to handle all kinds of content.

NETWORK Interconnected webs of conventional twisted-pair telephone wire, coaxial cable, fiber optic cable, cellular, broadcast, and microwave systems, plus satellite links will enable content to travel across the country on the information highway.

APPLICATIONS Application software will make content accessible. Expect to see entertainment on demand, medical consultations, home management systems, electronic newspapers, home shopping, business services, interactive education, and more.

CONSUMER DEVICES Videophones, personal computers, personal digital assistants, two-way and traditional television, cellular, traditional, and "smart" telephones — myriad devices will use the applications to deliver the content to consumers.

1833	1837	1845	1866	1866	1867	1876	1877	1889	1890	1895	1899
...ytical Engine	Telegraph	Rotary Printing Press	Experimental Wireless	Transatlantic Telegraph Cable	Typewriter	Telephone	Phonograph	Punch Card Tabulating Machine	Motion Pictures	Wireless Telegraph	Magnetic Voice Recorder
...rles Babbage	*Samuel F.B. Morse*	*Richard M. Hoe*	*Mahlon Loomis*	*Cyrus West Field, Samuel Canning, Daniel Gooch*	*Christopher L. Sholes*	*Alexander Graham Bell*	*Thomas Edison*	*Herman Hollerith*	*William Friese-Greene*	*Guglielmo Marconi*	*Vladimar Poulsen*

Chronological chart of company history, from Nippon Paper Industries corporate profile.

日本製紙社の会社案内より、同社の歴史を表した年表。

Japan 1993
CD: Tetsuya Ohta
AD: Tetsuya Ohta
D: Tetsuya Ohta
CL: Nippon Paper Industries

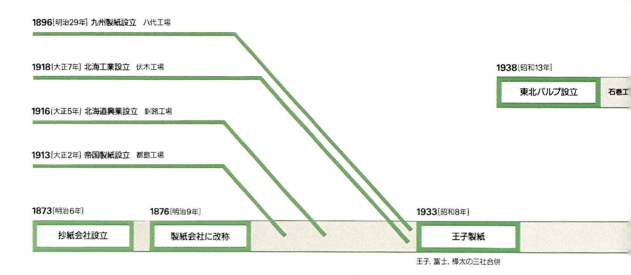

1896[明治29年] 九州製紙設立　八代工場

1918[大正7年] 北海工業設立　伏木工場

1916[大正5年] 北海道興業設立　釧路工場

1913[大正2年] 帝国製紙設立　都島工場

1938[昭和13年]
東北パルプ設立　石巻工

1873[明治6年]
抄紙会社設立

1876[明治9年]
製紙会社に改称

1933[昭和8年]
王子製紙
王子、富士、樺太の三社合併

1937[昭和12年] 新日本レイヨン産業設立　江津工場

1944[昭和19年] 島根化学工業に社名変更

1946[昭和21年]
山陽パルプ設立

1938[昭和13年]
國策パルプ工業設立

1940[昭和15年] 大日本再生製紙設立　勇払工場

Relationship diagram of international symbols, from Visual Message magazine.

「ビジュアルメッセージ」誌より、国際単位（SI）の関係図。

Japan 1993
CD: Tetsuya Ohta
AD: Tetsuya Ohta
D: Tetsuya Ohta
CL: Visual Message

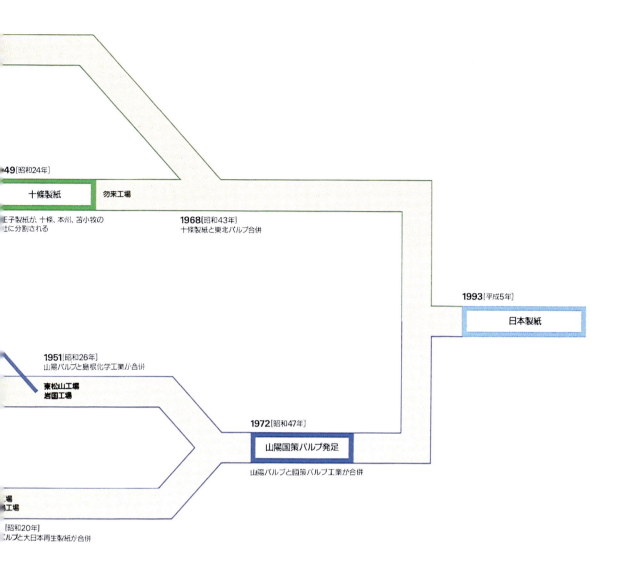

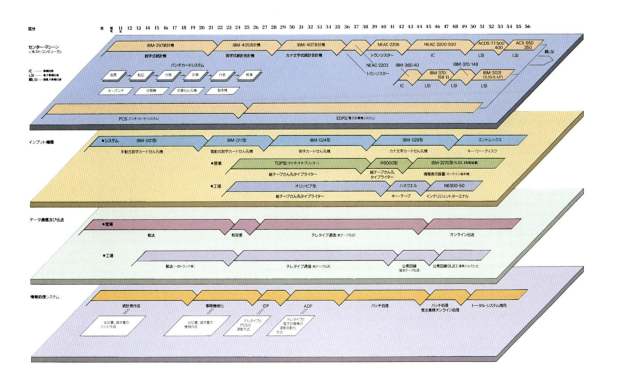

Chronological chart showing changes in information processing equipment. From Takeda Chemical Industries brochure '200 Years History of Takeda Chemical Industries'.

武田薬品工業社の発行した「武田薬品200年史」より、情報処理機器の変遷を表した年表。

Japan　1983
CD: Tetsuya Ohta
AD: Tetsuya Ohta
D: Tetsuya Ohta
CL: Takeda Chemical Industries

Chronological chart illustrating developments in science and technology associated with optics. From 'Principia', quarterly magazine of Ishikawajima-Harima Heavy Industries.

石川島播磨重工業社発行の「季刊プリンキピア」より、光にまつわる科学技術の発展を表した年表。

Japan 1994
CD: Takashi Yonezawa
AD: Yukimasa Matsuda
D: Satoru Kawaharada
CL: IHI

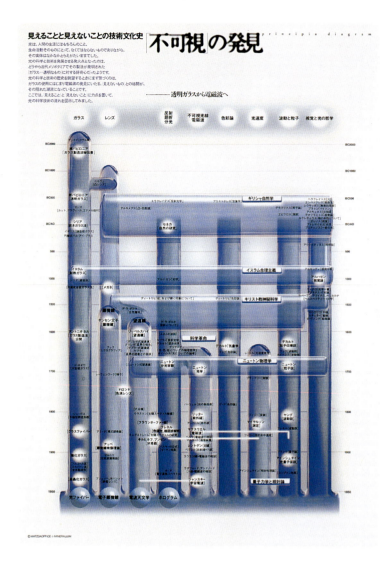

Chronological chart illustrating the development of cyberspace technology, from Intercommunication magazine, a publication of NTT Publishing Co., Ltd.

NTT 出版社の「インターコミュニケーション」誌より、サイバースペースに関する技術の発展を表した年表。

Japan 1993
CD: Takao Shiga
AD: Yukimasa Matsuda
CL: NTT Publishing Co., Ltd.

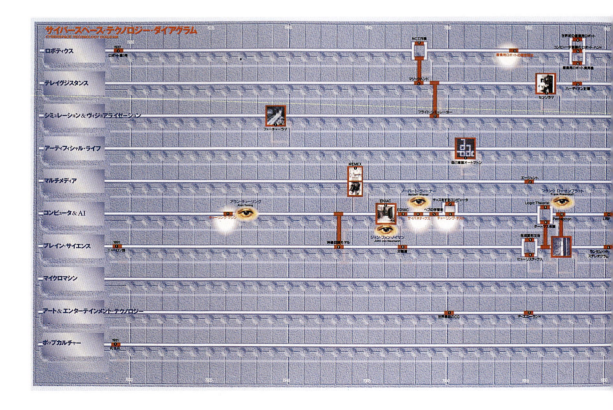

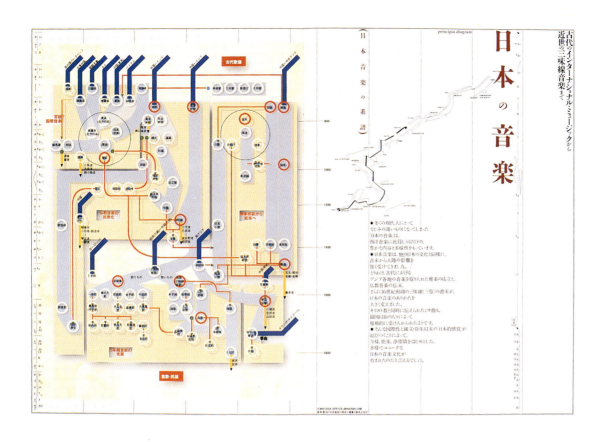

Chronological chart illustrating the origins and development of Japanese music. From 'Principia', quarterly magazine of Ishikawajima-Harima Heavy Industries.

石川島播磨重工業社発行の「季刊プリンビキア」より、日本音楽の系譜を表した年表。

Japan 1993
CD: Takashi Yonezawa
AD: Yukimasa Matsuda
D: Satoru Kawaharada
CL: IHI

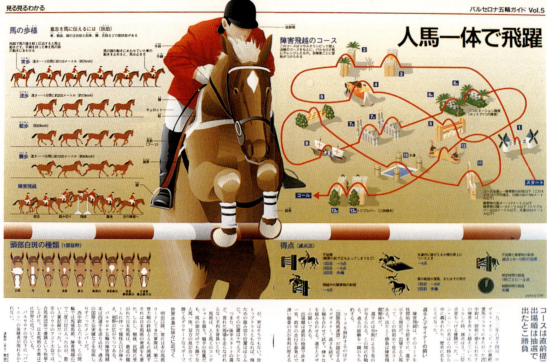

人馬一体で飛躍

冬季五輪の花形 アルペンスキー

1
Topic illustration of Olympic equestrian event from Asahi Shimbun's AERA magazine.

朝日新聞社の「アエラ」誌より、オリンピックの種目「障害飛越」についての主題図。

Japan　1992
AD: Hiroyuki Kimura
D: Hiroyuki Kimura/
Hiroko Enomoto/Sachiko Hagiwara/
Yuko Minoura/Takeshi Kamoi
CL: Asahi Shimbun

2
Topic illustration on alpine skiing, the main attraction of the Winter Olympics. From Asahi Shimbun's AERA magazine.

朝日新聞社の「アエラ」誌より、冬期オリンピックの花形種目、アルペンスキーに関する主題図。

Japan　1994
AD: Hiroyuki Kimura
D: Hiroyuki Kimura/Sachiko Hagiwara
CL: Asahi Shimbun

1
Topic illustration on Japanese bath salts, from Asahi Shimbun's AERA magazine.

朝日新聞社の「アエラ」誌より、日本の入浴剤に関する主題図。

Japan　1994
AD: Hiroyuki Kimura
D: Hiroyuki Kimura/Sachiko Hagiwara
CL: Asahi Shimbun

2
Topic illustration using a chessboard to show the location worldwide of 'overseas Chinese'. From View magazine, published by Kodansha.

講談社の「ヴューズ」誌より、チェス盤をモチーフにして世界の華僑の分布を表した主題図。

Japan　1994
AD: Hiroyuki Kimura
D: Hiroyuki Kimura/Hiroko Enomoto
CL: Kodansha Ltd.

Functional diagram explaining how to use dental floss correctly. From CLAUDIA magazine.

「クローディアマガジン」より、デンタルフロスの正しい使い方を表す機能図。

Brazil　　1993
AD: Márcia Zoladz
I: Marco Mancini
DF: CLAUDIA Art Department
CL: Revista CLAUDIA, Editora Abril S/A

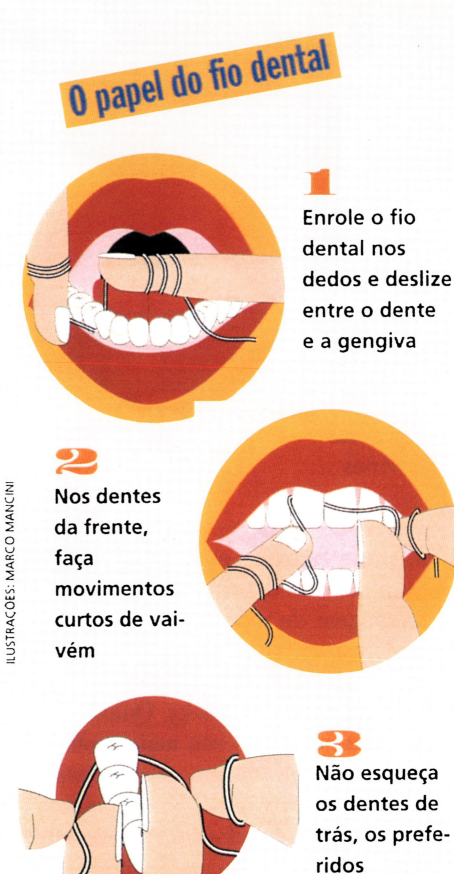

O papel do fio dental

1

Enrole o fio dental nos dedos e deslize entre o dente e a gengiva

2

Nos dentes da frente, faça movimentos curtos de vai-vém

ILUSTRAÇÕES: MARCO MANCINI

3

Não esqueça os dentes de trás, os preferidos pelas cáries

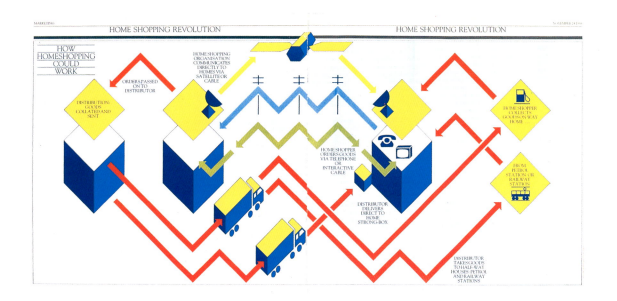

HOW HOMESHOPPING COULD WORK

DISTRIBUTION: GOODS COLLATED AND SENT

ORDERS PASSED ON TO DISTRIBUTOR

HOME SHOPPING ORGANISATION COMMUNICATES DIRECTLY TO HOMES VIA SATELLITE OR CABLE

HOME SHOPPER ORDERS GOODS VIA TELEPHONE OR INTERACTIVE CABLE

DISTRIBUTOR DELIVERS DIRECT TO HOME STRONG-BOX

DISTRIBUTOR TAKES GOODS TO HALF-WAY HOUSES: PETROL AND RAILWAY STATIONS

HOME SHOPPER COLLECTS GOODS ON WAY HOME ...

FROM PETROL STATION OR RAILWAY STATION

Relationship diagram showing how home shopping could work. From Marketing magazine.

「マーケティングマガジン」より、ホームショッピングの仕組みについての関係図。

U.K.
AD: Roland Schenk/Mark Porter
I: Michael Robinson
CL: Haymarket Magazine

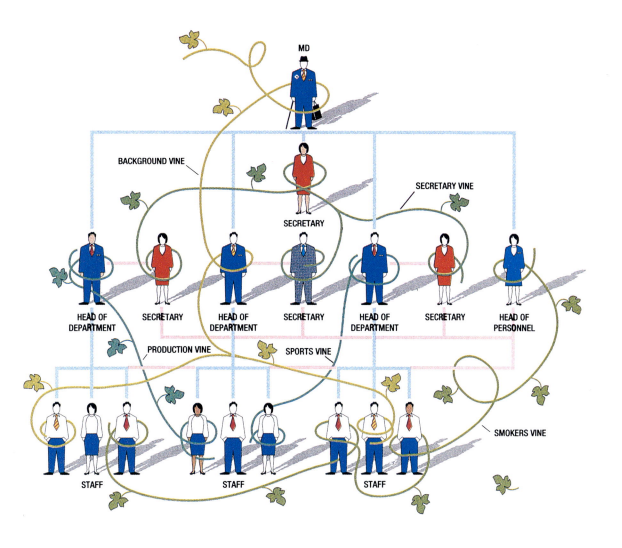

MD

BACKGROUND VINE

SECRETARY VINE

SECRETARY

HEAD OF DEPARTMENT

SECRETARY

HEAD OF DEPARTMENT

SECRETARY

HEAD OF DEPARTMENT

SECRETARY

HEAD OF PERSONNEL

PRODUCTION VINE

SPORTS VINE

SMOKERS VINE

STAFF

STAFF

STAFF

Diagram illustrating the alternative routes of communication in offices known as 'the grape vine'. From Intercity magazine.

「インターシティマガジン」より、オフィスには、情報を伝えるルートが複数あり、"ぶどうのつる"と呼ばれていることを表す組織図。

U.K.
AD: Neil Braidwood
I: Michael Robinson
CL: Redwood Publishing

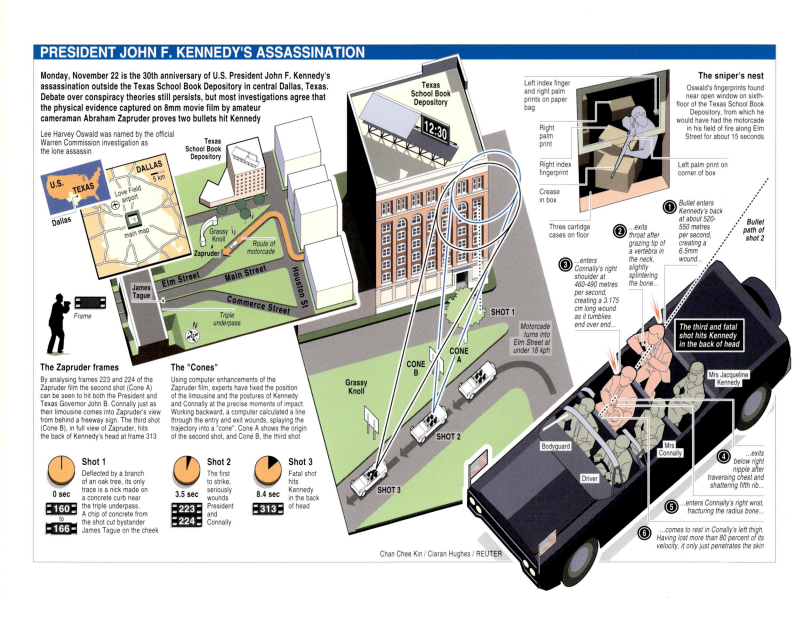

PRESIDENT JOHN F. KENNEDY'S ASSASSINATION

Monday, November 22 is the 30th anniversary of U.S. President John F. Kennedy's assassination outside the Texas School Book Depository in central Dallas, Texas. Debate over conspiracy theories still persists, but most investigations agree that the physical evidence captured on 8mm movie film by amateur cameraman Abraham Zapruder proves two bullets hit Kennedy

Lee Harvey Oswald was named by the official Warren Commission investigation as the lone assassin

DALLAS
5 km

U.S.
TEXAS

Dallas

Love Field airport

main map

Texas School Book Depository

Grassy Knoll

Route of motorcade

Zapruder

Elm Street

Main Street

Houston St

James Tague

Commerce Street

Frame

Triple underpass

N

Texas School Book Depository

12:30

The sniper's nest
Oswald's fingerprints found near open window on sixth-floor of the Texas School Book Depository, from which he would have had the motorcade in his field of fire along Elm Street for about 15 seconds

Left index finger and right palm prints on paper bag

Right palm print

Right index fingerprint

Crease in box

Three cartidge cases on floor

Left palm print on corner of box

SHOT 1

Motorcade turns into Elm Street at under 16 kph

CONE B

CONE A

Grassy Knoll

SHOT 2

SHOT 3

Bullet path of shot 2

① Bullet enters Kennedy's back at about 520-550 metres per second, creating a 6.5mm wound...

② ...exits throat after grazing tip of a vertebra in the neck, slightly splintering the bone...

③ ...enters Connally's right shoulder at 460-490 metres per second, creating a 3.175 cm long wound as it tumbles end over end...

The third and fatal shot hits Kennedy in the back of head

Mrs Jacqueline Kennedy

Bodyguard

Driver

Mrs Connally

④ ...exits below right nipple after traversing chest and shattering fifth rib...

⑤ ...enters Connally's right wrist, fracturing the radius bone...

⑥ ...comes to rest in Conally's left thigh. Having lost more than 80 percent of its velocity, it only just penetrates the skin

The Zapruder frames

By analysing frames 223 and 224 of the Zapruder film the second shot (Cone A) can be seen to hit both the President and Texas Governor John B. Connally just as their limousine comes into Zapruder's view from behind a freeway sign. The third shot (Cone B), in full view of Zapruder, hits the back of Kennedy's head at frame 313

The "Cones"

Using computer enhancements of the Zapruder film, experts have fixed the position of the limousine and the postures of Kennedy and Connally at the precise moments of impact. Working backward, a computer calculated a line through the entry and exit wounds, splaying the trajectory into a "cone". Cone A shows the origin of the second shot, and Cone B, the third shot

Shot 1
0 sec
160 to 166
Deflected by a branch of an oak tree, its only trace is a nick made on a concrete curb near the triple underpass. A chip of concrete from the shot cut bystander James Tague on the cheek

Shot 2
3.5 sec
223 224
The first to strike, seriously wounds President and Connally

Shot 3
8.4 sec
313
Fatal shot hits Kennedy in the back of head

Chan Chee Kin / Ciaran Hughes / REUTER

Topic illustration on the assassination of US president John F.Kennedy. Reuters news agency.

アメリカ大統領、ジョン・F・ケネディー暗殺事件についての主題図。

U.K.   1993
CD: Chan Chee Kin/Ciaran Hughes
AD: Chan Chee Kin
D: Chan Chee Kin/Ciaran Hughes
I: Chan Chee Kin/Ciaran Hughes
DF: Reuters News Graphics Service

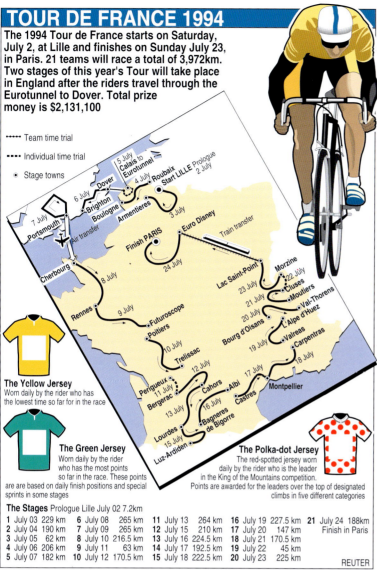

TOUR DE FRANCE 1994

The 1994 Tour de France starts on Saturday, July 2, at Lille and finishes on Sunday July 23, in Paris. 21 teams will race a total of 3,972km. Two stages of this year's Tour will take place in England after the riders travel through the Eurotunnel to Dover. Total prize money is $2,131,100

····· Team time trial

---- Individual time trial

• Stage towns

5 July Calais to Eurotunnel
5 July Dover
4 July Roubaix
Start LILLE Prologue 2 July
6 July Brighton
Boulogne
Armentieres
3 July
7 July Portsmouth
Air transfer
Finish PARIS
Euro Disney
Train transfer
Cherbourg
8 July
Morzine
22 July
Lac Saint-Point
23 July
Cluses
Moutiers
21 July
Rennes
9 July
Val-Thorens
20 July
Futuroscope
L'Alpe d'Huez
Poitiers
Bourg d'Oisans
Valreas
19 July
Carpentras
Trelissac
10 July
12 July
18 July
Perigueux
11 July
Cahors
Albi
Montpellier
Bergerac
Castres
17 July
13 July
16 July
Bagneres de Bigorre
Lourdes
15 July
Luz-Ardiden

The Yellow Jersey
Worn daily by the rider who has the lowest time so far for in the race

The Green Jersey
Worn daily by the rider who has the most points so far in the race. These points are are based on daily finish positions and special sprints in some stages

The Polka-dot Jersey
The red-spotted jersey worn daily by the rider who is the leader in the King of the Mountains competition. Points are awarded for the leaders over the top of designated climbs in five different categories

The Stages Prologue Lille July 02 7.2km

1 July 03	229 km	6 July 08	265 km	11 July 13	264 km	16 July 19	227.5 km	21 July 24	188km
2 July 04	190 km	7 July 09	265 km	12 July 15	210 km	17 July 20	147 km	Finish in Paris	
3 July 05	62 km	8 July 10	216.5 km	13 July 16	224.5 km	18 July 21	170.5 km		
4 July 06	206 km	9 July 11	63 km	14 July 17	192.5 km	19 July 22	45 km		
5 July 07	182 km	10 July 12	170.5 km	15 July 18	222.5 km	20 July 23	225 km		

REUTER

Source : Societe du Tour de France

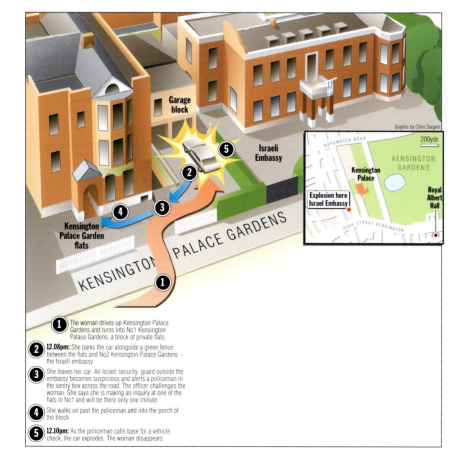

Garage block

Graphic by Chris Sargent

5

Israeli Embassy

2

4

3

Kensington Palace Garden flats

KENSINGTON PALACE GARDENS

1

BAYSWATER ROAD
200yds
KENSINGTON GARDENS
Kensington Palace
Explosion here Israel Embassy
Royal Albert Hall
HIGH STREET KENSINGTON

① The woman drives up Kensington Palace Gardens and turns into No1 Kensington Palace Gardens, a block of private flats

② **12.08pm:** She parks the car alongside a green fence between the flats and No2 Kensington Palace Gardens — the Israeli embassy

③ She leaves her car. An Israeli security guard outside the embassy becomes suspicious and alerts a policeman in the sentry box across the road. The officer challenges the woman. She says she is making an inquiry at one of the flats in No1 and will be there only one minute

④ She walks on past the policeman and into the porch of the block

⑤ **12.10pm:** As the policeman calls base for a vehicle check, the car explodes. The woman disappears

Topic illustration of the 16th stage of the 1994 Tour de France cycle race combined with a profile of one of the participating teams. From Reuters news agency.

ロイターズ・ニューズ・エージェンシーより、1994年ツール・ド・フランス自転車レースの第16ステージの解説と、参加チームのプロフィールが一緒になっている主題図。

U.K.   1994
I: Peter Sullivan
CL: Reuters News Graphics Service

Topic illustration of the car bombing of the Israeli embassy, London. From The Sunday Times newspaper.

「サンデー・タイムス」紙より、ロンドン、イスラエル大使館の自動車爆破事件についての主題図。

U.K.   1994
D: Chris Sargent
I: Chris Sargent
CL: The Sunday Times
© THE SUNDAY TIMES, LONDON. 1994

Illustration of a pharmaceutical manufacturing and distribution case study. From Wellcome plc 1993 annual report.

ウェルコム社の1993年アニュアルレポートより、薬品製造、及びその流通経路のケース・スタディを表す主題図。

U.K.   1993
CD: Jonathan Davis
D: Sally Maine
P: Mcintyre Photography
DF: Michael Peters Limited
CL: Wellcome Plc

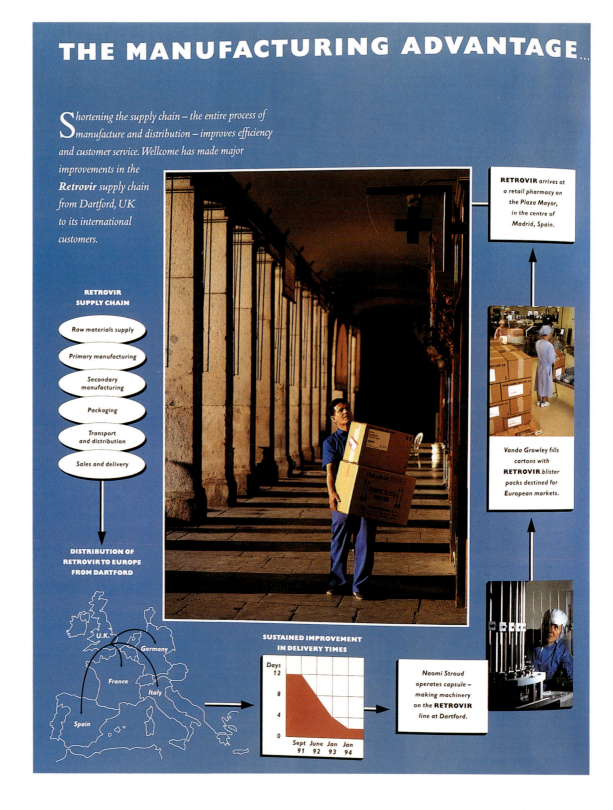

THE MANUFACTURING ADVANTAGE...

*Shortening the supply chain – the entire process of manufacture and distribution – improves efficiency and customer service. Wellcome has made major improvements in the **Retrovir** supply chain from Dartford, UK to its international customers.*

RETROVIR SUPPLY CHAIN

- Raw materials supply
- Primary manufacturing
- Secondary manufacturing
- Packaging
- Transport and distribution
- Sales and delivery

DISTRIBUTION OF RETROVIR TO EUROPE FROM DARTFORD

U.K.
Germany
France
Italy
Spain

RETROVIR *arrives at a retail pharmacy on the Plaza Mayor, in the centre of Madrid, Spain.*

*Vanda Growley fills cartons with **RETROVIR** blister packs destined for European markets.*

SUSTAINED IMPROVEMENT IN DELIVERY TIMES

Days
12
8
4
0
Sept June Jan Jan
91   92   93   94

*Naomi Stroud operates capsule – making machinery on the **RETROVIR** line at Dartford.*

Diagram illustrating changes to update sign language. From Details magazine.

「ディテールズ・マガジン」より、手話が時代に応じて変化していることを表す主題図。

U.S.A.   1994
AD: Markus Kiersztan
D: Nigel Holmes
I: Nigel Holmes
CL: Details Magazine

Signs of the Times

American Sign Language goes P.C.

How do you say "Japanese" in sign language? For years, the word was represented by twisting the little finger at the corner of the eye—a reference to the stereotypical feature of slanted eyes. Today, as American Sign Language absorbs the influences of multi-culturalism, signs that perpetuate ethnic and sexual stereotypes are dropping out of use. "Japanese" is now signed with Japan's own sign for the word, a gesture representing the shape of the Japanese islands. "African American," which was once signed by flattening the nose, also uses a map-drawing motion. "Gay," once represented by a limp-wristed, effeminate movement, is now signed by finger-spelling the word or placing the sign for the letter q—for queer—on the chin. "The deaf community has been looking for independence and a real identity," says Frederic A. Jondreau, director of the American Sign Language Institute in Manhattan. "By recognizing the individuality of other groups, they're showing a desire to be seen that way themselves."

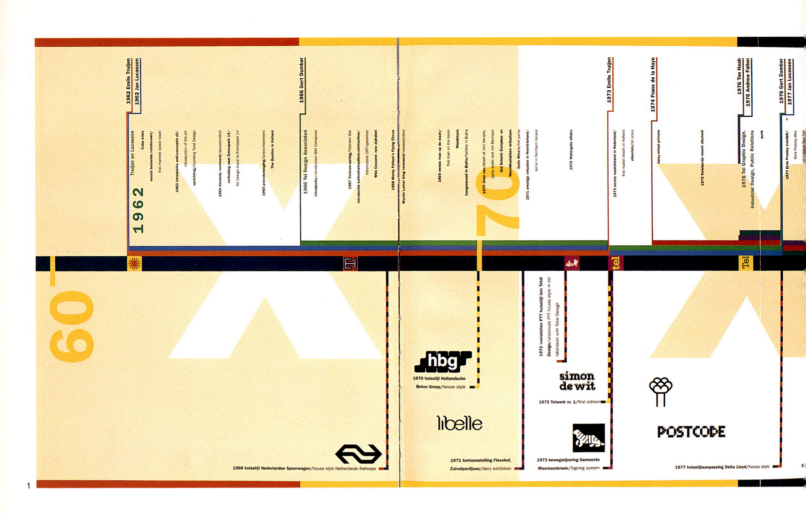

1

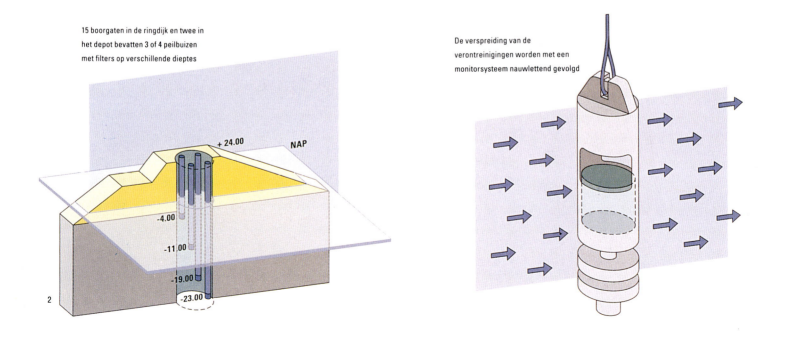

15 boorgaten in de ringdijk en twee in
het depot bevatten 3 of 4 peilbuizen
met filters op verschillende dieptes

De verspreiding van de
verontreinigingen worden met een
monitorsysteem nauwlettend gevolgd

2

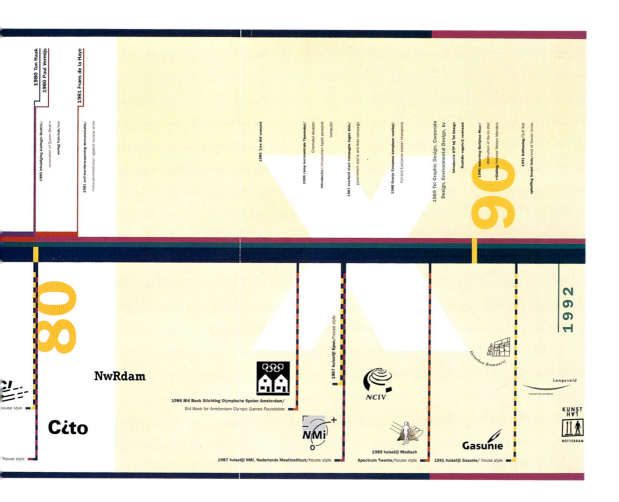

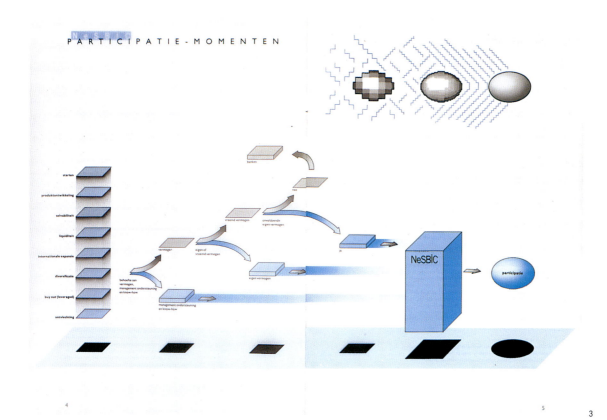

1
Chronological chart showing a design office's significant logos and changes in management and house style, together with important world events. From a Tel Design brochure.

テル・デザイン社のパンフレットより、同社の代表的なロゴデザインと経営方法、及び会社の方針の変化を世界の出来事とともに表した年表。

Netherlands   1992
CD: Gert Kootstra
AD: Gert Kootstra
D: Katrina Burns
DF: Tel Design

2
Functional diagram illustrating underwater filtration and monitoring techniques for an offshore civil engineering project. From a Rotterdam Department of Public Works public information brochure.

ロッテルダム市公共事業部の広報誌より、沖合いでの土木工事で実際に行なわれた水中ろ過、及び監視技術についての機能図。

Netherlands   1990
CD: Paul Vermijs
AD: Paul Vermijs
D: Stephan van Rijt
DF: Tel Design
CL: Department of Public Works,
City of Rotterdam

3
Flow chart illustrating how venture capital projects come about. From a NeSBIC corporate brochure.

NeSBIC社のパンフレットより、ベンチャー・キャピタルのプロジェクトがどのような経過をたどって持ち上がるのかを表すフローチャート。

Netherlands   1984
CD: Paul Vermijs
AD: Paul Vermijs
D: Paul Vermijs
DF: Tel Design
CL: NeSBIC

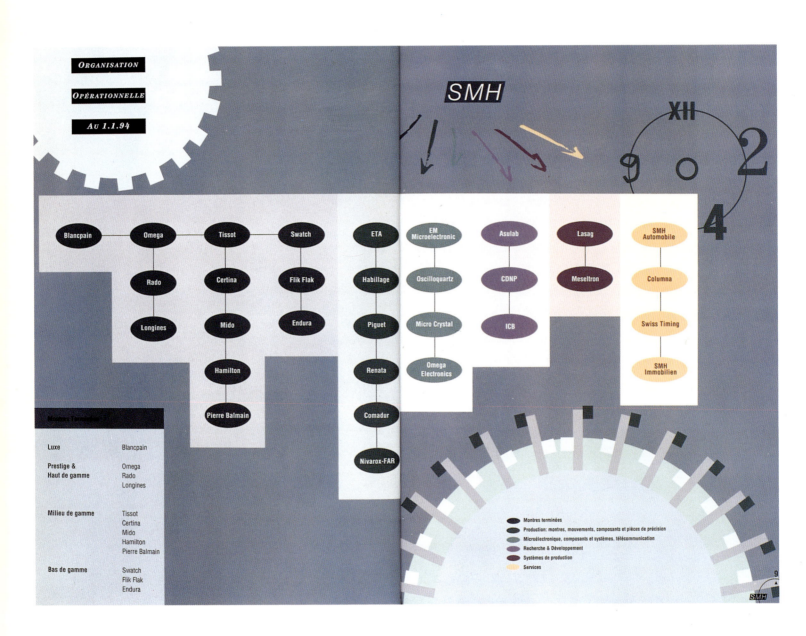

Organization chart of a Swiss watch
enterprise. From 1993 SMH annual report.

SMH社の1993年アニュアルレポートより、
スイスの時計メーカーの会社組織図。

Switzerland   1994
CD: Oscar Ribes
AD: Oscar Ribes
CL: SMH

Communi-Card

This card has been prepared to assist you in communicating with your family, friends and hospital staff.

Estos dibujos se han preparados para que usted se pueda comunicar con su familia, sus amistades, y los empleados del hospital.

Yes / Sí									No

Yes / Sí — Afraid/Sad *Miedo/Triste* — Angry/Upset *Enojado/Nervioso* — Drowsy/Tired *Soñoliento/Cansado* — Dizzy *Mareado* — Doctor *Médico* — Nurse *Enfermera* — Family/Friends *Familia/Amigos* — Clergy *Clerico* — No

Pain/Ache *Dolor* — Vomit/Full Stomach *Vómito/Estomago lleno* — Difficulty Breathing *Dificultad en Respirar* — Suction *Succión* — Intravenous *Intravenosa* — Lower/Raise Bed *Subir/Bajar la Cama* — Turn Me Over *Dar Vuelta de Lado a Lado* — In/Out of Bed *Entrar a/Salir de la Cama* — Please Leave *Por Favor Despídase* — House *Casa*

Medicine/Laxative *Medicina/Laxante* — Toilet/Commode *Servicio Sanitario* — Wash *Lavarse* — Shave/Hair Care *Afeitarse/Cuidado de Pelo* — Mouth Care *Higiene Oral* — Lotion *Crema* — Pillow/Blanket *Almohada/Frazada* — Drink *Bebida* — Food *Alimento* — Time *Hora*

Dentures *Dentadura* — Eyeglasses *Espejuelos* — Hearing Aid *Audifono de Oir* — Robe/Slippers *Bata de Casa/Chancletas* — Pajamas *Pijama* — Telephone *Teléfono* — Television *Televisión* — Money *Dinero* — Mail *Cartas* — Reading Material *Algo para Leer*

Visual aid card to assist communication between patients and hospital staff with no common language. From Mt. Sinai Medical Center.

マウント・シナイ・メディカルセンターより、言語が通じない時に患者と病院関係者がコミュニケーション手段として使用する機能図。

U.S.A.   1990-1993
CD: Richard Poulin
AD: Richard Poulin
D: Richard Poulin/J. Graham Hanson
DF: Richard Poulin Design Group Inc.
CL: Mt. Sinai Medical Center

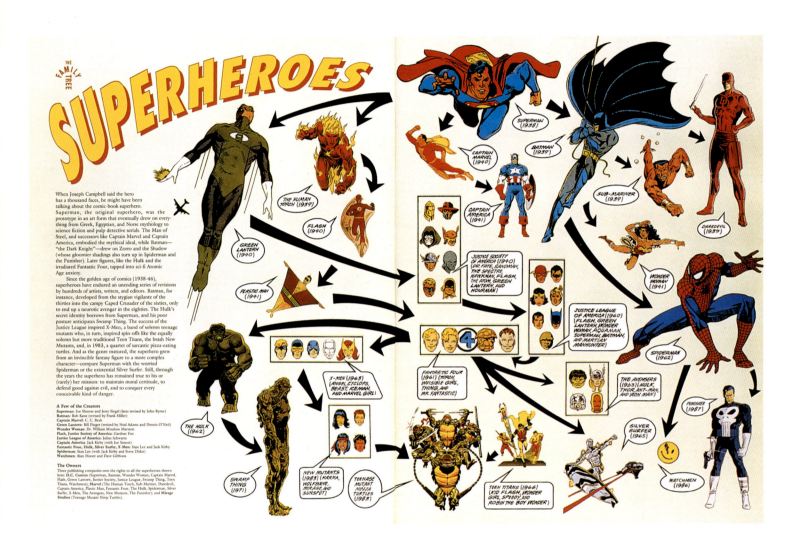

Flow chart illustrating the relations between generations of comic-book super heroes. From Wigwag magazine.

「ウィグワグ・マガジン」より、人気マンガの主人公の世代関係を表すフローチャート。

U.S.A. 1990
AD: Paul Davis
D: Alexandra Ginns

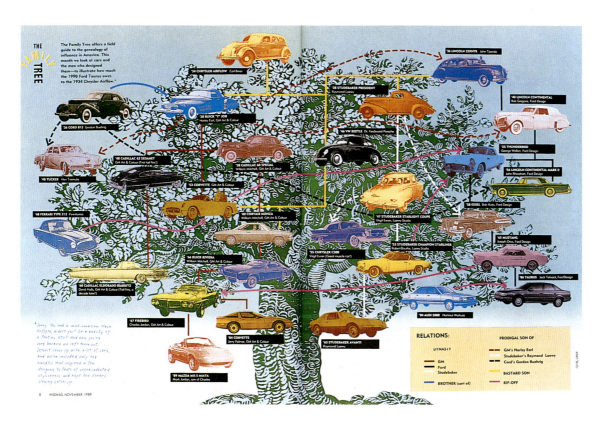

Genealogical chart showing how earlier generations of cars and their designers have influenced later models. From Wigwag magazine.

「ウィグワグ・マガジン」より、初期の自動車とその設計者がいかに後世のモデルに影響を与えたかを表す系統図。

U.S.A.   1989
AD: Paul Davis
I: Gene Greif

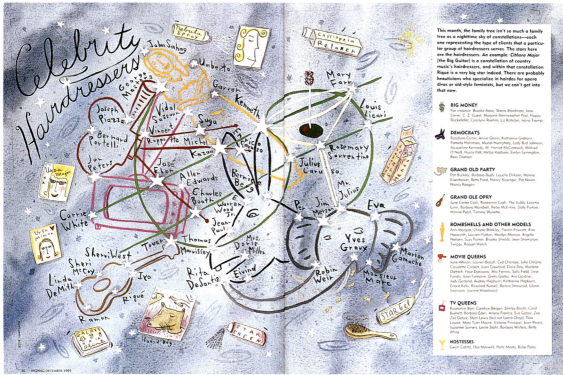

Diagram showing 'constellations' of celebrity hairdressers who serve certain categories of clients. From Wigwag magazine.

「ウィグワグ・マガジン」より、顧客の特長によって、人気美容師を星座にたとえた関係図。

U.S.A.   1989
AD: Paul Davis
I: Jessie Hartland

Topic illustration using a game board layout to show how waste management involves everybody. From Garbage magazine.

「ガーベジ・マガジン」より、ゴミ処理問題がいかに多くの人々にかかわっているかを、ゲーム盤をモチーフに表した主題図。

U.S.A.　1991
AD: Rob George
D: Scott MacNeill
I: Scott MacNeill-MacNeill & Macintosh
CL: Old House Journal Corp.

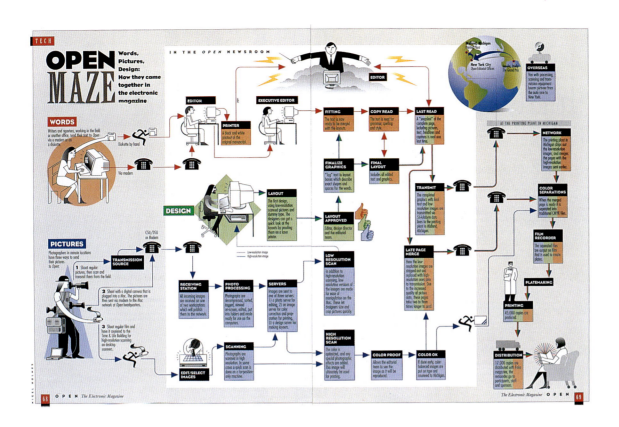

Flow chart explaining how a magazine issue is created, electronically processed and printed. From Open magazine.

「オープン・マガジン」より、雑誌の編集や電子製版の工程を表したフローチャート。

U.S.A.　1993
CD: Michael Grossman
AD: Michael Grossman
D: Nigel Holmes
I: Nigel Holmes
CL: Time Warner

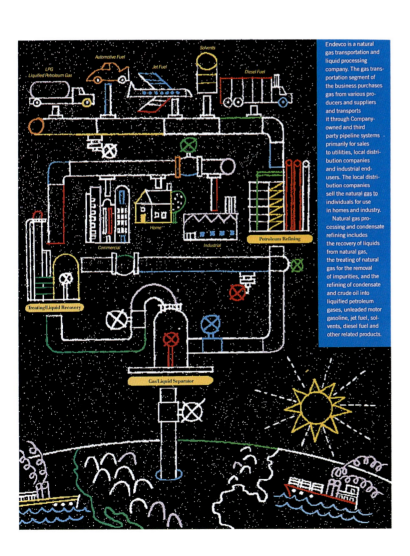

Topic illustration showing processing and uses of natural gas. From an Endevco, Inc. annual report.

エンデブコ社のアニュアルレポートより、天然ガスの加工処理法と用途を表した主題図。

U.S.A.　1992
AD: Joe Rattan
D: Joe Rattan/Greg Morgan
I: Linda Helton
CW: Lynn Thomas
DF: Joseph Rattan Design
CL: Endevco, Inc.

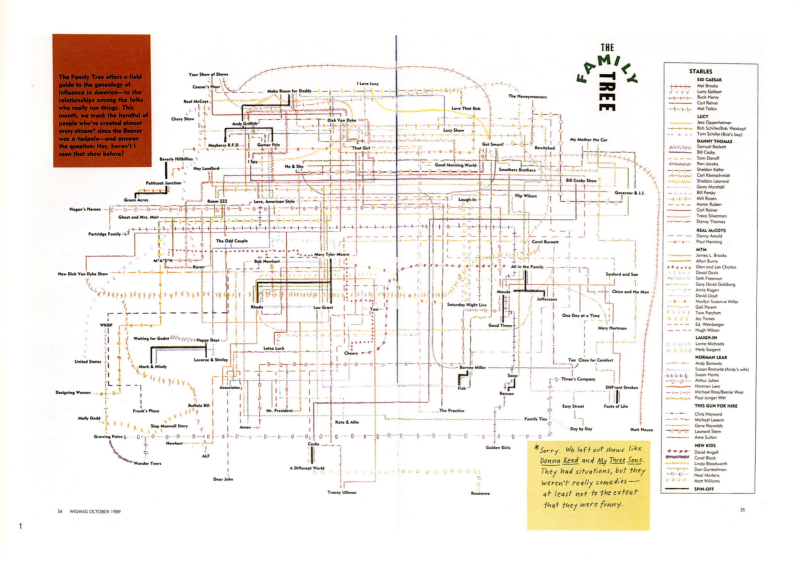

The Family Tree offers a field guide to the genealogy of influence in America—to the relationships among the folks who really run things. This month, we track the handful of people who've created almost every sitcom* since the Beaver was a tadpole—and answer the question: Hey, haven't I seen that show before?

THE FAMILY TREE

*Sorry. We left out shows like Donna Reed and My Three Sons. They had situations, but they weren't really comedies—at least not to the extent that they were funny.

STABLES

SID CAESAR
Mel Brooks
Larry Gelbart
Buck Henry
Carl Reiner
Mel Tolkin

LUCY
Jess Oppenheimer
Bob Schiller/Bob Weiskopf
Tom Schiller (Bob's boy)

DANNY THOMAS
Samuel Beckett
Bill Cosby
Sam Denoff
Ron Jacobs
Sheldon Keller
Carl Kleinschmidt
Sheldon Leonard
Garry Marshall
Bill Persky
Milt Rosen
Aaron Ruben
Carl Reiner
Treva Silverman
Danny Thomas

REAL McCOYS
Danny Arnold
Paul Henning

MTM
James L. Brooks
Allan Burns
Glen and Les Charles
David Davis
Seth Freeman
Gary David Goldberg
Amie Kogen
David Lloyd
Marilyn Suzanne Miller
Gail Parent
Tom Patchett
Jay Tarses
Ed. Weinberger
Hugh Wilson

LAUGH-IN
Lorne Michaels
Herb Sargent

NORMAN LEAR
Andy Borowitz
Susan Borowitz (Andy's wife)
Susan Harris
Arthur Julian
Norman Lear
Michael Ross/Bernie West
Paul Junger Witt

THIS GUN FOR HIRE
Chris Hayward
Michael Leeson
Gene Reynolds
Leonard Stern
Ame Sultan

NEW KIDS
David Angell
Carol Black
Linda Bloodworth
Dan Guntzelman
Neal Marlens
Matt Williams

SPIN-OFF

1

1
Genealogical chart showing interrelations between generations of US TV programs. From Wigwag magazine.

「ウィグワグ・マガジン」より、アメリカの
テレビ番組の世代間における相互関係を表す
フローチャート。

U.S.A.   1989
AD: Paul Davis

2
Flow chart illustrating the buying process related to the mom/child relationship. From an advertising agency's brochure.

広告代理店のパンフレットより、母子関係
とショッピング行為の相関関係を説明する
フローチャート。

U.S.A.   1993
CD: Carlos Segura
AD: Jon Stepping
D: Jon Stepping
I: Jon Stepping
DF: Segura Inc.
CL: DDB Needham

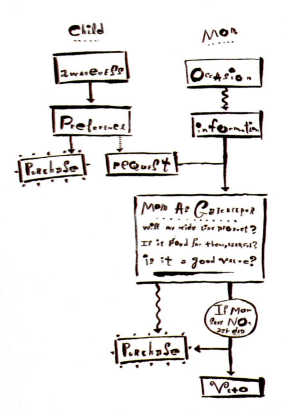

2

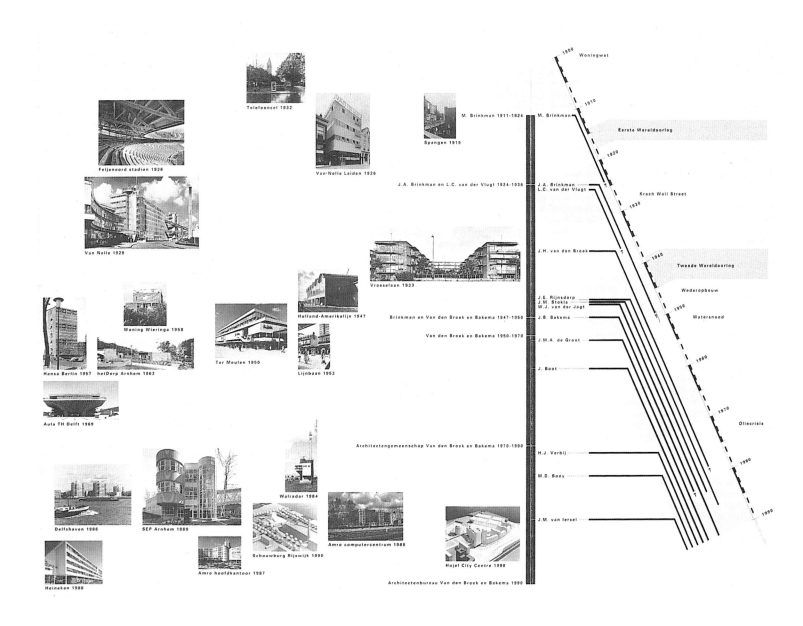

Telefooncel 1932

Van·Nelle Leiden 1926

M. Brinkman 1911-1924   M. Brinkman

Spangen 1919

Feijenoord stadion 1936

J.A. Brinkman en L.C. van der Vlugt 1924-1936   J.A. Brinkman
L.C. van der Vlugt

Van Nelle 1929

J.H. van den Broek

Vroeselaan 1933

Woning Wieringa 1958

Holland-Amerikalijn 1947

J.E. Rijnsdorp
J.M. Stokla
W.J. van der Jagt

Brinkman en Van den Broek en Bakema 1947-1950   J.B. Bakema

Hansa Berlin 1957   hetDorp Arnhem 1963

Ter Meulen 1950

Van den Broek en Bakema 1950-1970   J.M.A. de Groot

Lijnbaan 1953

J. Boot

Aula TH Delft 1969

Architectengemeenschap Van den Broek en Bakema 1970-1990   H.J. Verbij

Walradar 1984

M.D. Booy

Delfshaven 1986   SEP Arnhem 1989

Amro computercentrum 1988

J.M. van Iersel

Schouwburg Rijswijk 1990

Amro hoofdkantoor 1987

Hotel City Centre 1990

Heineken 1988

Architectenbureau Van den Broek en Bakema 1990

1900   Woningwet

1910

Eerste Wereldoorlog

1920

Krach Wall Street

1930

1940   Tweede Wereldoorlog

Wederopbouw

1950

Watersnood

1960

1970   Oliecrisis

1980

1990

Chronological chart showing a Dutch architectural practice's major projects and principal architects, together with world events, from 1911 to 1990. From a Van den Broek en Bakema corporate brochure.

Van den Broek en Bakema社のパンフレットより、1911年から1990年までのオランダ建築様式の主な設計プロジェクトと代表的な建築物を、世界の出来事とともに表した年表。

Netherlands   1990
CD: Ronald van Lit
AD: Ronald van Lit
D: Ronald van Lit
DF: Tel Design
CL: Van den Broek en Bakema Architects

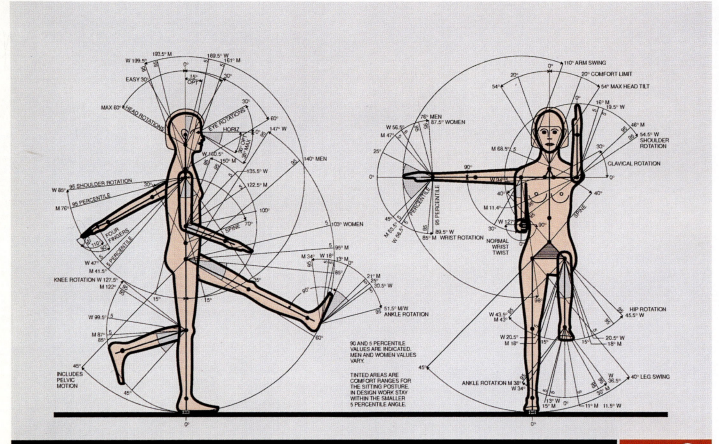

ANGLE MOVEMENTS OF BODY COMPONENTS   DRAWING 16

Functional diagrams illustrating the dimensions of the human body and its range of movements. From 'The Measure of Man and Woman'.

「ザ・メジャー・オブ・マン・アンド・ウーマン」より、人体の大きさと動作の範囲を表した機能図。

U.S.A.   1993
CD: James Ryan
AD: Alvin Tilley
D: Rebecca Welles
I: Alvin Tilley and Microcolor, Inc.
DF: Henry Dreyfuss Associates
CL: Henry Dreyfuss Associates & Whitney Library of Design

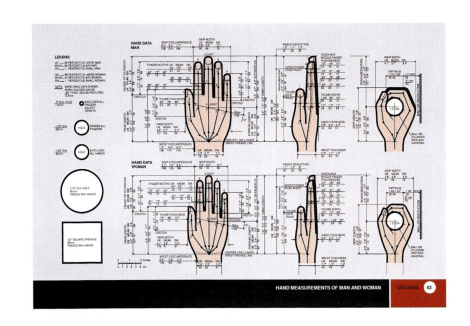

HAND MEASUREMENTS OF MAN AND WOMAN   DRAWING 42

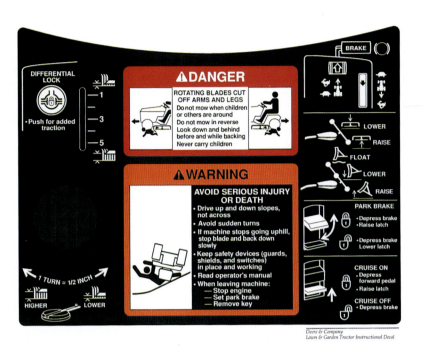

Deere & Company
Lawn & Garden Tractor Instructional Decal

US and European versions of a functional diagram illustrating the operation and safety precautions of a Deere & Co. garden tractor, appearing on the product and in the owner's manual.

庭園用トラクターの製品本体、及び使用者マニュアルに記載されている運転方法と注意事項についてのアメリカ、ヨーロッパ向けの機能図。

U.S.A.　　1992
CD: William E. Crookes
D: Dan Nickles/Jim Weitz/Roslind Skirm
I: Richard Schwamb/Nick Taylor/
Kent Hicks
DF: Henry Dreyfuss Associates
CL: Deere & Co.

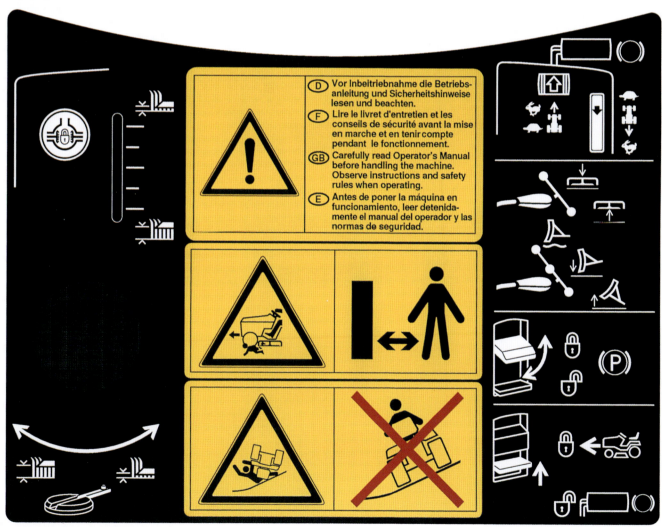

Deere & Company
Lawn & Garden Tractor Instructional Decal

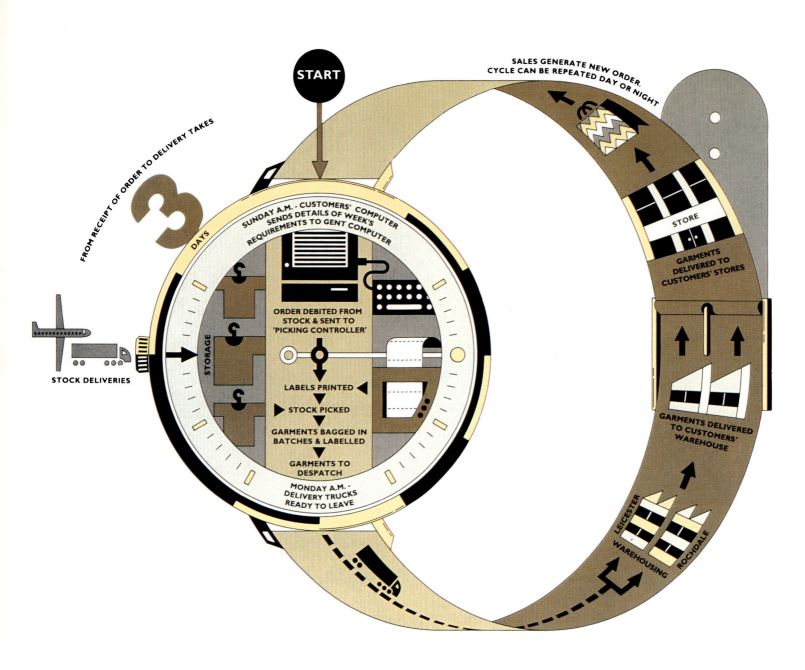

START

FROM RECEIPT OF ORDER TO DELIVERY TAKES

3

DAYS

SUNDAY A.M. - CUSTOMERS' COMPUTER SENDS DETAILS OF WEEK'S REQUIREMENTS TO GENT COMPUTER

ORDER DEBITED FROM STOCK & SENT TO 'PICKING CONTROLLER'

LABELS PRINTED

STOCK PICKED

GARMENTS BAGGED IN BATCHES & LABELLED

GARMENTS TO DESPATCH

MONDAY A.M. - DELIVERY TRUCKS READY TO LEAVE

STORAGE

STOCK DELIVERIES

SALES GENERATE NEW ORDER. CYCLE CAN BE REPEATED DAY OR NIGHT

STORE

GARMENTS DELIVERED TO CUSTOMERS' STORES

GARMENTS DELIVERED TO CUSTOMERS' WAREHOUSE

LEICESTER WAREHOUSING

ROCHDALE

Flow charts of processes involved in clothing manufacture, stressing speed as the most important factor. From SR Gent annual report.

SRジェント社のアニュアルレポートより、アパレル業界の生産工程を表すフローチャート。速さが最も重要であることを強調している。

U.K.   1993
CD: Lou Grainger
AD: Lou Grainger
D: Lou Grainger
I: Tilly Northedge
DF: Addison Design Company Ltd.
CL: SR Gent

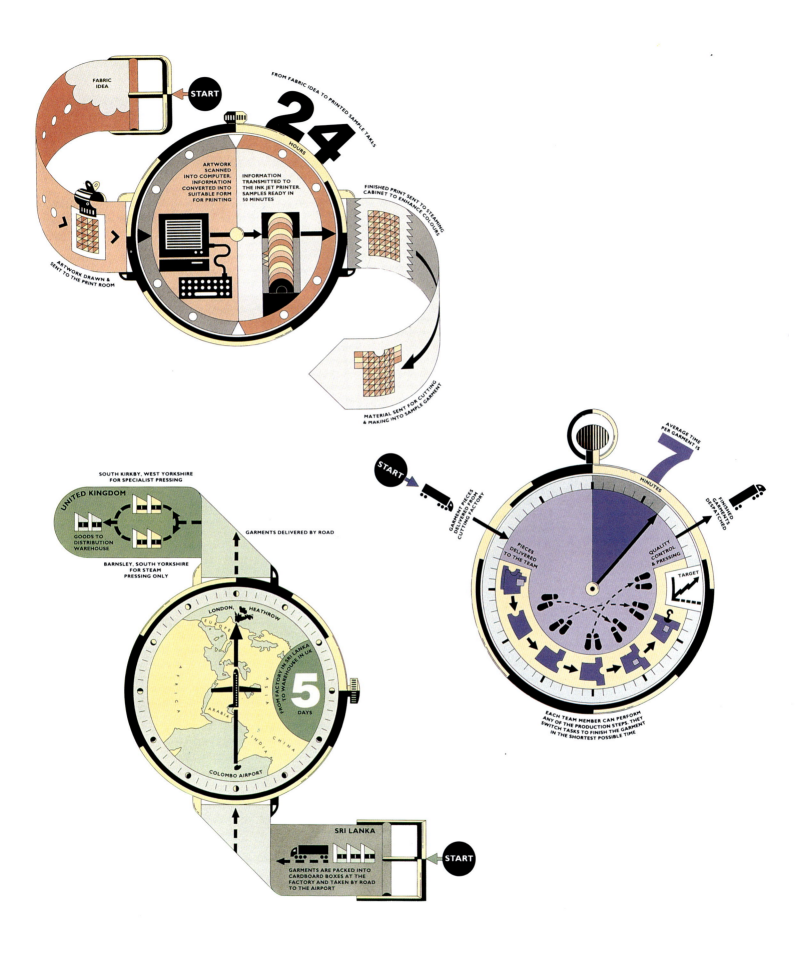

FABRIC
IDEA

START

FROM FABRIC IDEA TO PRINTED SAMPLE TAKES

24 HOURS

ARTWORK
SCANNED
INTO COMPUTER.
INFORMATION
CONVERTED INTO
SUITABLE FORM
FOR PRINTING

INFORMATION
TRANSMITTED TO
THE INK JET PRINTER.
SAMPLES READY IN
50 MINUTES

FINISHED PRINT SENT TO STEAMING
CABINET TO ENHANCE COLOURS

ARTWORK DRAWN &
SENT TO THE PRINT ROOM

MATERIAL SENT FOR CUTTING
& MAKING INTO SAMPLE GARMENT

SOUTH KIRKBY, WEST YORKSHIRE
FOR SPECIALIST PRESSING

UNITED KINGDOM

GOODS TO
DISTRIBUTION
WAREHOUSE

BARNSLEY, SOUTH YORKSHIRE
FOR STEAM
PRESSING ONLY

GARMENTS DELIVERED BY ROAD

LONDON, HEATHROW

EUROPE

AFRICA

ARABIA

ASIA

INDIA

CHINA

FROM FACTORY IN SRI LANKA
TO WAREHOUSE IN UK

5 DAYS

COLOMBO AIRPORT

SRI LANKA

START

GARMENTS ARE PACKED INTO
CARDBOARD BOXES AT THE
FACTORY AND TAKEN BY ROAD
TO THE AIRPORT

START

GARMENT PIECES
DELIVERED FROM
CUTTING FACTORY

AVERAGE TIME
PER GARMENT IS

7 MINUTES

FINISHED
GARMENTS
DESPATCHED

PIECES
DELIVERED
TO THE TEAM

QUALITY
CONTROL
& PRESSING

TARGET

EACH TEAM MEMBER CAN PERFORM
ANY OF THE PRODUCTION STEPS. THEY
SWITCH TASKS TO FINISH THE GARMENT
IN THE SHORTEST POSSIBLE TIME

Functional diagram showing the role of intermediate-level vision. From American Scientist magazine.

「アメリカン・サイエンティスト・マガジン」より、インターミディエイト・レベルでの視覚機能を表す機能図。

U.S.A.　1994
AD: Linda K.Huff
D: Leif H.Finkel/Aaron Cox
I: Aaron Cox
CL: Sigma Xi

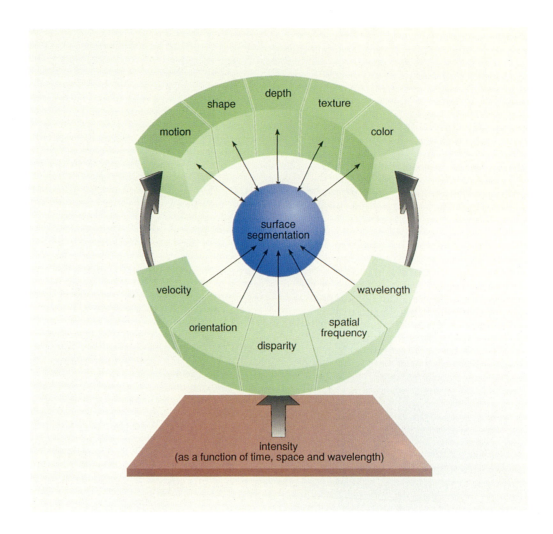

Genealogical chart illustrating the Sherman paradox-the probability of contracting a disease increases in successive generations. From American Scientist magazine.

「アメリカン・サイエンティスト・マガジン」より、シャーマン・パラドックスの系統図。世代を追うにつれて病気にかかる確率が増すことを表す。

U.S.A.　1994
AD: Linda K.Huff
D: Michelle Hoffman/
Edward D.Roberts III
I: Edward D.Roberts III
CL: Sigma Xi

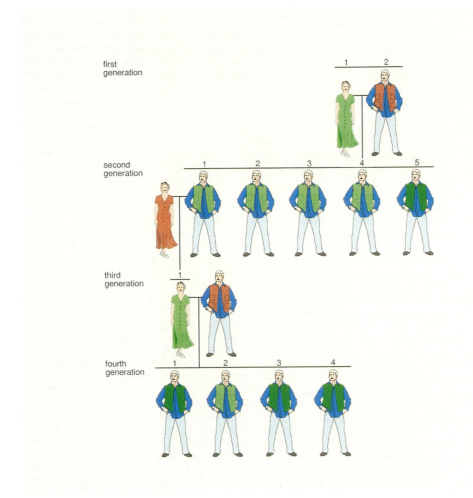

3 Maps 地図

Maps show spatial information in a two-dimensional area. Besides usual maps, there are floor plans showing layouts inside buildings. Maps of the universe are included in the section on scientific illustrations.

地図は一定の空間を平面に表したものである。ここでは一般的な地図以外にも、建物内部の案内図（フロアー・マップ）も地図の領域とした。宇宙空間を表した図は科学イラストレーションの領域としてある。

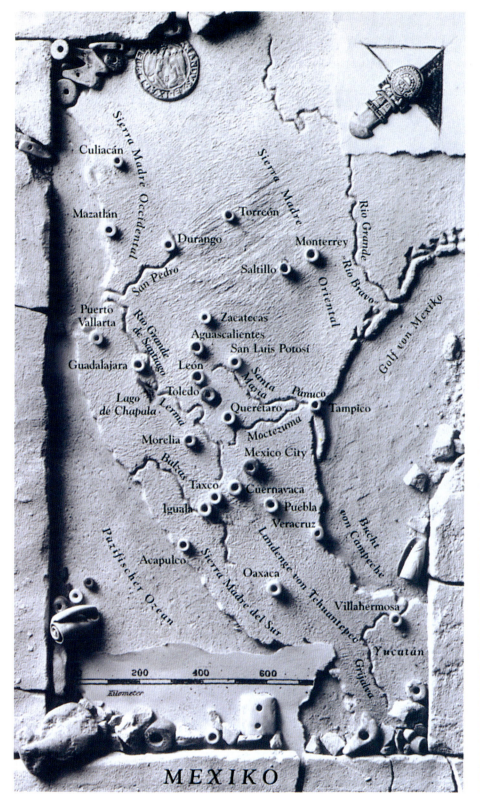

MEXIKO

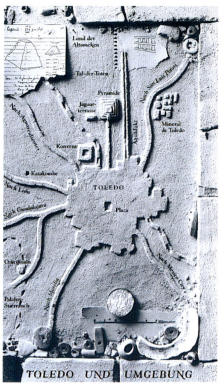

TOLEDO UND UMGEBUNG

PLAZA DE TOLEDO

Maps used to illustrate James A. Michener's novel 'Mexico', published by Gustav Luebbe Verlag GmbH.

グスタフ・ルエッブ・ヴェーラグ社刊行、ジェームズ・A・ミシェナー著の小説「メキシコ」の解説用に制作された地図。

Germany 1994
CD: Arno Haering
AD: Achim Kiel
P: Jutta Bruedern
I: Achim Kiel
DF: Pencil Corporate Art
CL: Gustav Luebbe Verlag GmbH

Natural gas produced in Canada reaches New Jersey Natural Gas via the Tennessee Gas Pipeline. We take this gas in the northern part of our utility's service territory.

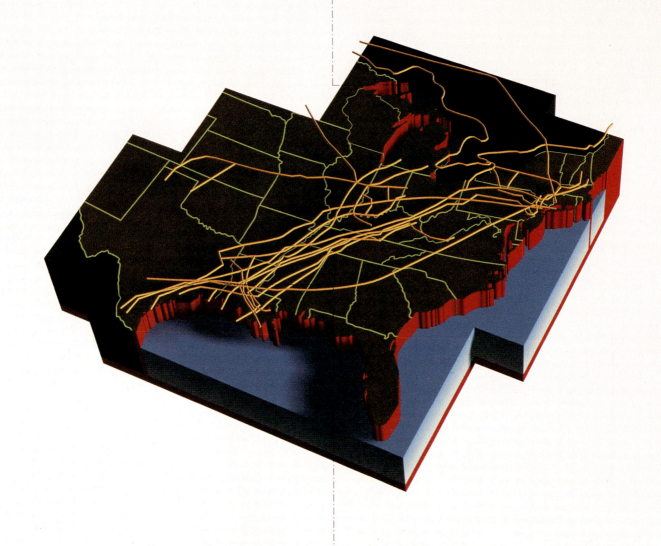

In 1988, New Jersey Natural Gas took gas from six suppliers. Today, we purchase gas supplies produced in the Gulf of Mexico, Midcontinent, and Canada from over 25 different producers and marketers.

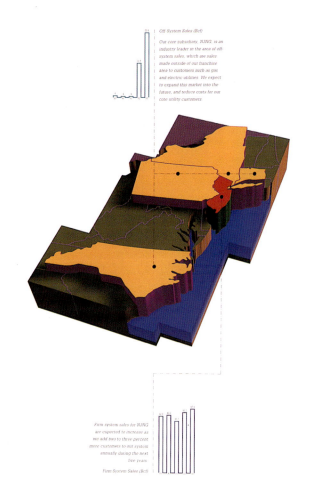

Off-System Sales (Bcf)

Our core subsidiary, NJNG, is an industry leader in the area of off-system sales, which are sales made outside of our franchise area to customers such as gas and electric utilities. We expect to expand this market into the future, and reduce costs for our core utility customers.

Firm system sales for NJNG are expected to increase as we add two to three percent more customers to our system annually during the next five years.

Firm System Sales (Bcf)

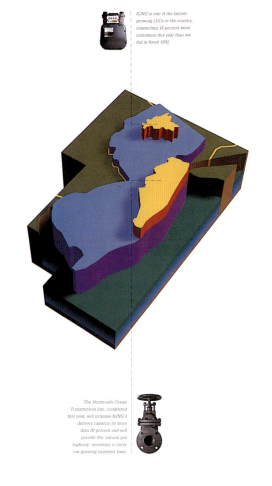

NJNG is one of the fastest-growing LDCs in the country, connecting 18 percent more customers this year than we did in fiscal 1992.

The Monmouth-Ocean Transmission line, completed this year, will increase NJNG's delivery capacity by more than 30 percent and will provide the 'natural gas highway' necessary to serve our growing customer base.

Federal Energy Regulatory Commission Order 636 completes the transition of the natural gas industry to a more competitive, market-based environment. The full unbundling of the merchant and transportation services of interstate pipelines mandated by Order 636 radically changes the structure of the industry as we know it.

Incentive regulation will help NJNG manage risk and reduce our dependence on future price increases. Incentive regulation will help companies at the retail level respond more creatively to the changes occurring in the natural gas market place.

Maps illustrating an energy distributor's pipeline network and service territories. From New Jersey Resources Corporation 1993 annual report.

ニュージャージー・リソーシス社の1993年アニュアルレポートより、エネルギー供給会社のパイプライン・ネットワークとサービス地域を表すマップ・イラストレーション。

U.S.A.　1993
AD: Roger Cook/Don Shanosky
D: Cathryn Cook
I: Stacey Lewis
DF: Cook and Shanosky Associates, Inc.
CL: New Jersey Resources Corporation

Location map of a redeveloped commercial
block in Montreal, Canada, from a real estate
promotional brochure.

不動産プロモーション用パンフレットより、
カナダ、モントリオール市の再開発商業地域
の所在地図。

Canada   1991
CD: Ghyslaine Fallu
AD: Denis Desrocher
D: Tam Tam
I: Tam Tam
DF: Tam Tam
CL: Centre de Commerce Mondial de Montreal

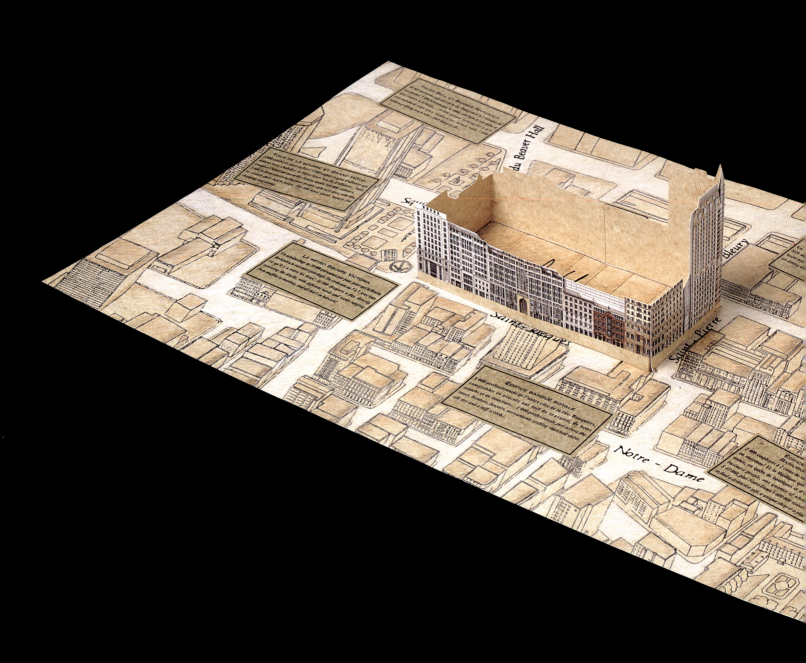

GROSS-BRITANNIEN (heute)

Map used to illustrate Barbara Erskine's novel 'Kingdom of Shadows', published by Gustav Luebbe Verlag GmbH.

グスタフ・ルエッブ・ヴェーラグ社刊行、バーバラ・アースキン著の小説「キングダム・オブ・シャドウズ」の解説用に制作された地図。

Germany   1992
CD: Arno Haering
AD: Achim Kiel
P: Uwe Brandes
I: Achim Kiel
DF: Pencil Corporate Art
CL: Gustav Luebbe Verlag GmbH

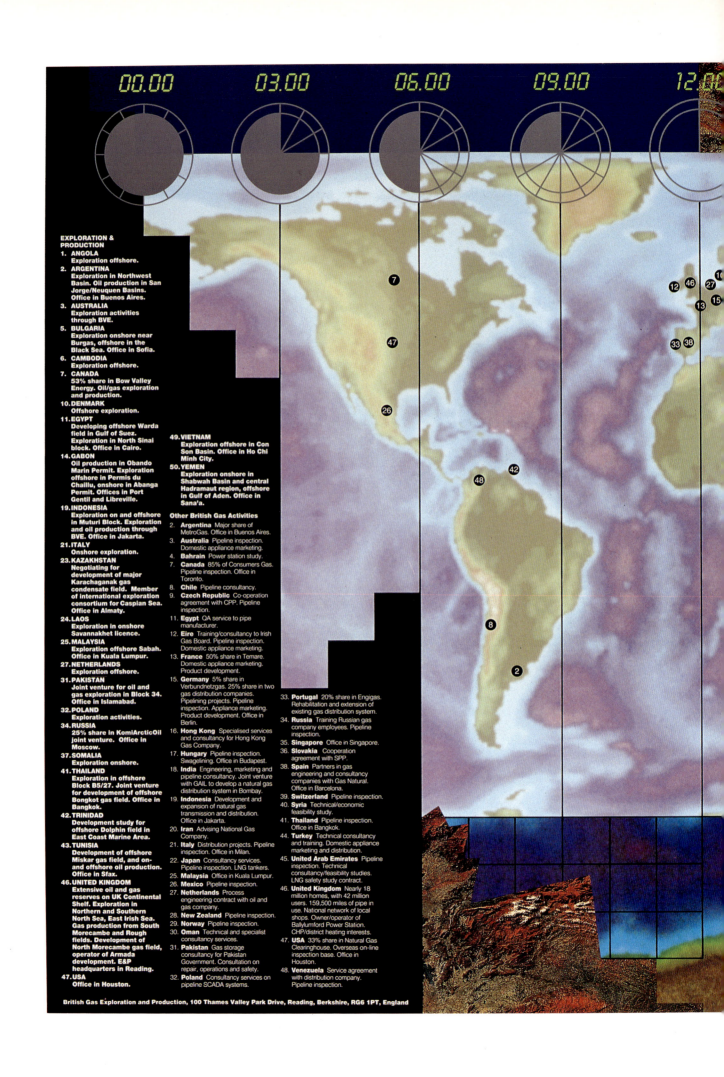

00.00 03.00 06.00 09.00 12.0

EXPLORATION & PRODUCTION

1. **ANGOLA**
   Exploration offshore.
2. **ARGENTINA**
   Exploration in Northwest Basin. Oil production in San Jorge/Neuquen Basins. Office in Buenos Aires.
3. **AUSTRALIA**
   Exploration activities through BVE.
5. **BULGARIA**
   Exploration onshore near Burgas, offshore in the Black Sea. Office in Sofia.
6. **CAMBODIA**
   Exploration offshore.
7. **CANADA**
   53% share in Bow Valley Energy. Oil/gas exploration and production.
10. **DENMARK**
    Offshore exploration.
11. **EGYPT**
    Developing offshore Warda field in Gulf of Suez. Exploration in North Sinai block. Office in Cairo.
14. **GABON**
    Oil production in Obando Marin Permit. Exploration offshore in Permis du Chaillu, onshore in Abanga Permit. Offices in Port Gentil and Libreville.
19. **INDONESIA**
    Exploration on and offshore in Muturi Block. Exploration and oil production through BVE. Office in Jakarta.
21. **ITALY**
    Onshore exploration.
23. **KAZAKHSTAN**
    Negotiating for development of major Karachaganak gas condensate field. Member of international exploration consortium for Caspian Sea. Office in Almaty.
24. **LAOS**
    Exploration in onshore Savannakhet licence.
25. **MALAYSIA**
    Exploration offshore Sabah. Office in Kuala Lumpur.
27. **NETHERLANDS**
    Exploration offshore.
31. **PAKISTAN**
    Joint venture for oil and gas exploration in Block 34. Office in Islamabad.
32. **POLAND**
    Exploration activities.
34. **RUSSIA**
    25% share in KomiArcticOil joint venture. Office in Moscow.
37. **SOMALIA**
    Exploration onshore.
41. **THAILAND**
    Exploration in offshore Block B5/27. Joint venture for development of offshore Bongkot gas field. Office in Bangkok.
42. **TRINIDAD**
    Development study for offshore Dolphin field in East Coast Marine Area.
43. **TUNISIA**
    Development of offshore Miskar gas field, and on- and offshore oil production. Office in Sfax.
46. **UNITED KINGDOM**
    Extensive oil and gas reserves on UK Continental Shelf. Exploration in Northern and Southern North Sea, East Irish Sea. Gas production from South Morecambe and Rough fields. Development of North Morecambe gas field, operator of Armada development. E&P headquarters in Reading.
47. **USA**
    Office in Houston.

49. **VIETNAM**
    Exploration offshore in Con Son Basin. Office in Ho Chi Minh City.
50. **YEMEN**
    Exploration onshore in Shabwah Basin and central Hadramaut region, offshore in Gulf of Aden. Office in Sana'a.

Other British Gas Activities

2. **Argentina** Major share of MetroGas. Office in Buenos Aires.
3. **Australia** Pipeline inspection. Domestic appliance marketing.
4. **Bahrain** Power station study.
7. **Canada** 85% of Consumers Gas. Pipeline inspection. Office in Toronto.
8. **Chile** Pipeline consultancy.
9. **Czech Republic** Co-operation agreement with CPP. Pipeline inspection.
11. **Egypt** QA service to pipe manufacturer.
12. **Eire** Training/consultancy to Irish Gas Board. Pipeline inspection. Domestic appliance marketing.
13. **France** 50% share in Temare. Domestic appliance marketing. Product development.
15. **Germany** 5% share in Verbundnetzgas. 25% share in two gas distribution companies. Pipelining projects. Pipeline inspection. Appliance marketing. Product development. Office in Berlin.
16. **Hong Kong** Specialised services and consultancy for Hong Kong Gas Company.
17. **Hungary** Pipeline inspection. Swagelining. Office in Budapest.
18. **India** Engineering, marketing and pipeline consultancy. Joint venture with GAIL to develop a natural gas distribution system in Bombay.
19. **Indonesia** Development and expansion of natural gas transmission and distribution. Office in Jakarta.
20. **Iran** Advising National Gas Company.
21. **Italy** Distribution projects. Pipeline inspection. Office in Milan.
22. **Japan** Consultancy services. Pipeline inspection. LNG tankers.
25. **Malaysia** Office in Kuala Lumpur.
26. **Mexico** Pipeline inspection.
27. **Netherlands** Process engineering contract with oil and gas company.
28. **New Zealand** Pipeline inspection.
29. **Norway** Pipeline inspection.
30. **Oman** Technical and specialist consultancy services.
31. **Pakistan** Gas storage consultancy for Pakistan Government. Consultation on repair, operations and safety.
32. **Poland** Consultancy services on pipeline SCADA systems.

33. **Portugal** 20% share in Engigas. Rehabilitation and extension of existing gas distribution system.
34. **Russia** Training Russian gas company employees. Pipeline inspection.
35. **Singapore** Office in Singapore.
36. **Slovakia** Cooperation agreement with SPP.
38. **Spain** Partners in gas engineering and consultancy companies with Gas Natural. Office in Barcelona.
39. **Switzerland** Pipeline inspection.
40. **Syria** Technical/economic feasibility study.
41. **Thailand** Pipeline inspection. Office in Bangkok.
44. **Turkey** Technical consultancy and training. Domestic appliance marketing and distribution.
45. **United Arab Emirates** Pipeline inspection. Technical consultancy/feasibility studies. LNG safety study contract.
46. **United Kingdom** Nearly 18 million homes, with 42 million users. 159,500 miles of pipe in use. National network of local shops. Owner/operator of Ballylumford Power Station. CHP/district heating interests.
47. **USA** 33% share in Natural Gas Clearinghouse. Overseas on-line inspection base. Office in Houston.
48. **Venezuela** Service agreement with distribution company. Pipeline inspection.

British Gas Exploration and Production, 100 Thames Valley Park Drive, Reading, Berkshire, RG6 1PT, England

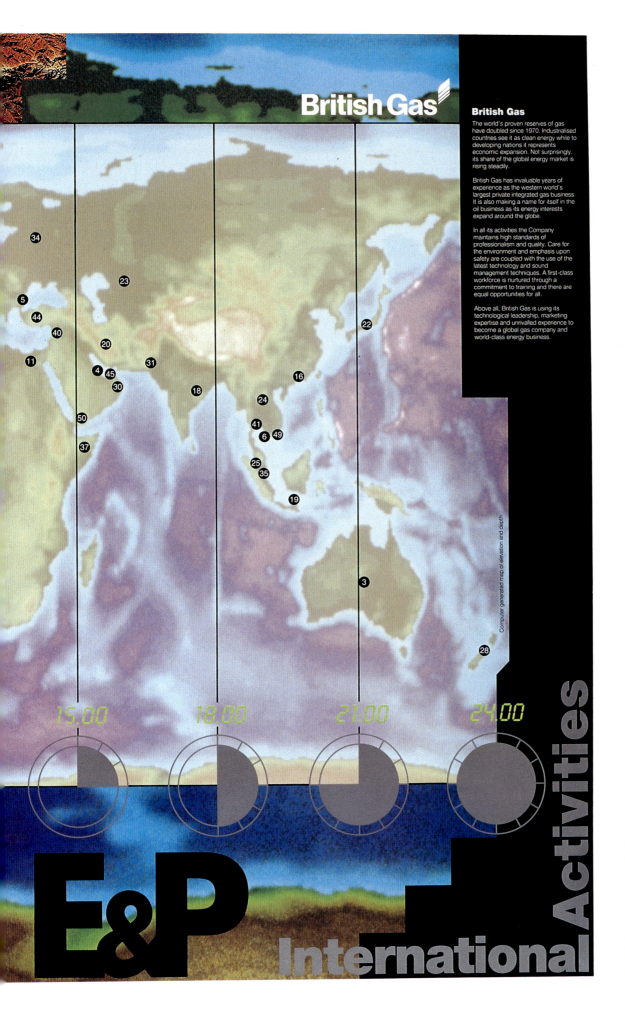

British Gas

British Gas

The world's proven reserves of gas have doubled since 1970. Industrialised countries see it as clean energy while to developing nations it represents economic expansion. Not surprisingly, its share of the global energy market is rising steadily.

British Gas has invaluable years of experience as the western world's largest private integrated gas business. It is also making a name for itself in the oil business as its energy interests expand around the globe.

In all its activities the Company maintains high standards of professionalism and quality. Care for the environment and emphasis upon safety are coupled with the use of the latest technology and sound management techniques. A first-class workforce is nurtured through a commitment to training and there are equal opportunities for all.

Above all, British Gas is using its technological leadership, marketing expertise and unrivalled experience to become a global gas company and world-class energy business.

Computer generated map of elevation and depth

15.00 18.00 21.00 24.00

E&P

International Activities

Map showing global locations and activities of British Gas. From a British Gas E & P leaflet.

ブリティッシュガスE&P社のパンフレットより、同社の海外拠点とその活動について表す地図。

U.K.   1993
CD: Geoff Aldridge
D: Sally Mcintosh
DF: Communication by Design Ltd, London
CL: British Gas E & P

Map showing location of a biotechnology company's international partners and availability of its products. From Centocor, Inc. 1992 annual report.

セントコー社の1992年アニュアルレポートより、同バイオテクノロジー会社の海外提携先と、商品を取り扱っている地域を表す世界地図。

U.S.A. 1993
CD: Joel Katz
D: Kimberly Mollo/Joel Katz
I: Kimberly Mollo/David Schpok/Joel Katz
DF: Paradigm:design
CL: Centocor, Inc.

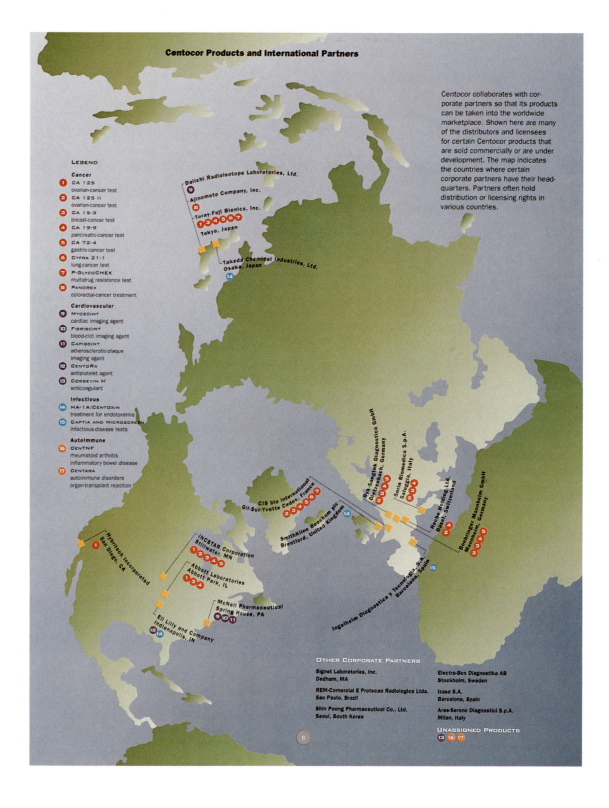

Centocor Products and International Partners

Centocor collaborates with corporate partners so that its products can be taken into the worldwide marketplace. Shown here are many of the distributors and licensees for certain Centocor products that are sold commercially or are under development. The map indicates the countries where certain corporate partners have their headquarters. Partners often hold distribution or licensing rights in various countries.

LEGEND

Cancer
1 CA 125 ovarian-cancer test
2 CA 125 II ovarian-cancer test
3 CA 15-3 breast-cancer test
4 CA 19-9 pancreatic-cancer test
5 CA 72-4 gastric-cancer test
6 CYFRA 21-1 lung-cancer test
7 P-GLYCOCHEK multidrug resistance test
8 PANOREX colorectal-cancer treatment

Cardiovascular
9 MYOSCINT cardiac imaging agent
10 FIBRISCINT blood-clot imaging agent
11 CAPISCINT atherosclerotic-plaque imaging agent
12 CENTORx antiplatelet agent
13 CORSEVIN M anticoagulant

Infectious
14 HA-1A/CENTOXIN treatment for endotoxemia
15 CAPTIA AND MICROSCREEN infectious-disease tests

AutoImmune
16 CENTNF rheumatoid arthritis inflammatory bowel disease
17 CENTARA autoimmune disorders organ-transplant rejection

Daiichi Radioisotope Laboratories, Ltd.
9
Ajinomoto Company, Inc.
8
Toray-Fuji Bionics, Inc.
1 3 4 5 6 7
Tokyo, Japan
Takeda Chemical Industries, Ltd. Osaka, Japan
14

Byk-Sangtek Diagnostica GmbH Dietzenbach, Germany
Sorin Biomedica S.p.A. Saluggia, Italy
4
Roche Holding Ltd. Basel, Switzerland
4
Boehringer Mannheim GmbH Mannheim, Germany
4 5 2

CIS bio International Gif-Sur-Yvette Cedex, France
2 3 4 5 6 7

SmithKline Beecham plc Brentford, United Kingdom
14

Ingelheim Diagnostica y Tecnologia S.A. Barcelona, Spain
15

Hybritech Incorporated San Diego, CA
1

INCSTAR Corporation Stillwater, MN
1 2 3 4 5

Abbott Laboratories Abbott Park, IL
1 3 4

McNeil Pharmaceutical Spring House, PA
9 10 11

Eli Lilly and Company Indianapolis, IN
12 14

OTHER CORPORATE PARTNERS

Signet Laboratories, Inc. Dedham, MA

REM-Comercial E Protecao Radiologica Ltda. Sao Paulo, Brazil

Shin Poong Pharmaceutical Co., Ltd. Seoul, South Korea

Electra-Box Diagnostika AB Stockholm, Sweden

Izasa S.A. Barcelona, Spain

Ares-Serono Diagnostici S.p.A. Milan, Italy

UNASSIGNED PRODUCTS
13 16 17

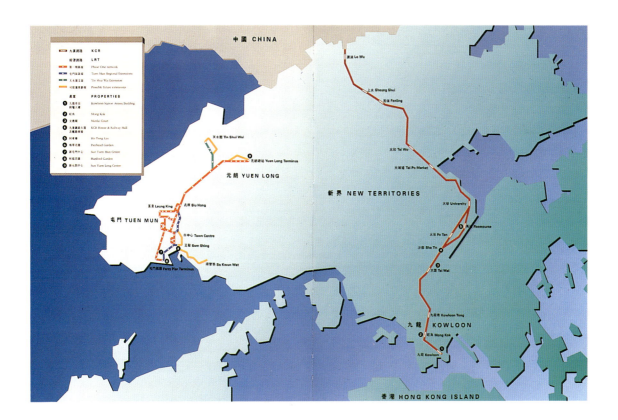

Map showing rail network and company properties. From Kowloon-Canton Railway Corporation 1992 annual report.

九龍広東鉄道会社の1992年アニュアルレポートより、同社の路線図と会社所有地を表した地図。

Hong Kong 1992
CD: Kan Tai-keung
AD: Eddy Yu Chi Kong
D: Eddy Yu Chi Kong
DF: Kan Tai-keung Design & Associates Ltd.
CL: Kowloon-Canton Railway Corporation

1) Ares Services S.A. serves as Executive Headquarters of the Group.
2) Inter-Lab Ltd. (formerly Inter-Yeda Ltd.) is 100% owned by Interpharm Laboratories Ltd. which is 76.3% owned by the Group.
3) InterPharm Industries, Ltd. is 100% owned by both InterPharm Laboratories Ltd. and Inter-Lab Ltd. which are 76.3% owned by the Group.
4) This company is the holding company for most of the Group's Italian subsidiaries.
5) 73.3% of the shares of this company are held, directly or indirectly, by Istituto Farmacologico Serono S.p.A. (IFS), which in turn is 68.4% owned by the Group.
6) Industria Farmaceutica Serono S.p.A. and Calibis S.p.A. are wholly owned subsidiaries of IFS which, in turn, is 68.4% owned by the Group.

7) 42.9% of the shares of Ares-Serono Diagnostici S.p.A. are indirectly owned by IFS which, in turn, is 68.4% owned by the Group. The remaining 57.1% of the shares are owned by the Group.
8) Istituto di Ricerca Cesare Serono S.p.A. is 100% owned by IFS and its wholly owned subsidiaries which, in turn, are 68.4% owned by the Group.
9) 100% of the shares of this company are held, directly or indirectly, by IFS, which in turn is 68.4% owned by the Group.
10) 51% of the shares are owned by IFS which, in turn, is 68.4% owned by the Group. The remaining 49% of the shares are owned by the Group.
11) Bourn-Hall Clinic is a clinic specialized in the treatment of infertility.
12) Serono Laboratories Inc. sold its diagnostic assets and liabilities to Serono Diagnostics, Inc. in 1993.

Location map of pharmaceutical group's associates and subsidiaries. From Ares-Serono 1993 annual report.

アレス・セロノ社の1993年アニュアルレポートより、同製薬会社グループの関連会社、及び子会社の所在地を表した地図。

Switzerland 1994
CD: Oscar Ribes
AD: Oscar Ribes
CL: Ares Serono

Maps showing location of a German
bank's branch offices, from Vereinsbank
1993 annual report.

Vereins銀行の1993年アニュアルレポートよ
り、支店の所在地図。

Switzerland   1994
CD: Gottschalk+Ash Int'l
D: Fritz Gottschalk/ Heather LaFleur
CL: Vereinsbank, München

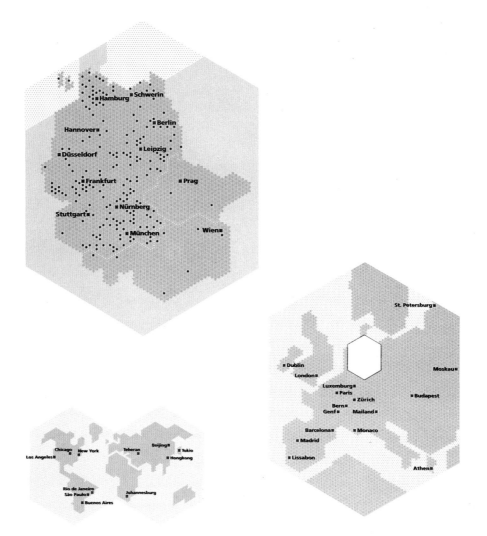

Location map of facilities of a US long-term
health care company. From Hillhaven
Corporation 1993 annual report.

ヒルヘブン社の1993年アニュアルレポート
より、長期療養施設の所在地図。

U.S.A.   1993
AD: Jack Anderson
D: Jack Anderson/Mary Hermes
I: Todd Connor/Georgia Deaver
DF: Hornall Anderson Design Works
CL: Hillhaven Corporation

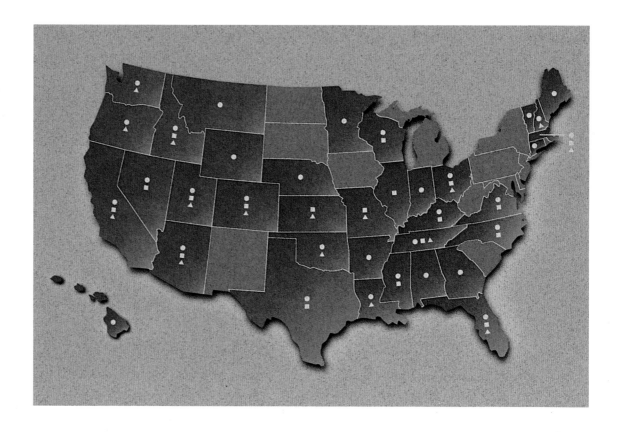

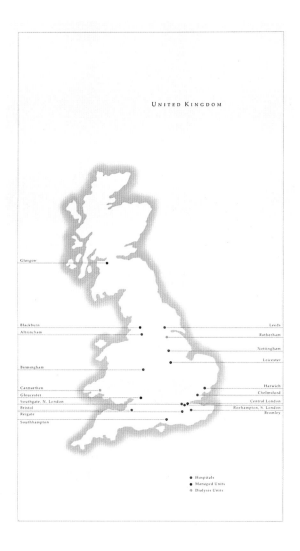

UNITED KINGDOM

Glasgow

Blackburn   Leeds
Altrincham   Rotherham
                                             Nottingham
                                             Leicester
Birmingham

Carmarthen   Harwich
Gloucester   Chelmsford
Southgate, N. London   Central London
Bristol   Roehampton, S. London
Reigate   Bromley
Southhampton

  • Hospitals
  • Managed Units
  ○ Dialysis Units

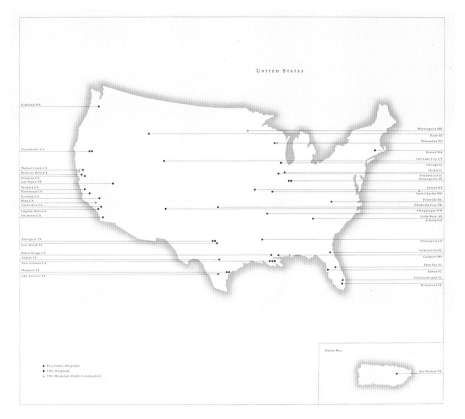

UNITED STATES

Kirkland WA

                                             Minneapolis MN
                                             Boise ID
                                             Milwaukee WI
Sacramento CA   Boston MA
                                             Salt Lake City UT
Walnut Creek CA   Chicago IL
Belmont Hills CA   Skokie IL
Fremont CA   Streamwood IL
Las Vegas NV   Indianapolis IN
Ventura CA   Lenexa KS
Rosemead CA   Saint Charles MO
Fontana CA   Pineville NC
Brea CA   Oklahoma City OK
Santa Ana CA   Albuquerque NM
Laguna Hills CA   Little Rock AR
Encinitas CA   Atlanta GA

Arlington TX   Shreveport LA
Fort Worth TX
Baton Rouge LA   Jacksonville FL
Austin TX   Gulfport MS
New Orleans LA   Palm Bay FL
Houston TX   Tampa FL
San Antonio TX   Fort Lauderdale FL
                                             Hollywood FL

  • Psychiatric Hospitals
  • THC Hospitals
  ○ THC Hospitals Under Construction

Puerto Rico

                                             Rio Piedras PR

Location maps of Community Psychiatric Center health facilities in UK (above) and US and Puerto Rico (below). From Community Psychiatric Center 1993 annual report.

コミュニティー・サイキアトリック・センターの1993年アニュアルレポートより、同センターのイギリス（上）、及びアメリカとプエルトリコ（下）における所在地図。

U.S.A.   1993
AD: Jim Berte
D: Maria Dellota/Jim Berte
DF: Runyan Hinsche Associates
CL: Community Psychiatric Center

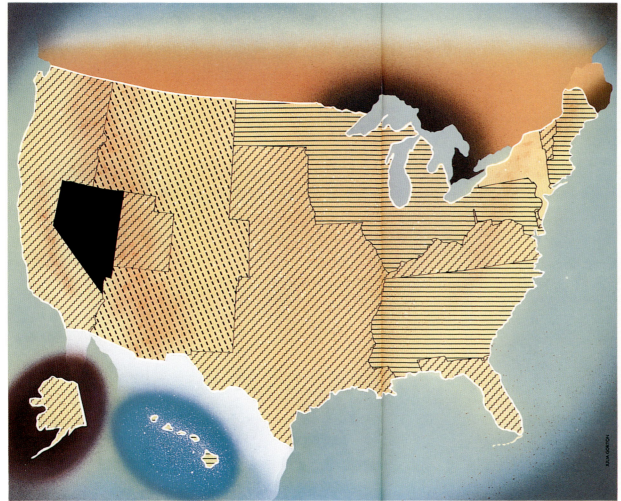

GEOGRAPHY

Deaths by suicide (annually) per
100,000 residents. As a point of
comparison, keep in mind that Nevada
is the fastest-growing state in the
country, while everyone is supposedly
dying to leave New York.

	under 8
	8–13
	13.1–17
	17.1–24
	over 24

Ala.	12.4
Alaska	14.8
Ariz.	19.3
Ark.	13.5
Cal.	14.7
Colo.	17.6
Conn.	9.6
Del.	13.3
D.C.	12.0
Fla.	16.0
Ga.	13.0
Hawaii	10.0
Idaho	17.7
Ill.	11.0
Ind.	11.7
Iowa	12.9
Kans.	13.6
Ky.	14.2
La.	14.2
Me.	11.1
Md.	12.2
Mass.	9.2
Mich.	12.3
Minn.	12.8
Miss.	11.1
Mo.	14.2
Mont.	21.7
Neb.	14.3
Nev.	24.1
N.H.	13.0
N.J.	7.6
N.M.	19.4
N.Y.	7.6
N.C.	12.2
N.D.	10.8
Ohio	11.6
Okla.	14.6
Oreg.	16.7
Pa.	12.2
R.I.	10.2
S.C.	11.4
S.D.	14.3
Tenn.	12.9
Tex.	13.6
Utah	14.7
Vt.	14.0
Va.	14.1
Wash.	15.3
W.Va.	14.2
Wis.	12.5
Wyo.	19.1
U.S.	12.8

29

Map comparing suicide rates in US
states. From Wigwag magazine.

「ウィグワグ・マガジン」より、自殺発生率を
アメリカの州別に比較する地図。

U.S.A.   1990
AD: Paul Davis
I: Julia Gorton

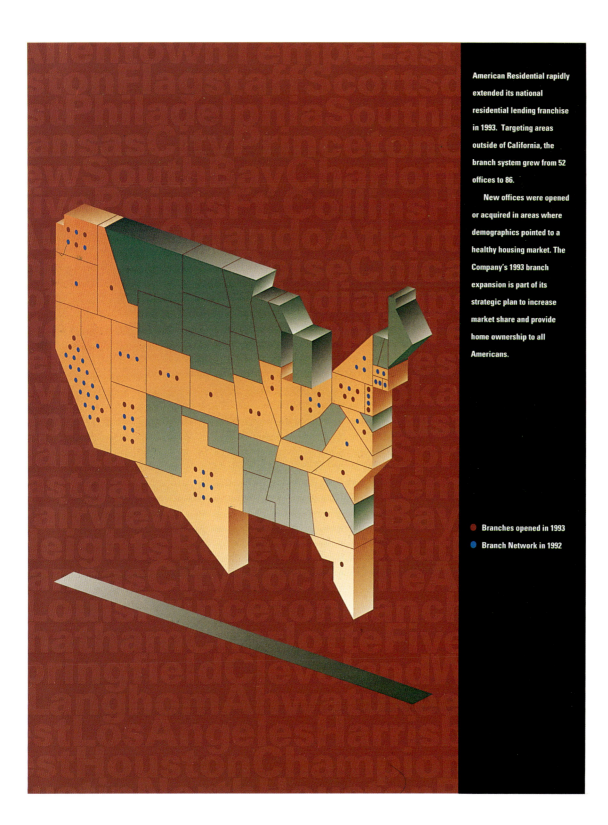

American Residential rapidly extended its national residential lending franchise in 1993. Targeting areas outside of California, the branch system grew from 52 offices to 86.

New offices were opened or acquired in areas where demographics pointed to a healthy housing market. The Company's 1993 branch expansion is part of its strategic plan to increase market share and provide home ownership to all Americans.

● Branches opened in 1993
● Branch Network in 1992

Map of branch network and new branches. From American Residential Holding Corporation 1993 annual report.

アメリカン・レジデンシャル・ホールディング社の1993年アニュアルレポートより、同社の支社ネットワークと新支社を示す地図。

U.S.A.   1993
CD: Carl Seltzer
AD: Carl Seltzer
D: Carl Seltzer/Luis Alvarado
DF: Carl Seltzer Design Office
CL: American Residential Holding Corp.

Map showing numbers of endangered species in US states. From Details magazine.

「ディテールズ・マガジン」より、絶滅の危機
に瀕している動物の種の数を州別に表した
アメリカの地図。

U.S.A.　　1994
AD: Markus Kiersztan
D: Nigel Holmes
I: Nigel Holmes
CL: Details Magazine

Map comparing state laws prohibiting certain sexual activities in the US. From Details magazine.

「ディテールズ・マガジン」より、特定の性
的行為を禁止する州法を比較したアメリカ
の地図。

U.S.A.　　1993
AD: BW Honeycutt
D: Nigel Holmes
I: Nigel Holmes
CL: Details Magazine

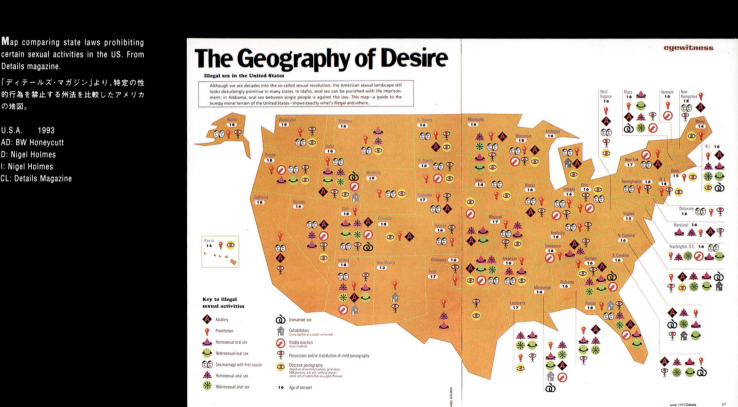

FLORIDA
GEORGIA
Little St. Simons
Useppa
Little Palm
Deep Water Cay
BAHAMAS

GULF OF MEXICO

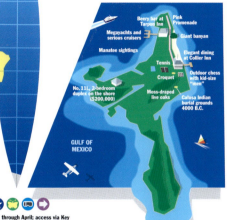

USEPPA ISLAND CLUB

Posh and exclusive, this mangrove cay has a fitness center, tennis and croquet, sailing, and a colorful history: The Calusa Indians, to whose shell middens the island owes its height, predated the club's robber baron founders by 6,000 years, and Useppa was a CIA staging area for the Bay of Pigs in '61. Now about 100 airy, latticed, privately owned cottages distinguish the 100 acres where Rothschilds and Roosevelt once angled for tarpon. The season runs from mid-September to mid-June; access via Fort Myers (813-283-1061; from $100 per day for nonmembers).

Beery bar at Tarpon Inn
Pink Promenade
Megayachts and serious cruisers
Giant banyan
Manatee sightings
Elegant dining at Collier Inn
Tennis
Croquet
Outdoor chess with kid-size "men"
No. 11L, 2-bedroom duplex on the shore ($200,000)
Moss-draped live oaks
Calusa Indian burial grounds 4000 B.C.

LITTLE PALM ISLAND

Truman fished here, though it's hard to picture Harry among the bronzed, the bikini-clad, and the bird-loving who flock to this five-acre dot awash in AAA diamonds and *Mobil Travel Guide* stars. Then again, Harry might feel right at home: plenty of bucks stop here. The duplexes are thatched and the suites are pastel, but the food can be pretentious and the massages cost $70, so use your Jacuzzi instead. The best weather occurs from around Christmas through April; access via Key West (800-343-8567; 60 guests; doubles from $495, two-night minimum).

Day-trippers confined to restaurant and boutique
15-minute boat ride from Little Torch Key
On stilts, suite 13 has hammock, outdoor shower, rocking chaise
Rent Sun Cat for silent birding
Pool
Staff headquarters
Rooms 17–24 are most private
Snorkeling boat to Looe Key reef departs at 10:30
7½-minute round-the-island walk
Jamaican palms shade interior. Mangrove flats, alive with red-billed ibis, willets, and plovers, fringe coast

LITTLE ST. SIMONS ISLAND

Homo sapiens is as happy in this wilderness as the local rara avis are. Piney high ground and marshy sloughs are offset by such indulgences as roaring fires, hearty meals, and jolly cocktail hours. The family Berolzheimer opened the 1917 Hunting Lodge and two handsome new four-bedroom houses to 24 guests—birders, wildlife enthusiasts, fishermen, crabbers, horseback riders, boaters, and seashell collectors. Spring and fall are the best seasons; access via Jacksonville, Florida (912-638-7472; doubles from $300, two-night minimum).

The Backbone: High dune trail to green marsh
Gators at Myrtle Pond
Sancho Panza Beach
Best view of marshes from River Lodge room 2 and Cedar House 4; better rooms in Hunting Lodge
Herd of 640 fallow deer
Crab for hors d'oeuvres in Mosquito Creek
Wooden shade hut
7 miles of brown beach
Main Beach
HAMPTON RIVER
Morning birding in marshes, afternoon birding in trees
Pine forest
ATLANTIC OCEAN
43 loggerhead turtles laid eggs at Rainbow Beach last May, June, and July

DEEP WATER CAY CLUB

The bonefish-rich waters off Grand Bahama harbor this esteemed 33-year-old club, owned by Tennessee anglers. But the weathered nine-bedroom complex, with monogrammed linens, chummy dinners, and an honor bar, has a lot more amenities than most fishing camps. It's a great family resort, and perfect for father-son fishing excursions. The best weather occurs in October and November and from March into June; access via West Palm Beach (407-684-3958 in Fla.; $995 per person, three-night minimum).

5-minute boat ride to McClean's Town
Grouper, grilled snapper; fix-your-own drinks at the clubhouse
Jetty
Squirrel-tailed lizards on sandy paths
Small pool
Airstrip
Fleets of the world's fastest fish
Room 7: Embroidered white shams, 9 pillows
Wooden chaises shaded by thatch
2½ miles of grainy walking sand
NORTHWEST PROVIDENCE CHANNEL
Thrift Harbor Creek: Drift-snorkel at ebb tide

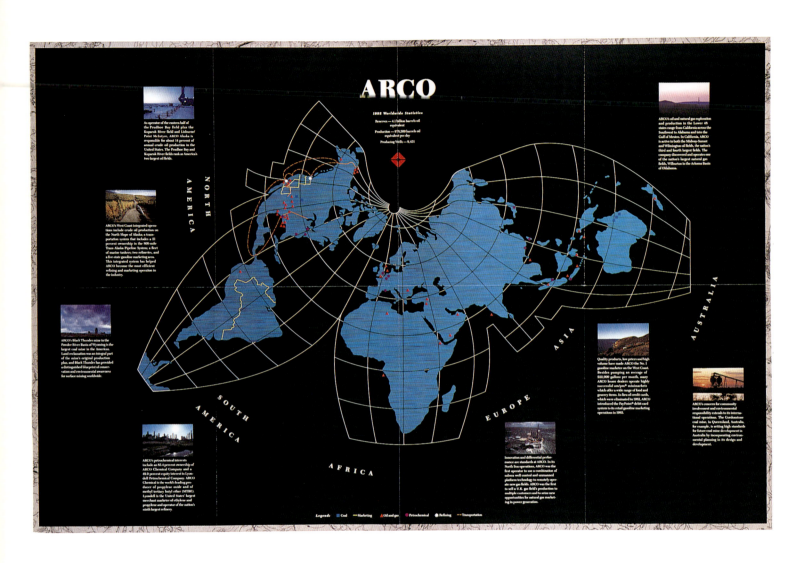

Map illustrating an energy company's
activities. From Arco 1992 annual report.

アルコ社の1992年アニュアルレポートより、
エネルギー会社の活動内容を表す地図。

U.S.A.   1992
CD: Ron Jefferies
AD: Ron Jefferies/Scott Lambert
D: Scott Lambert
I: Scott Lambert
DF: The Jefferies Association
CL: Arco

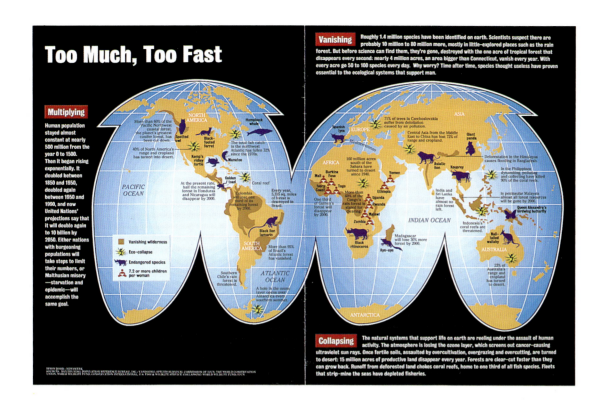

Too Much, Too Fast

Multiplying

Human population stayed almost constant at nearly 500 million from the year 0 to 1500. Then it began rising exponentially. It doubled between 1850 and 1950, doubled again between 1950 and 1990, and now United Nations' projections say that it will double again to 10 billion by 2050. Either nations with burgeoning populations will take steps to limit their numbers, or Malthusian misery —starvation and epidemic—will accomplish the same goal.

Vanishing

Roughly 1.4 million species have been identified on earth. Scientists suspect there are probably 10 million to 80 million more, mostly in little-explored places such as the rain forest. But before science can find them, they're gone, destroyed with the one acre of tropical forest that disappears every second: nearly 4 million acres, an area bigger than Connecticut, vanish every year. With every acre go 50 to 100 species every day. Why worry? Time after time, species thought useless have proven essential to the ecological systems that support man.

Collapsing

The natural systems that support life on earth are reeling under the assault of human activity. The atmosphere is losing the ozone layer, which screens out cancer-causing ultraviolet sun rays. Once fertile soils, assaulted by overcultivation, overgrazing and overcutting, are turned to desert: 15 million acres of productive land disappear every year. Forests are clear-cut when they can grow back. Runoff from deforested land chokes coral reefs, home to one third of all fish species. Fleets that strip-mine the seas have depleted fisheries.

World map highlighting ecological hot spots. From Newsweek magazine.

「ニューズウィーク・マガジン」より、生態学上危険な地域を表した世界地図。

U.S.A.   1992
AD: Patricia Bradbury
D: Dixon Rohr
I: Dixon Rohr
DF: Newsweek
CL: Newsweek

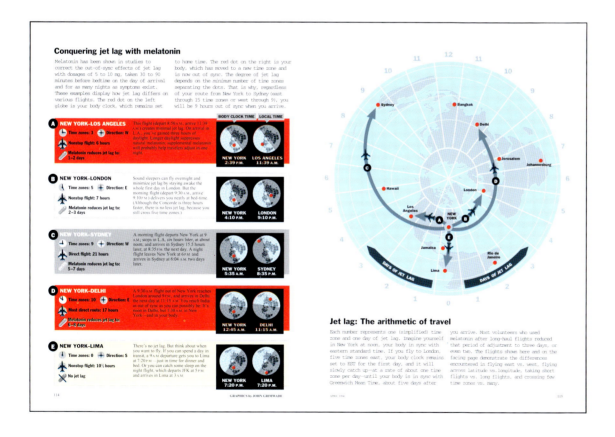

Conquering jet lag with melatonin

Melatonin has been shown in studies to correct the out-of-sync effects of jet lag with dosages of 5 to 10 mg, taken 30 to 90 minutes before bedtime on the day of arrival and for as many nights as symptoms exist. These examples display how jet lag differs on various flights. The red dot on the left globe is your body clock, which remains set to home time. The red dot on the right is your body, which has moved to a new time zone and is now out of sync. The degree of jet lag depends on the *minimum* number of time zones separating the dots. That is why, regardless of your route from New York to Sydney (east through 15 time zones or west through 9), you will be 9 hours out of sync when you arrive.

A NEW YORK–LOS ANGELES
Time zones: 3   Direction: W
Nonstop flight: 6 hours
Melatonin reduces jet lag to: 1–2 days

This flight (depart 8:30 A.M., arrive 11:39 A.M.) creates minimal jet lag. On arrival in L.A., you've gained three hours of daylight. Longer daylight suppresses natural melatonin; supplemental melatonin will probably help travelers adjust in one night.

BODY CLOCK TIME — NEW YORK 2:39 P.M.   LOCAL TIME — LOS ANGELES 11:39 A.M.

B NEW YORK–LONDON
Time zones: 5   Direction: E
Nonstop flight: 7 hours
Melatonin reduces jet lag to: 2–3 days

Sound sleepers can fly overnight and minimize jet lag by staying awake the whole first day in London. But the morning flight (depart 9:30 A.M., arrive 9:10 P.M.) delivers you neatly at bed-time. (Although the Concorde is three hours faster, there is no less jet lag, because you still cross five time zones.)

NEW YORK 4:10 P.M.   LONDON 9:10 P.M.

C NEW YORK–SYDNEY
Time zones: 9   Direction: W
Direct flight: 21 hours
Melatonin reduces jet lag to: 5–7 days

A morning flight departs New York at 9 A.M.; stops in L.A. six hours later, at noon, and arrives in Sydney 15.5 hours later, at 8:35 P.M. the next day. A night flight leaves New York at 6 P.M. and arrives in Sydney at 6:04 A.M. two days later.

NEW YORK 5:35 A.M.   SYDNEY 8:35 P.M.

D NEW YORK–DELHI
Time zones: 10   Direction: E
Most direct route: 17 hours
Melatonin reduces jet lag to: 6–8 days

A 9:30 A.M. flight out of New York reaches London around 9 P.M., and arrives in Delhi the next day at 11:15 A.M. You reach India as out of sync as you can possibly be; it's noon in Delhi, but 1:30 A.M. in New York—and your body.

NEW YORK 12:45 A.M.   DELHI 11:15 A.M.

E NEW YORK–LIMA
Time zones: 0   Direction: S
Nonstop flight: 10½ hours
No jet lag

There's no jet lag. But think about when you want to fly. If you can spend a day in transit, a 9 A.M. departure gets you to Lima at 7:20 P.M.—just in time for dinner and bed. Or you can catch some sleep on the night flight, which departs JFK at 5 P.M. and arrives in Lima at 3 A.M.

NEW YORK 7:20 P.M.   LIMA 7:20 P.M.

Jet lag: The arithmetic of travel

Each number represents one (simplified) time zone and one day of jet lag. Imagine yourself in transit, in New York at noon, your body in sync with eastern standard time. If you fly to London, five time zones east, your body clock remains set to EST for the first day, and it will slowly catch up—at a rate of about one time zone per day—until your body is in sync with Greenwich Mean Time, about five days after you arrive. Most volunteers who used melatonin after long-haul flights reduced that period of adjustment to three days, or even two. The flights shown here and on the facing page demonstrate the differences encountered in flying east vs. west, flying across latitude vs. longitude, taking short flights vs. long flights, and crossing few time zones vs. many.

114   GRAPHICS by JOHN GRIMWADE   APRIL 1994   115

Map showing flights from New York of various lengths with likely number of days of jet lag. From Conde Nast Traveler magazine.

「コンデ・ナスト・トラベラー・マガジン」より、ニューヨークからの飛行距離と、時差ボケの解消にかかるおおよその日数を表す地図。

U.S.A.   1994
CD: Diana LaGuardia
I: John Grimwade
CL: Conde Nast Traveler

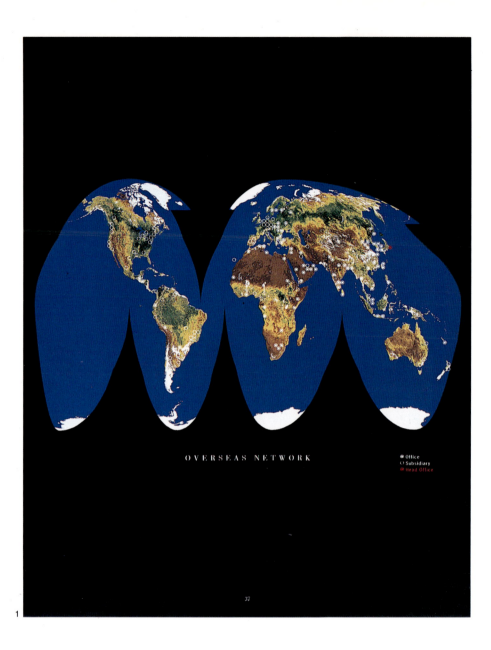

OVERSEAS NETWORK

● Office
○ Subsidiary
● Head Office

37

1
Map illustrating trading giant's worldwide business strategy, from Mitsubishi Corporation corporate profile.

三菱商事社の会社案内より、同社の世界戦略を表した世界地図。

Japan   1994
D: Gento Matsumoto
DF: Saru Brunei Co., Ltd.
CL: Mitsubishi Corporation

New York

Lake Erie

Ohio

25
Three Rivers Pipeline

Penns

36

West Virginia   Maryland

New Mexico

11

Mexico

● **Pipeline Systems**
1. Ada
2. Beaumont
3. Blanton
4. Brazoria
5. Chalybeate Springs
6. Champion
7. Citgo Refining
8. Claiborne
9. Diboll
10. Dubach/Calhoun
11. El Paso
12. Elm Grove
13. Excelsior
14. Garvin County NGL
15. Gregg County
16. Jasper
17. Leaf River
18. Matagorda
19. Mississippi Fuel

20. Mountain Creek
21. Nacogdoches
22. Panola County
23. Shelby County
24. Taylor Packing
25. Three Rivers Pipeline
26. Proposed Cornerstone Pipeline
27. Proposed Mississippi Fuel Expansion

■ **Compressor Stations**
1. Ada
8. Claiborne
28. Clarke County
10. Dubach/Calhoun
12. Elm Grove
29. Rankin County
39. Baxterville

2

NORTH AMERICA
Limits: $420.9 million
Clients: 40
Locations: Canada, United States

Centre Ca
pro
geogr

3

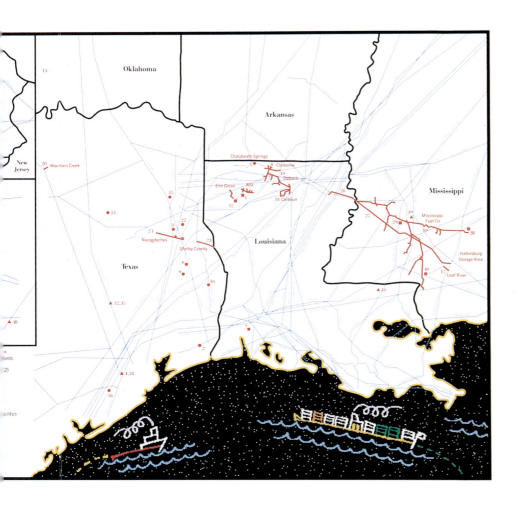

2
Map of natural gas pipelines and processing facilities. From an Endevco, Inc. annual report.

エンデブコ社のアニュアルレポートより、天然ガスのパイプラインと生産施設を表した地図。

U.S.A.   1992
AD: Joe Rattan
D: Joe Rattan/Greg Morgan
I: Linda Helton
CW: Lynn Thomas
DF: Joseph Rattan Design
CL: Endevco, Inc.

3
Maps showing geographic zones of operation of a reinsurance company. From a Centre Cat capabilities brochure.

センター・キャット社の業務案内より、同保険会社の活動区域を表す地図。

U.S.A.   1994
CD: Andy Blankenburg
AD: Andy Blankenburg/Carol Layton
D: David Weinstock
DF: WYD Design Inc.
CL: Centre Cat Limited

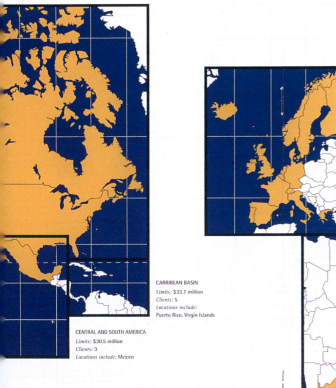

CARRIBEAN BASIN
Limits: $33.7 million
Clients: 5
Locations include:
Puerto Rico, Virgin Islands

CENTRAL AND SOUTH AMERICA
Limits: $30.5 million
Clients: 3
Locations include: Mexico

EUROPE
Limits: $66.9 million
Clients: 10
Locations include:
France, Germany, Norway, U.K.

AFRICA
Centre Cat plans to accept risks in this region as of October 1994.
Locations:
South Africa

Worldwide, we have the capacity to commit up to
$75 million of limit in each of 36 underwriting *zones.*
Individual clients have received *commitments*
of up to $60 million of limit in a single zone.

EAST ASIA
Limits: $35.4 million
Clients: 4
Locations include: Japan

AUSTRALIA AND NEW ZEALAND
Limits: $136.6 million
Clients: 9
Locations: Australia, New Zealand

...ty is limited not by contract,
...eding company, but by
...es containing a small number
...supported by *large* limits.

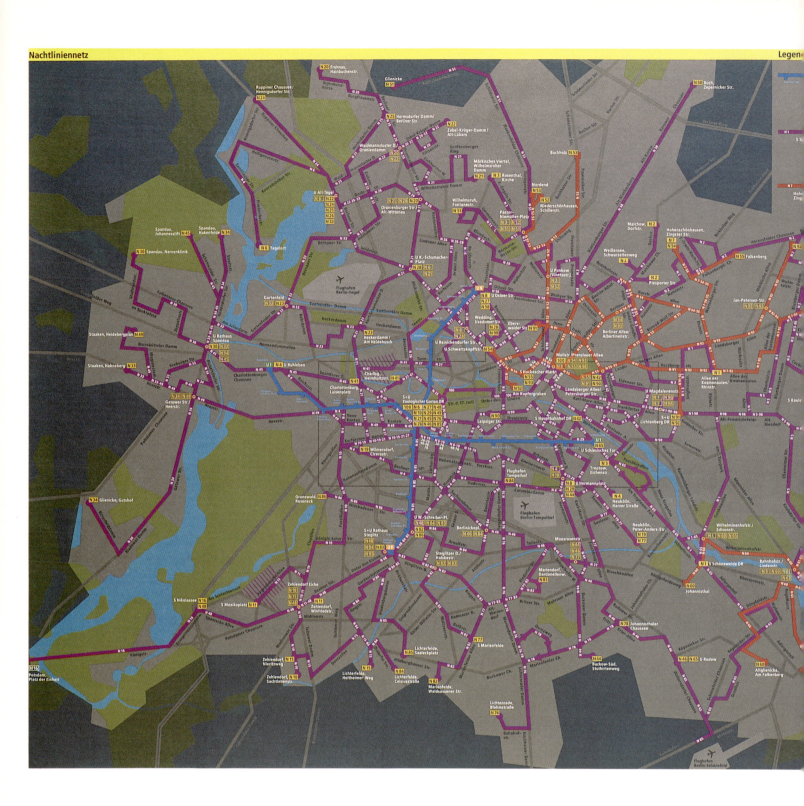

Map of nighttime bus routes, Berlin, for
public display.
公共案内用、ベルリンの夜間バス路線図。

Germany   1991
D: Jens Kreitmeyer
DF: Metadesign Berlin
CL: Berliner Verkehrs-Betriebe

Stand: 31. Mai 1992

Nachtliniennetz Stadt Potsdam

Map of nighttime bus and tramway routes, Potsdam, for public display.

公共案内用、ポツダムの夜間バスと市電の路線図。

Germany   1991
D: Brigitte Hartwig
DF: Metadesign Berlin
CL: Verkehrsbetrieb Potsdam

Location/access map for a property in Vaihingen, Stuttgart. From real estate promotional material.

不動産販売資料より、シュタットガルト、ヴァイヒンゲンにある不動産の所在地図。

Germany   1994
CD: Udo Würth
AD: Udo Würth
D: Udo Würth
P: Udo Würth
I: Udo Würth
DF: Faktor Büro Für Gestaltung
CL: Wieler Objektbau, Immobilienanlagen

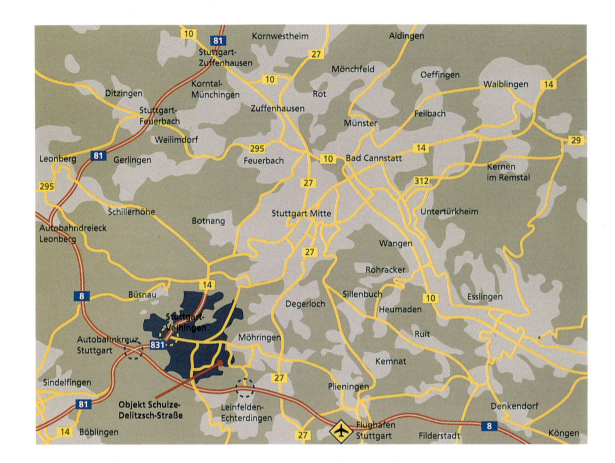

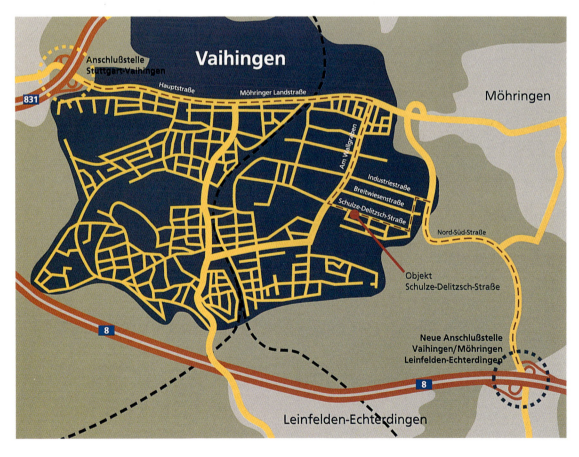

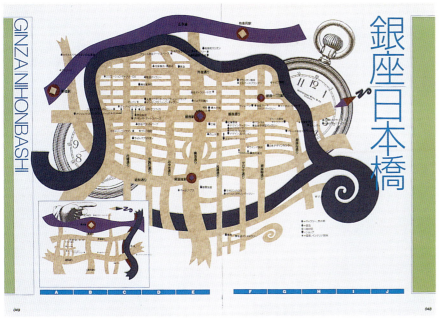

Location maps of design shops in Tokyo, from 'Designers' Workshop' magazine, published by Bijutsu Shuppan-Sha, Ltd.

美術出版社の「デザインの現場」誌より、東京のデザインショップの所在地図。

Japan 1993
CD: Nobuko Shimuta
AD: Nobuo Nakagaki
D: Youichi Matsuda
I: Tsukushi
CL: Bijutsu Shuppan-Sha, Ltd.

Guide map explaining access to an exhibition on book design at seven levels: from planet to land mass, metropolis, street, building, exhibition site and finally to the books.

ブックデザイン展の会場・展示品へのアクセスを惑星、列島、都市、街路、建築、室内、図書の7つの視点の跳躍によって表したガイドマップ。

Japan   1994
CD: Gow Michiyoshi
D: Kazusada Mukai
I: Kazusada Mukai/Tokuji Utsu
CL: The Michiyoshi Gow Book Design
Exhibition Executive Committee

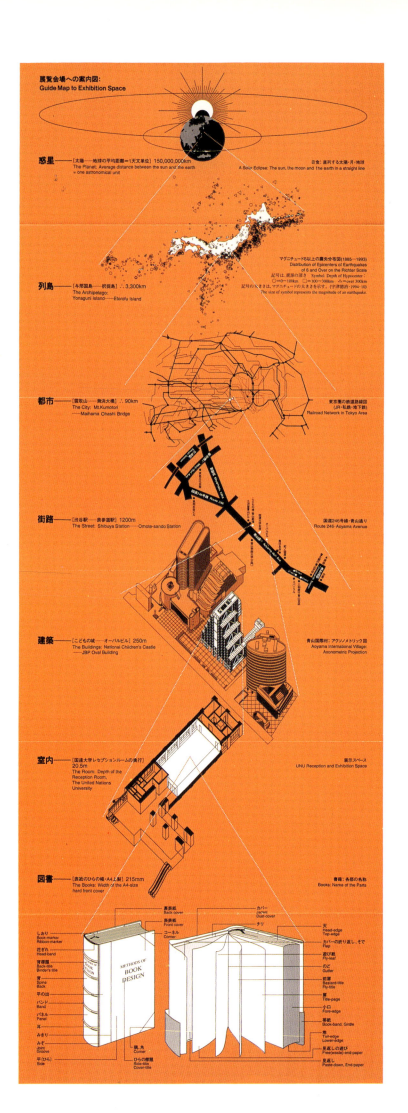

展覧会場への案内図:
Guide Map to Exhibition Space

惑星 — [太陽——地球の平均距離=1天文単位] 150,000,000km
The Planet: Average distance between the sun and the earth = one astronomical unit

日食: 直列する太陽・月・地球
A Solar Eclipse: The sun, the moon and the earth in a straight line

列島 — [与那国島——択捉島] ∴ 3,300km
The Archipelago:
Yonaguni Island——Etorofu Island

マグニチュード6以上の震央分布図(1885—1993)
Distribution of Epicenters of Earthquakes
of 6 and Over on the Richter Scale
記号は、震源の深さ Symbol: Depth of Hypocenter
○=0〜100km ○=100〜300km ○=over 300km
記号の大きさは、マグニチュードの大きさを示す。（宇津徳治・1994・10）
The size of symbol represents the magnitude of an earthquake.

都市 — [雲取山——舞浜大橋] ∴ 90km
The City: Mt.Kumotori
——Maihama Ohashi Bridge

東京圏の鉄道路線図
(JR・私鉄・地下鉄)
Railroad Network in Tokyo Area

街路 — [渋谷駅——表参道駅] 1200m
The Street: Shibuya Station——Omote-sando Station

国道246号線・青山通り
Route 246・Aoyama Avenue

建築 — [こどもの城——オーバルビル] 250m
The Buildings: National Children's Castle
——JBP Oval Building

青山国際村: アクソノメトリック図
Aoyama International Village:
Axonometric Projection

室内 — [国連大学レセプションルームの奥行] 20.5m
The Room: Depth of the Reception Room, The United Nations University

展示スペース
UNU Reception and Exhibition Space

図書 — [表紙のひらの横・A4上製] 215mm
The Books: Width of the A4-size hard front cover

書籍: 各部の名称
Books: Name of the Parts

しおり
Book-marker
Ribbon-marker
花ぎれ
Head-band
背標題
Back-title
Binder's title
背
Spine
Back
平の出
バンド
Band
パネル
Panel
耳
みぞ
みぞ
Joint
Groove
平(ひら)
Side

裏表紙
Back cover
表表紙
Front cover
コーネル
Corner

METHODS OF
BOOK
DESIGN

展・角
Corner
ひらの標題
Side-title
Cover-title

カバー
Jacket
Dust-cover
チリ

天
Head-edge
Top-edge
カバーの折り返し、そで
Flap
遊び紙
Fly-leaf
のど
Gutter
前扉
Bastard-title
Fly-title
扉
Title-page
小口
Fore-edge
帯紙
Book-band, Girdle
地
Tail-edge
Lower-edge
見返しの遊び
Free(waste)-and-paper
見返し
Paste-down, End-paper

World map drawn with place names, from Kodansha publicity material.

講談社の新聞広告より、文字で表現された世界地図。

Japan   1993
CD: Norio Nakamura
AD: Norio Nakamura
D: Norio Nakamura
CL: Kodansha Ltd.

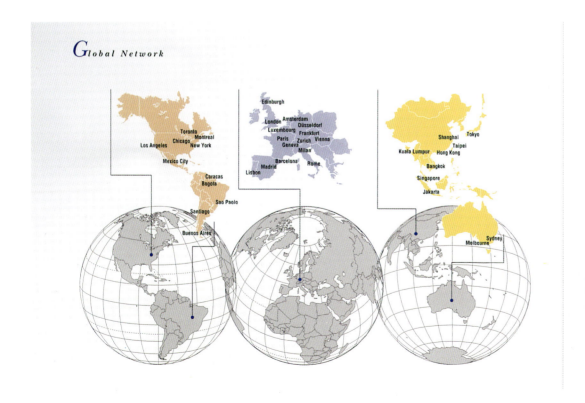

Global Network

Cartographic representation of corporation's global network. From a C. J. Lawrence/Deutsche Bank Securities Corporation capabilities book.

C. J. ローレンス/ドイツ銀行証券会社の業務案内より、同社のグローバル・ネットワークを表す世界地図。

U.S.A.   1994
CD: Steve Ferrari
D: Sue Balle
I: Scott Walters
DF: The Graphic Expression
CL: C.J. Lawrence/
Deutsche Bank Securities Corporation

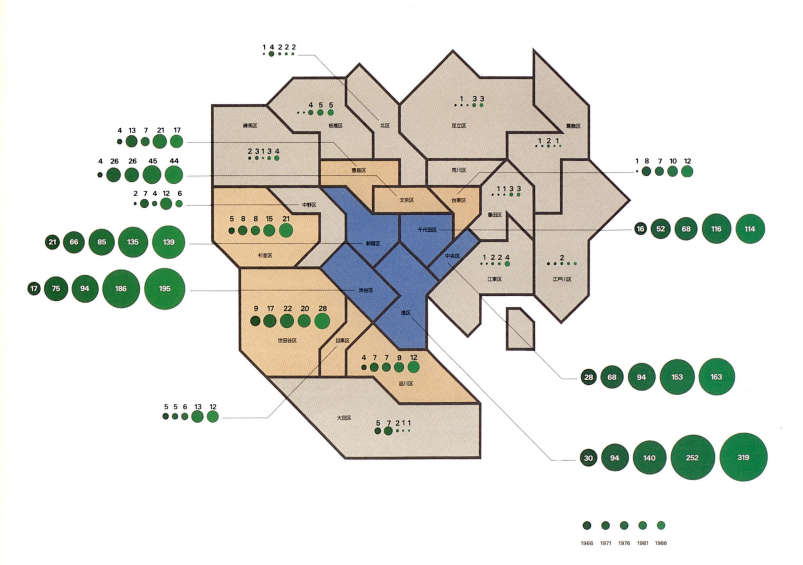

練馬区 1 4 2 2 2

板橋区 4 5 5

北区

足立区 1 3 3

葛飾区

荒川区 1 2 1

4 13 7 21 17

豊島区 2 3 1 3 4

文京区

台東区 1 8 7 10 12

中野区 2 7 4 12 6

墨田区 1 1 3 3

千代田区

新宿区 5 8 8 15 21

16 52 68 116 114

21 66 85 135 139

中央区

17 75 94 186 195

港区 1 2 2 4 江東区

2 江戸川区

9 17 22 20 28

世田谷区

目黒区

品川区 4 7 7 9 12

28 68 94 153 163

5 5 6 13 12

大田区

5 7 2 1 1

30 94 140 252 319

1966   1971   1976   1981   1986

Diagrammatic map of Tokyo, showing growth in the numbers of advertising productions, by ward. From Morisawa Corporation's 'Tategumi Yokogumi' publicity magazine.

モリサワ社のPR誌「たて組ヨコ組」より、東京における広告プロダクション数の推移をエリア別に表した地図。

Japan   1987
CD: Tetsuya Ohta
AD: Tetsuya Ohta
D: Tetsuya Ohta
CL: Morisawa

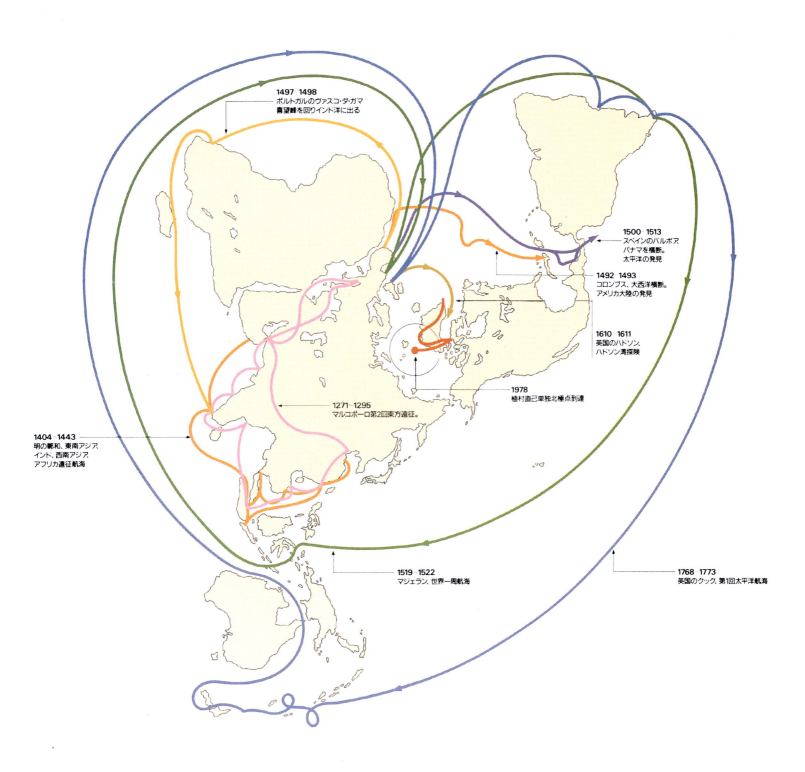

1497–1498
ポルトガルのヴァスコ・ダ・ガマ
喜望峰を回りインド洋に出る

1500–1513
スペインのバルボア
パナマを横断。
太平洋の発見

1492–1493
コロンブス、大西洋横断。
アメリカ大陸の発見

1610–1611
英国のハドソン、
ハドソン湾探険

1978
植村直己単独北極点到達

1271–1295
マルコポーロ第2回東方遠征。

1404–1443
明の鄭和、東南アジア
インド、西南アジア
アフリカ遠征航海

1519–1522
マジェラン、世界一周航海

1768–1773
英国のクック、第1回太平洋航海

Map using North Pole projection to illustrate
the history of voyages of discovery.

海洋探検と発見の歴史を北極点を中心に説
明した地図。

Japan   1992
CD: Tetsuya Ohta
AD: Tetsuya Ohta
D: Tetsuya Ohta
CL: Asahi Kaiyo Corporation

New York City guidebook and city map combined. That Van Dam Book.

ニューヨーク市のガイドブックと地図が1冊になっている、「ザット・ヴァン・ダム・ブック」。

U.S.A. 1993
CD: Stephan Van Dam
AD: Stephan Van Dam
D: G. Vollath/Steve Lawson/S. Van Dam
E: Stephan Van Dam
DF: Van Dam, Inc.
CL: Van Dam, Inc.

Guide map to cherry blossom viewing locations in Yokohama.

横浜のお花見ガイドマップ。

Japan 1994
AD: Kenzo Nakagawa
D: Hiroyasu Nobuyama/
Satoshi Morikami/Hiroyuki Inda
DF: NDC Graphics Inc.
CL: Tower Shop

Location maps of summertime firework displays in Japan's capital region.

首都圏各地で開催される花火大会のガイドマップ。

Japan 1982
AD: Nobuo Morishita
CL: PIA Corp.

Design for an in-vehicle automatic navigation device showing control panel and monitor screen. For Motorola, Inc.

モトローラ社、自動車ナビゲーションシステムのコントロール・パネルとモニター画面のデザイン。

U.S.A. 1992
AD: Aaron Marcus
D: Aaron Marcus/Grant Letz/
Greg Galle/Todd Blank
DF: AM+A
CL: Motorola, Inc.

Cartographic illustration for an essay on the Ottoman legacy. From Champion International's 'Subjective Reasoning' promotional feature.

チャンピオンズ・インターナショナル社発行の「サブジェクティヴ・リーズニング」より、オスマン・トルコ帝国の遺産に関する記事のためのイラストマップ。

U.S.A. 1993
AD: Paula Scher/William Drenttel
D: Michael Gericke
P: Christopher Morris/
Black Star (Bosnia Photo)
I: Hammond Inc.
DF: Pentagram Design
CL: Champion International

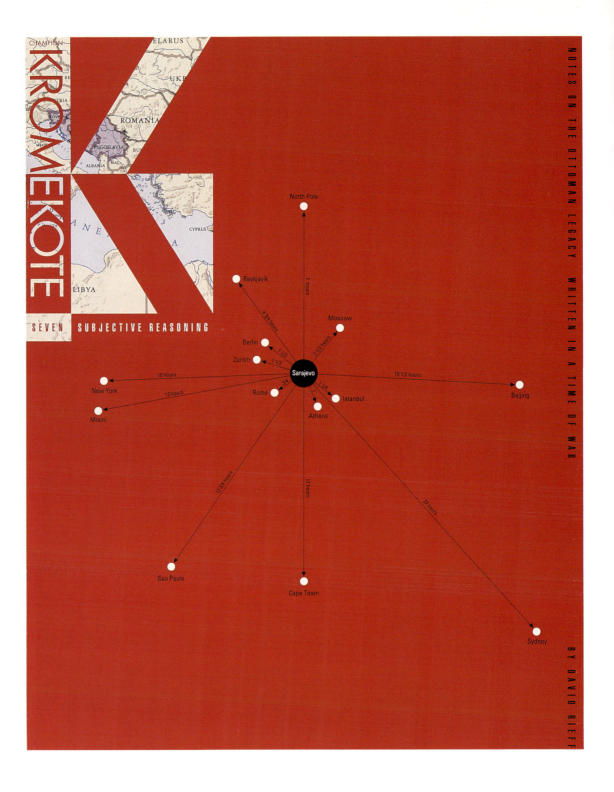

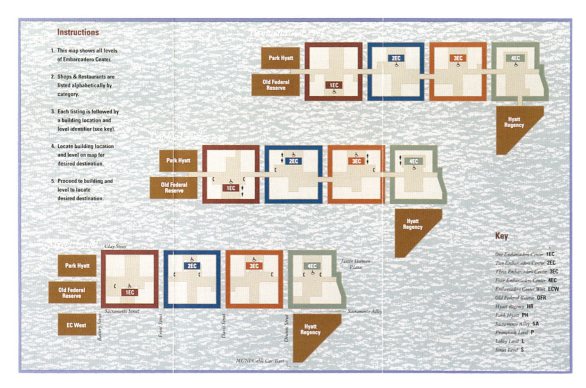

Layout and location map Embarcadero Center, San Francisco. From real estate promotional material.

不動産プロモーション用資料より、サンフランシスコ、エンバルカデロ・センターの平面図と所在地図。

U.S.A.   1993
CD: Richard Poulin
AD: Richard Poulin
D: Richard Poulin/J. Graham Hanson
DF: Richard Poulin Design Group Inc.
CL: Pacific Property Services, L.P., Ltd.

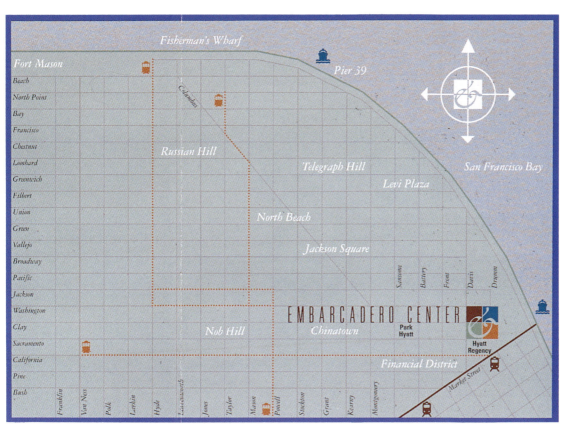

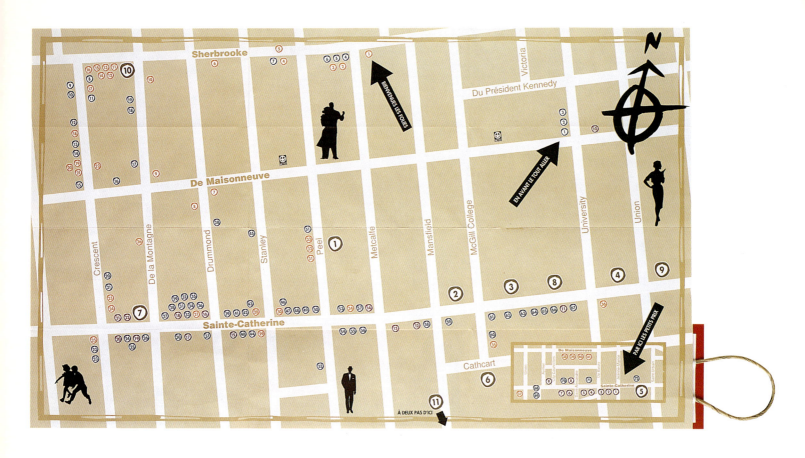

Map of shopping district of Montreal,
Canada, showing fashion retailers. From
a City of Montreal publication.

モントリオール市の広報誌より、カナダ、モ
ントリオール市のショッピング街にあるファ
ッション・ブティックの地図。

Canada   1991
CD: Ghyslaine Fallu
AD: Martin Beauvais
D: Tam Tam
P: Carl Lessard/Barry Harris/
Sofie Ricard/Linda Corbett
I: Louise Savoie
DF: Tam Tam
CL: Ville de Montreal

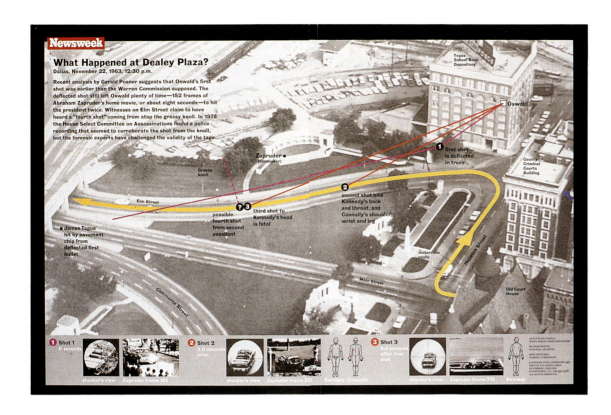

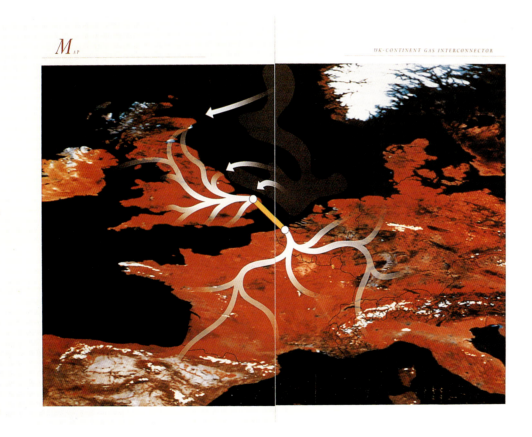

Illustration re-creating the events at Dealey Plaza leading up to the assassination of President John F. Kennedy. From Newsweek magazine.

「ニューズウィーク・マガジン」より、ディーリープラザにおける、アメリカ大統領ジョン・F・ケネディー暗殺事件の流れを再現した説明地図。

U.S.A.　1993
CD: Patricia Bradbury
AD: Bonnie Scranton
D: Bonnie Scranton
DF: Newsweek
CL: Newsweek

Map showing UK and continental Europe gas distribution through the Interconnector pipeline. From a UK-Continent Gas Interconnector brochure.

UKコンチネント・ガス・インターコネクター社のパンフレットより、英国とヨーロッパ大陸における同社のパイプラインによるガス供給を説明する地図。

U.K.　1993
CD: Geoff Aldridge
D: Duncan Wilson
I: Duncan Wilson
DF: Communication by Design Ltd,
London
CL: Interconnector Study Group

Plan of Duncan Aviation facility in Lincoln, Nebraska. From a Duncan Aviation brochure.

ダンカン航空会社のパンフレットより、ネブラスカ州リンカーンにある同社施設の平面図。

U.S.A.   1991
CD: Mitchell Mauk
AD: Mitchell Mauk
D: Mitchell Mauk
I: Mitchell Mauk
DF: Mauk Design
CL: Duncan Aviation

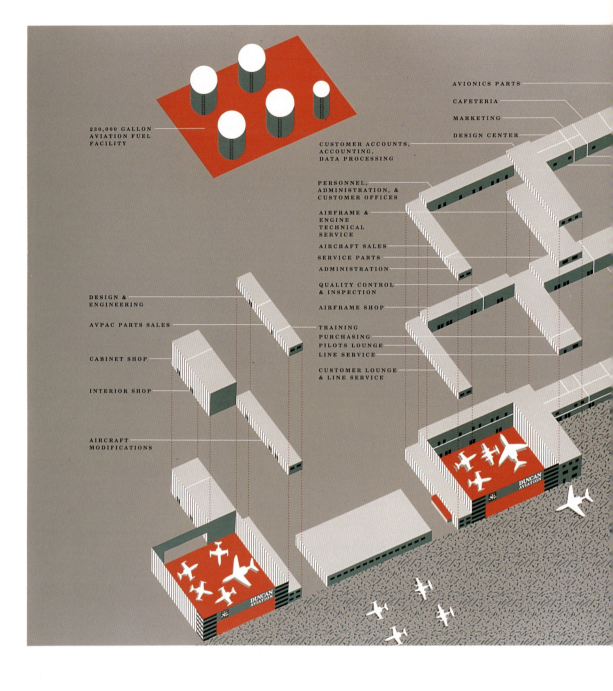

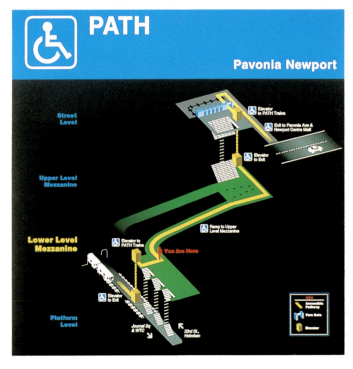

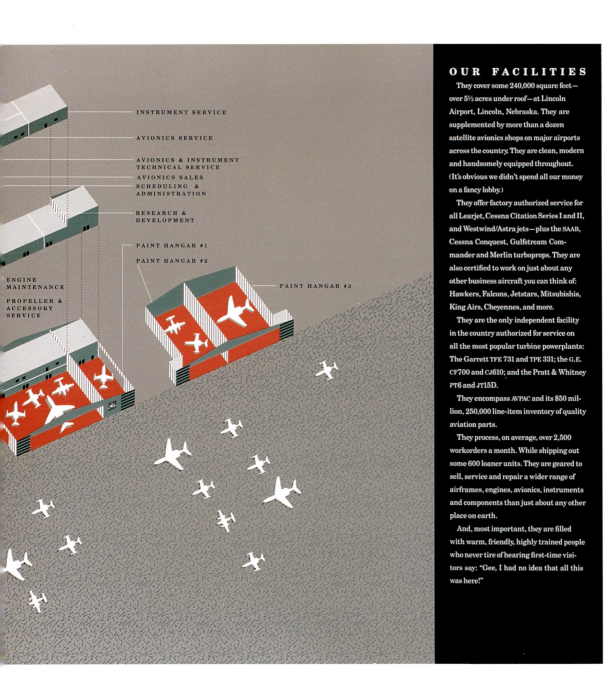

INSTRUMENT SERVICE

AVIONICS SERVICE

AVIONICS & INSTRUMENT
TECHNICAL SERVICE

AVIONICS SALES

SCHEDULING &
ADMINISTRATION

RESEARCH &
DEVELOPMENT

PAINT HANGAR #1

PAINT HANGAR #2

PAINT HANGAR #3

ENGINE
MAINTENANCE

PROPELLER &
ACCESSORY
SERVICE

OUR FACILITIES

They cover some 240,000 square feet—over 5½ acres under roof—at Lincoln Airport, Lincoln, Nebraska. They are supplemented by more than a dozen satellite avionics shops on major airports across the country. They are clean, modern and handsomely equipped throughout. (It's obvious we didn't spend all our money on a fancy lobby.)

They offer factory authorized service for all Learjet, Cessna Citation Series I and II, and Westwind/Astra jets—plus the SAAB, Cessna Conquest, Gulfstream Commander and Merlin turboprops. They are also certified to work on just about any other business aircraft you can think of: Hawkers, Falcons, Jetstars, Mitsubishis, King Airs, Cheyennes, and more.

They are the only independent facility in the country authorized for service on all the most popular turbine powerplants: The Garrett TFE 731 and TPE 331; the G.E. CF700 and CJ610; and the Pratt & Whitney PT6 and JT15D.

They encompass AVPAC and its $50 million, 250,000 line-item inventory of quality aviation parts.

They process, on average, over 2,500 workorders a month. While shipping out some 600 loaner units. They are geared to sell, service and repair a wider range of airframes, engines, avionics, instruments and components than just about any other place on earth.

And, most important, they are filled with warm, friendly, highly trained people who never tire of hearing first-time visitors say: "Gee, I had no idea that all this was here!"

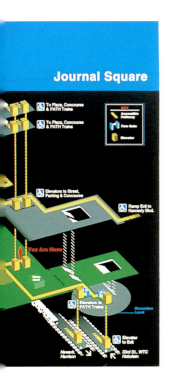

Pictograms for public display indicating elderly and disabled access at stations of the PATH light rail transit system between New York and New Jersey.

ニューヨークとニュージャージー間のPATH ライト電車乗換システムを導入している駅で 老人や身体障害者の乗換方法を表示するガイ ドマップ。

U.S.A.   1994
CD: Louis Nelson
AD: Jennifer Stoller
D: Christopher Rose
DF: Louis Nelson Associates
CL: Port Authority of
New York & New Jersey

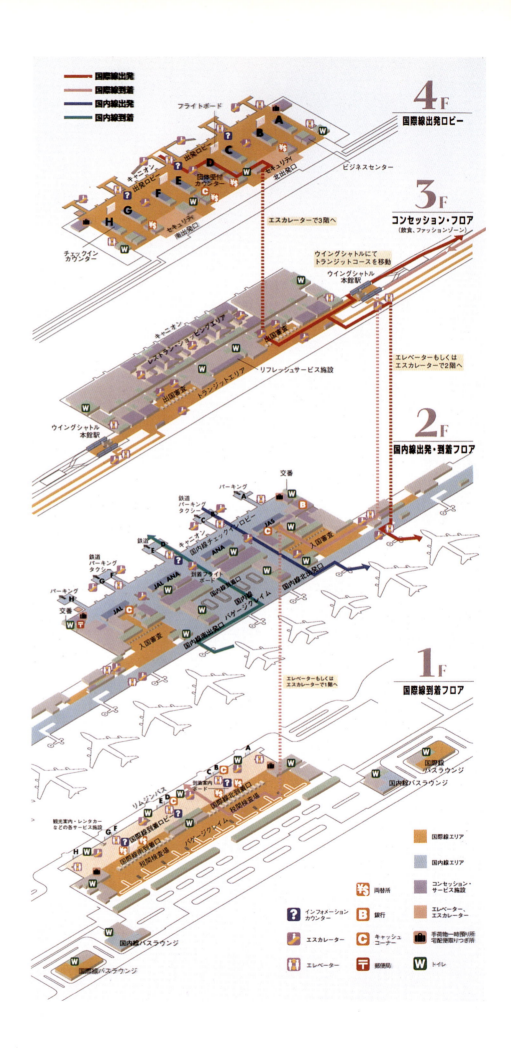

Floor plans of the Kansai International
Airport terminal building, from Flight
Guide '94 vol.90.

「フライトガイド'94 vol.90」より、関西新
国際空港ターミナルビルのフロア・ガイド。

Japan　1994
AD: Shigeru Nakato
D: Shigeru Nakato
CL: The Earth

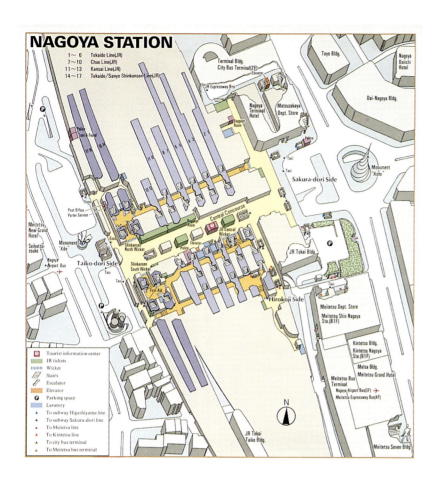

NAGOYA STATION

1～6	Tokaido Line(JR)
7～10	Chuo Line(JR)
11～13	Kansai Line(JR)
14～17	Tokaido/Sanyo Shinkansen Line(JR)

Toyo Bldg.

Nagoya Daiichi Hotel

Terminal Bldg.
City Bus Terminal(2F)
Elevator

JR Expressway Bus

Dai-Nagoya Bldg.

Nagoya Terminal Hotel

Matsuzakaya Dept. Store

Baggage Room

Police

Taxi

Taxi

Monument "Hizho"

Sakura-dori Side

Police
Lost & Found

Post Office
Porter Service

Baggage Room

JR Central Wicket

Central Concourse

Meitetsu New Grand Hotel

Seikatsu-souko

Monument "Kibo"

Shinkansen North Wicket

Police

Nagoya Airport Bus

Taiko-dori Side

Taxi

Taxi

Shinkansen South Wicket

First Ave

JR Tokai Bldg.

Hirokoji Side

Meitetsu Dept. Store

Meitetsu Shin Nagoya Sta.(B1F)

Kintetsu Bldg.

Kintetsu Nagoya Sta.(B1F)

Melsa Bldg.

Meitetsu Grand Hotel

Meitetsu Bus Terminal

Nagoya Airport Bus(3F)
Meitetsu Expressway Bus(4F)

JR Tokai Taiko Bldg.

Meitetsu Seven Bldg.

N

- Tourist information center
- JR tickets
- Wicket
- Stairs
- Escalator
- Elevator
- Parking space
- Lavatory
- To subway Higashiyama line
- To subway Sakura-dori line
- To Meitetsu line
- To Kintetsu line
- To city bus terminal
- To Meitetsu bus terminal

Guide to Nagoya station and its environs, from handbook for foreign visitors published by Nagoya Convention and Visitors Bureau.

名古屋観光コンベンションビューロー発行の「外国人受入施設登録店ガイドマップ」より、名古屋駅構内とその周辺を立体的に表現した案内図。

Japan 1993
CD: Toru Okude
AD: Masahito Kawashima
D: Kayo Hotta
I: Kayo Hotta
CL: Nagoya Convention and Visitors Bureau, Nagoya City

Floor guide for Kansai International Airport, published by PIA Corp.

ぴあ社発行の関西新国際空港フロア別ガイドマップ。

Japan
D: Nobuo Morishita/Kaori Ishikawa
CL: PIA Corp.

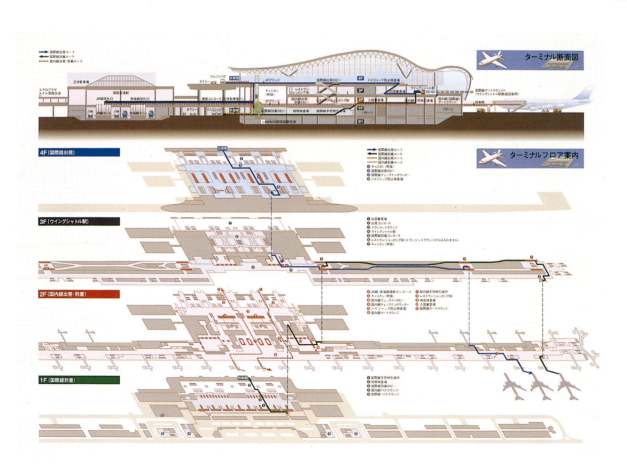

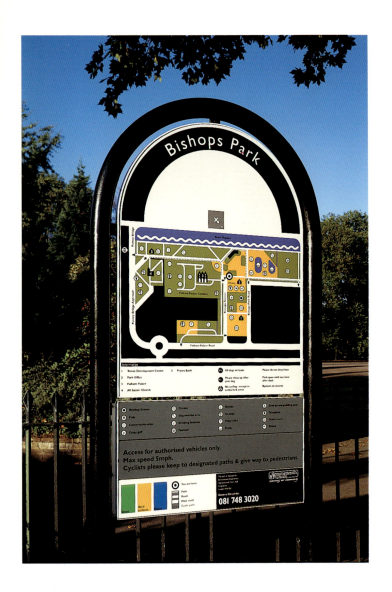

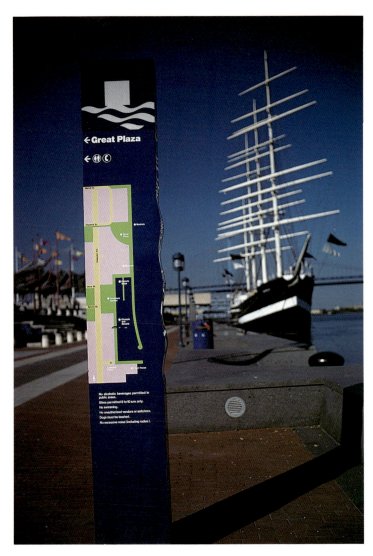

Diagrammatic layout indicating facilities
in a public park in West London.

ロンドン西部にある公園の施設案内図。

U.K.   1994
CD: Peter Grundy/Tilly Northedge
D: Peter Grundy/Tilly Northedge
I: Peter Grundy/Tilly Northedge
DF: Grundy & Northedge
CL: Hammersmith & Fulham Council

Design for a pylon at Penn's Landing,
Philadelphia, giving information for
visitors. North-south alignment of the
maps is reversed on opposing sides of
the pylon, for easier orientation.

フィラデルフィア、ベンズ・ランディング
にある観光客案内用パイロンのデザイン。
案内がわかりやすいように、南北それぞれ
の地図をパイロンの両面に配している。

U.S.A.   1986
CD: Joel Katz
D: Joel Katz/Jerome Cloud
DF: Katz Wheeler Design
CL: City of Philadelphia

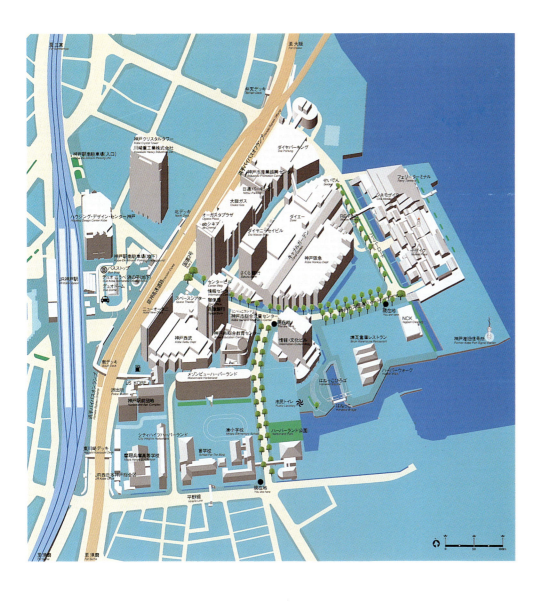

Location diagram for public display of Kobe's Harborland development, produced by the Housing and Urban Development Corporation.

住宅・都市整備公団発行の神戸ハーバーランド案内サイン地図。

Japan   1992
CD: Tokihiro Okuda
AD: Tokihiro Okuda/Nobuyuki Suehiro
D: Yuko Katsumata/Yumi Baba
DF: Community & Communication Co., Ltd.
CL: Housing and Urban Development Corporation

Level A . Lower A

On this level you will find: art and design from India, China, Japan and Korea; European art; the Cast Courts; and much more

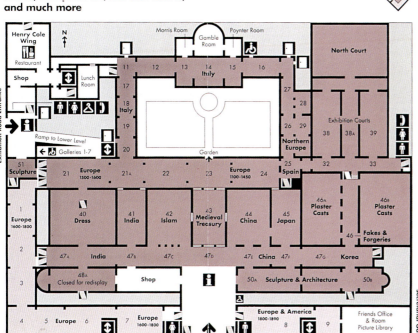

Plan of the layout of the Victoria & Albert Museum, London, from visitors' leaflet.

来館者用パンフレットより、ロンドン・ヴィクトリア・アルバート博物館の館内案内図。

U.K.   1994
CD: Peter Grundy/Tilly Northedge
AD: Peter Grundy/Tilly Northedge
D: Peter Grundy
I: Tilly Northedge
DF: Grundy & Northedge
CL: Victoria & Albert Museum

Guide to exhibits at a 'Tokyo Creative' event.
デザインとテクノロジーのイベント「東京
クリエイティブ」の会場ガイドマップ。

Japan   1992
AD: Gento Matsumoto
DF: Saru Brunei Co., Ltd.
CL: Tokyo Creative Committee

Farewell Happening,
Thursday, August 29
Renseignements généra
General information and
Assistance pour accomp
Accompanying persons a

❻ Bureau de poste (10h00
   Post office (10:00–14:0C

❼ Écouteurs pour interprét
   Headsets for interpretat

Bureaux / Offices

402A Secrétariat du congrès
      Congress secretariat

402B Services aux conférenciers
      Speakers centre

402C Interprètes
      Interpreters

405A Salle de presse
      Press room

317   ICOGRADA

318   Comité organisateur
      Organizing committee

Plan of Dubrovnik showing main tourist
attractions and also damage sustained
during 1991 shelling. From Conde Nast
Traveler magazine.
「コンデ・ナスト・トラベラー・マガジン」よ
り、デュブロフニクの主な観光スポットと
1991年の砲撃による被害地を示す市街地図。

U.S.A.   1994
CD: Diana LaGuardia
I: John Grimwade
CL: Conde Nast Traveler

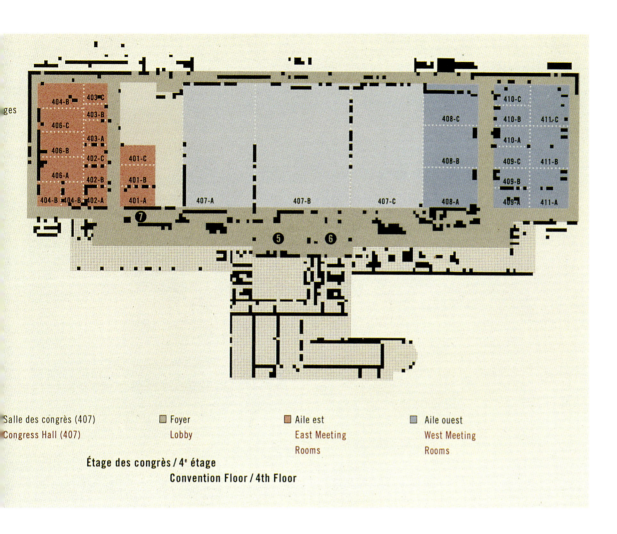

Salle des congrès (407)
Congress Hall (407)

☐ Foyer
   Lobby

☐ Aile est
   East Meeting
   Rooms

☐ Aile ouest
   West Meeting
   Rooms

Étage des congrès / 4ᵉ étage
Convention Floor / 4th Floor

Floor plan of the Montreal Convention Centre. From an ICOGRADA program.

ICOGRADAのプログラムより、モントリオール・コンベンション・センターのフロアー・マップ。

Canada   1991
AD: Malcolm Waddell
D: Sandy King
I: Sandy King
DF: Eskind Waddell
CL: ICOGRADA

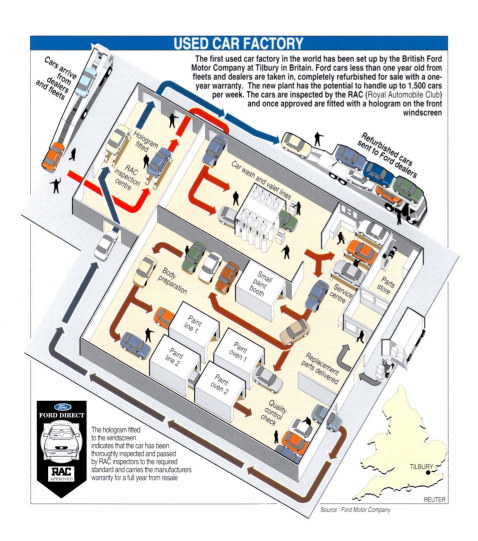

USED CAR FACTORY

The first used car factory in the world has been set up by the British Ford Motor Company at Tilbury in Britain. Ford cars less than one year old from fleets and dealers are taken in, completely refurbished for sale with a one-year warranty. The new plant has the potential to handle up to 1,500 cars per week. The cars are inspected by the RAC (Royal Automobile Club) and once approved are fitted with a hologram on the front windscreen

Cars arrive from dealers and fleets

Hologram fitted

RAC inspection centre

Car wash and valet lines

Refurbished cars sent to Ford dealers

Body preparation

Small paint booth

Service centre

Parts store

Paint line 1

Paint line 2

Paint oven 1

Paint oven 2

Replacement parts delivered

Quality control check

FORD DIRECT
RAC APPROVED

The hologram fitted to the windscreen indicates that the car has been thoroughly inspected and passed by RAC inspectors to the required standard and carries the manufacturers warranty for a full year from resale

TILBURY

REUTER

Source : Ford Motor Company

Layout of the world's first used car factory set up by the British Ford Motor Company. From Reuters news agency.

英国フォード社が世界で初めて建てた中古車整備工場の見取り図。

U.K.   1994
I: Peter Sullivan
CL: Reuters News Graphics Service

Guide map of outdoor leisure facilities in New Zealand.

ニュージーランド各地で楽しめるアウトドア・レジャーのガイドマップ。

Japan 1992
AD: Hiroyuki Kimura
D: Hiroyuki Kimura/Sachiko Hagiwara
CL: Yomiuri Shimbun

Map illustrating the policing of Sarajevo's partition. From The Sunday Times newspaper.

「ザ・サンデー・タイムズ」紙より、サラエボ分割統治後の各国の停戦監視団の配置図。

U.K. 1994
D: Phil Green
E: Phil Green
I: Phil Green
CL: The Sunday Times

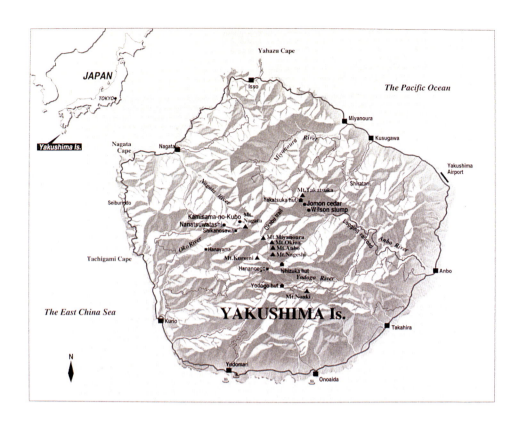

JAPAN

TOKYO

Yakushima Is.

The East China Sea

Yahazu Cape

Isso

Miyanoura

The Pacific Ocean

Kusugawa

Nagata Cape

Nagata

Miyanoura River

Yakushima Airport

Seiburindo

Mt.Takatsuka

Takatsuka hut

Shiratani

Jomon cedar

Wilson stump

Kamisama-no-Kubo

Mt. Nagata

Nanatsuwatashi

Shikanosawa

Okabu trail

Nagata River

Oko River

Mt.Miyanoura

Mt.Okina

Hanayama

Mt.Anbo

Mt.Nageshi

Logging railroad

Anbo River

Tachigami Cape

Mt.Kuromi

Hananoego

Ishizuka hut

Yodogo River

Anbo

Yodogo hut

Mt.Nanki

Kurio

YAKUSHIMA Is.

Takahira

Yudomari

Onoaida

N

Maps using 3-D effect to show topographical
features in the Japanese resort areas of
Yakushima (above) and Kamikochi (below).

屋久島（上）、及び上高地（下）の地形を立体
的に表現した地図。

Japan   1991-1992
AD: Hiroyuki Kimura
D: Hiroyuki Kimura/
Hiroko Enomoto/Sachiko Hagiwara
I: Koji Suzuki.
CL: Shogakukan Inc.

Map of Barcelona, Spain, showing the Olympic marathon course and tourist attractions, from AERA magazine, published by Asahi Shimbun.

朝日新聞社の「アエラ」誌より、バルセロナ・オリンピックのマラソンコースを観光案内もかねて表した地図。

Japan 1992
AD: Hiroyuki Kimura
D: Hiroyuki Kimura/Sachiko Hagiwara
CL: Asahi Shimbun

Diagrammatic layout of Kansai International Airport, from AERA magazine, published by Asahi Shimbun.

朝日新聞社の「アエラ」誌より、関西新国際空港の案内図。

Japan 1994
AD: Hiroyuki Kimura
D: Hiroyuki Kimura/Sachiko Hagiwara
CL: Asahi Shimbun

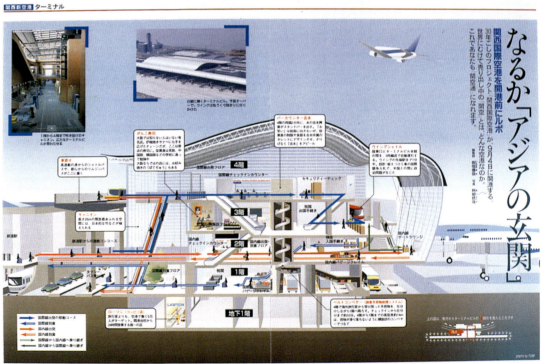

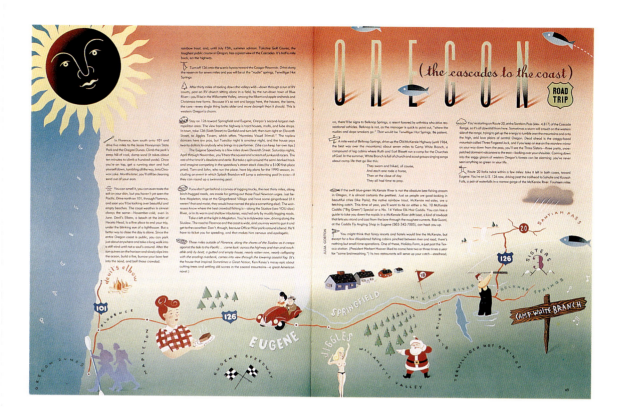

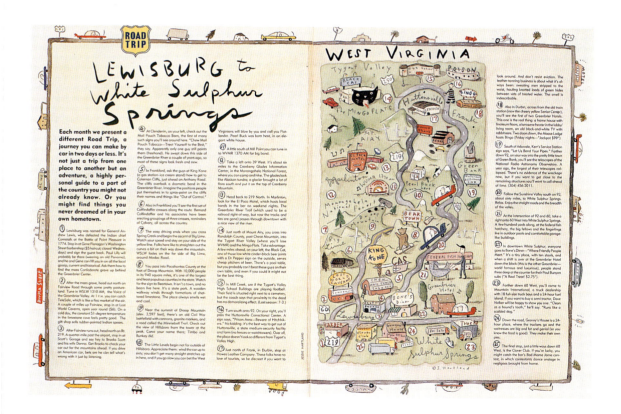

Illustrated map of a recommended road trip through West Virginia. From Wigwag magazine.

「ウィグワグ・マガジン」より、西バージニアのおすすめドライブコースのイラスト・マップ。

U.S.A.   1989
AD: Paul Davis
I: J. Hartland

Illustrated map of a recommended road trip through Oregon. From Wigwag magazine.

「ウィグワグ・マガジン」より、オレゴンのおすすめドライブコースのイラスト・マップ。

U.S.A.   1990
AD: Paul Davis
I: Julia Gorton

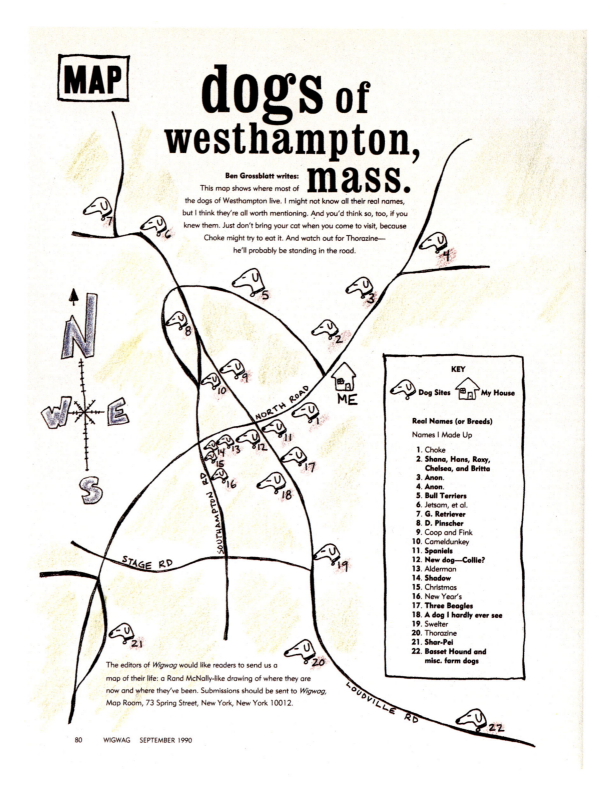

MAP

dogs of westhampton, mass.

Ben Grossblatt writes:
This map shows where most of the dogs of Westhampton live. I might not know all their real names, but I think they're all worth mentioning. And you'd think so, too, if you knew them. Just don't bring your cat when you come to visit, because Choke might try to eat it. And watch out for Thorazine— he'll probably be standing in the road.

NORTH ROAD
SOUTHAMPTON RD
STAGE RD
LOUDVILLE RD
ME

KEY

Dog Sites   My House

Real Names (or Breeds)
Names I Made Up

1. Choke
2. **Shana, Hans, Roxy, Chelsea, and Britta**
3. Anon.
4. Anon.
5. **Bull Terriers**
6. Jetsam, et al.
7. **G. Retriever**
8. **D. Pinscher**
9. Coop and Fink
10. Cameldunkey
11. **Spaniels**
12. **New dog—Collie?**
13. Alderman
14. **Shadow**
15. Christmas
16. New Year's
17. **Three Beagles**
18. **A dog I hardly ever see**
19. Swelter
20. Thorazine
21. **Shar-Pei**
22. **Basset Hound and misc. farm dogs**

The editors of *Wigwag* would like readers to send us a map of their life: a Rand McNally-like drawing of where they are now and where they've been. Submissions should be sent to *Wigwag*, Map Room, 73 Spring Street, New York, New York 10012.

Architectural, industrial and scientific illustrations 建築・工業・科学イラストレーション

This section has three subsections: diagrams showing the structures of buildings, illustrations of industrial products, and scientific illustrations. As those diagrams illustrating manufacturing processes or functions of particular products fit both here and in section 2, they have been included where thought most appropriate.

建物の構造を図解したもの、工業製品を図解したもの、科学的内容を図解したものの3つに分けてある。製品の生産工程や、機能を表した図は2章と4章で重複するが、見やすいように2つの章に分けて紹介した。

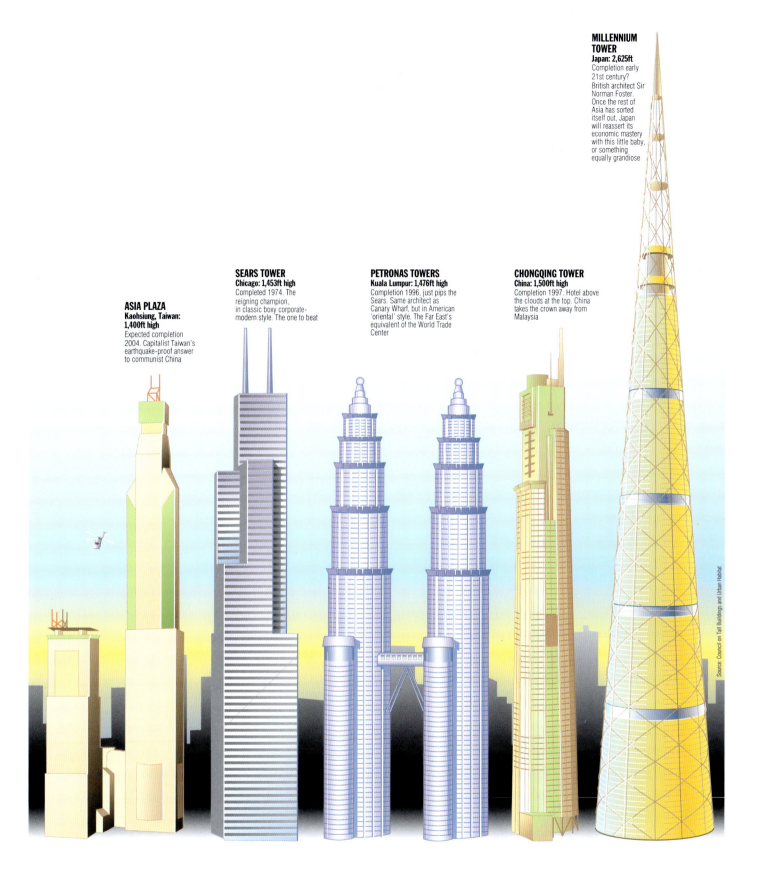

MILLENNIUM TOWER
Japan: 2,625ft
Completion early 21st century? British architect Sir Norman Foster. Once the rest of Asia has sorted itself out, Japan will reassert its economic mastery with this little baby, or something equally grandiose

ASIA PLAZA
Kaohsiung, Taiwan: 1,400ft high
Expected completion 2004. Capitalist Taiwan's earthquake-proof answer to communist China

SEARS TOWER
Chicago: 1,453ft high
Completed 1974. The reigning champion, in classic boxy corporate-modern style. The one to beat

PETRONAS TOWERS
Kuala Lumpur: 1,476ft high
Completion 1996, just pips the Sears. Same architect as Canary Wharf, but in American 'oriental' style. The Far East's equivalent of the World Trade Center

CHONGQING TOWER
China: 1,500ft high
Completion 1997. Hotel above the clouds at the top. China takes the crown away from Malaysia

Source: Council on Tall Buildings and Urban Habitat

Illustration showing the world's tallest buildings. From The Sunday Times newspaper.

「ザ・サンデー・タイムズ」紙より、世界で最も高いビルのイラストレーション。

U.K. 1994
I: Chris Sargent
CL: The Sunday Times
© THE SUNDAY TIMES, LONDON. 1994

Layout of a new gas-fired electricity generating station. From a Powergen brochure.

パワージェン社のパンフレットより、新火力発電所の見取り図。

U.K.   1993
CD: John Perlmutter
AD: John Perlmutter
I: Tilly Northedge
DF: Grundy & Northedge
CL: Uffindell & West

.... Site Layout

1. Administration Block
2. Control Room
3. Gas Reception Station
4. Gas Turbine House
5. Generator Transformer Gas Turbine
6. Boiler House
7. Steam Turbine House
8. Generator Transformer Steam Turbine
9. Cooling Towers
10. Settling Pond
11. Main Stacks
12. By-pass Stacks
13. Transformers
14. National Grid

Illustration of an 'intelligent building'. From United Technologies Journal.

「ユナイデッド・テクノロジー・ジャーナル」より、インテリジェント・ビルのイラスト。

U.K.
AD: Derek Birdsall
I: Michael Robinson
CL: United Technologies Corporation

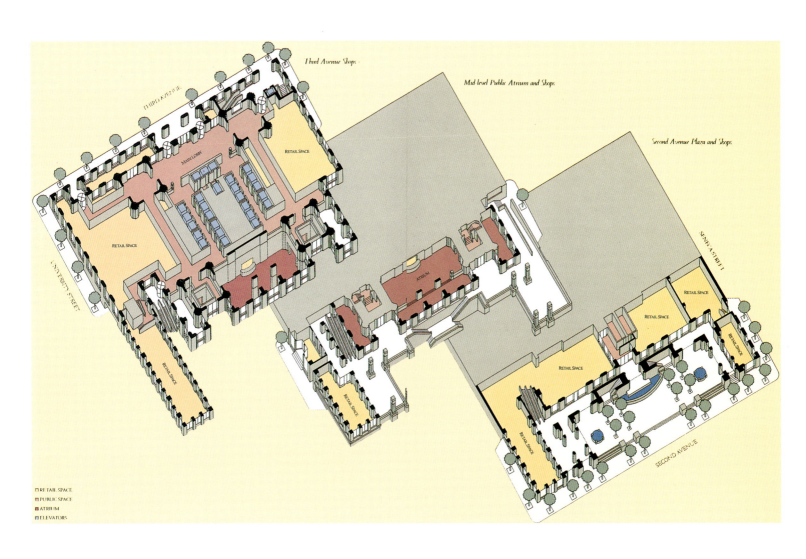

Layout diagram of Washington Mutual Tower building, from a real estate brochure.

不動産案内用パンフレットより、ワシント
ン・ミューチュアル・タワービルの見取図。

U.S.A. 1984
CD: Kathy Eitner
AD: Kathy Eitner
D: Guy Peckham
I: Guy Peckham
DF: The Rockey Company, Inc.
CL: Wright Runstad & Company

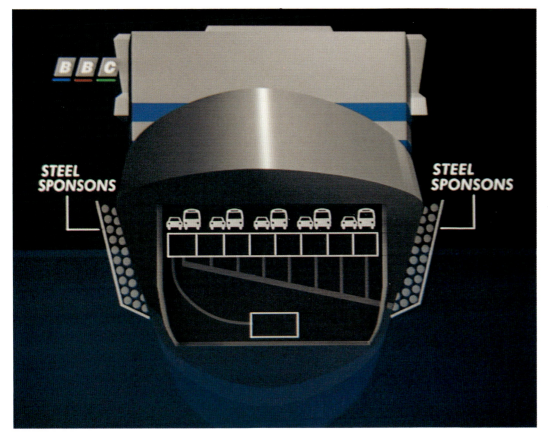

Illustration of a roll-on roll-off ferry. For BBC News broadcast.

BBCのニュース放送用に制作された、
カーフェリーのイラスト。

U.K. 1994
D: BBC News, Graphic Design
CL: BBC News & Current Affairs

Detailed study for Hamburg's Labour Museum. From a Pencil Art Editions publication.

ペンシル・アート・エディションズ社が制作したハンブルグ労働者博物館の詳細な設計図案。

Germany   1987
AD: Achim Kiel
I: Frank Giesselmann
DF: Pencil Corporate Art
CL: Technical University Brunswick

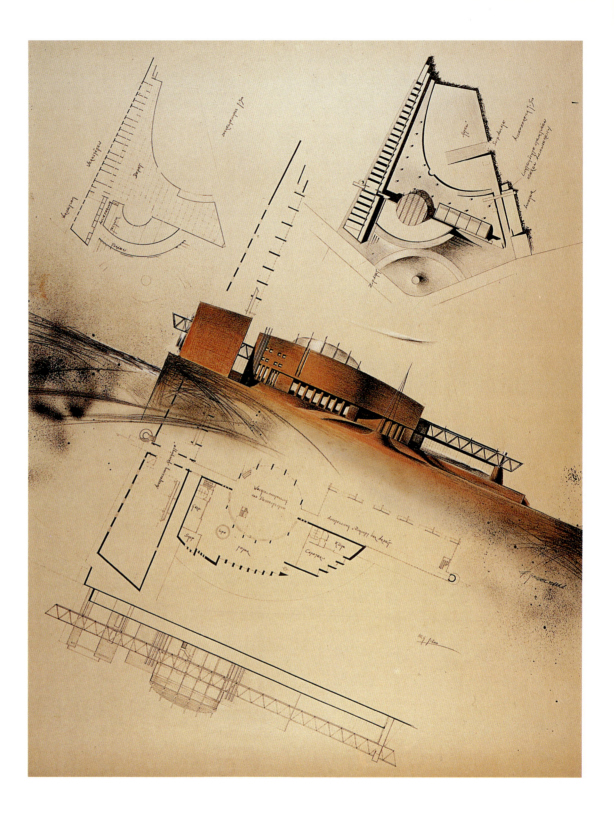

Colour etching of Hofbrauhaus Wolters, Braunschweig, Germany, part of a series on 19th century factory architecture. From an original print edition entitled 'Securing the Evidence.

「セキュアリング・ジ・エヴィデンス」と題された原版より、19世紀の工場建築を題材にしたシリーズのうち、ドイツ、ブローンズウィグにある「ホフブラウハウス・ウォルターズ」のカラーエッチング。

Germany 1985
AD: Achim Kiel
P: Uwe Brandes
I: Achim Kiel
DF: Pencil Corporate Art
CL: Pencil Art Editions

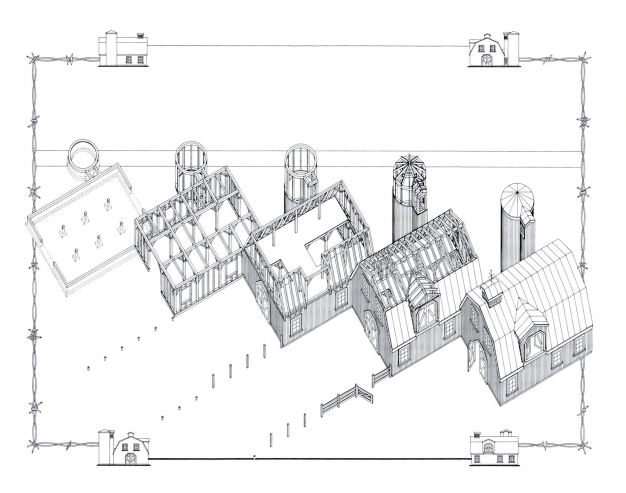

Illustration of stages in barn construction. From a design publication.

デザイン画集より、家畜小屋の建設工程図。

U.S.A. 1984
CD: Guy Peckham
AD: Guy Peckham
D: Guy Peckham
I: Guy Peckham
DF: Guy Peckham
CL: Guy Peckham

The inside of the New Classic computer.
From Macworld magazine.

「マックワールド・マガジン」より、ニュー・ク
ラシック・コンピューターの内部構造の図説。

U.S.A.　1993
AD: Kent Tayenaka
P: Luis Delgado
I: Arne Hurty
Captions: Galen Gruman
CL: Macworld Inc.

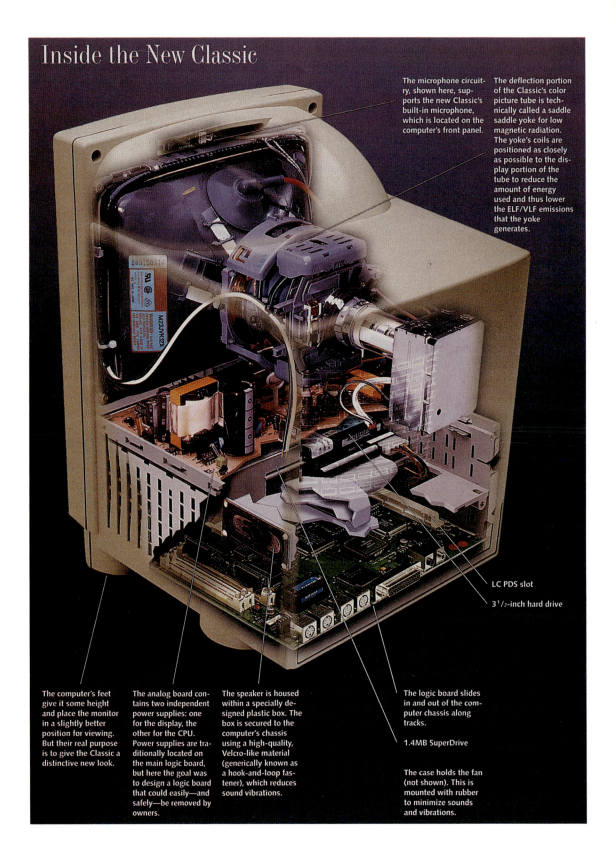

Inside the New Classic

The microphone circuit-
ry, shown here, sup-
ports the new Classic's
built-in microphone,
which is located on the
computer's front panel.

The deflection portion
of the Classic's color
picture tube is tech-
nically called a saddle
saddle yoke for low
magnetic radiation.
The yoke's coils are
positioned as closely
as possible to the dis-
play portion of the
tube to reduce the
amount of energy
used and thus lower
the ELF/VLF emissions
that the yoke
generates.

LC PDS slot

3¹/₂-inch hard drive

The computer's feet
give it some height
and place the monitor
in a slightly better
position for viewing.
But their real purpose
is to give the Classic a
distinctive new look.

The analog board con-
tains two independent
power supplies: one
for the display, the
other for the CPU.
Power supplies are tra-
ditionally located on
the main logic board,
but here the goal was
to design a logic board
that could easily—and
safely—be removed by
owners.

The speaker is housed
within a specially de-
signed plastic box. The
box is secured to the
computer's chassis
using a high-quality,
Velcro-like material
(generically known as
a hook-and-loop fas-
tener), which reduces
sound vibrations.

The logic board slides
in and out of the com-
puter chassis along
tracks.

1.4MB SuperDrive

The case holds the fan
(not shown). This is
mounted with rubber
to minimize sounds
and vibrations.

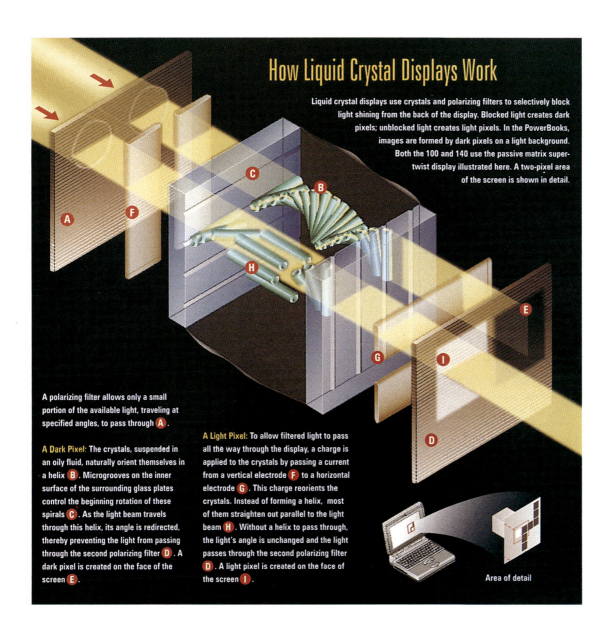

How Liquid Crystal Displays Work

Liquid crystal displays use crystals and polarizing filters to selectively block light shining from the back of the display. Blocked light creates dark pixels; unblocked light creates light pixels. In the PowerBooks, images are formed by dark pixels on a light background. Both the 100 and 140 use the passive matrix super-twist display illustrated here. A two-pixel area of the screen is shown in detail.

A polarizing filter allows only a small portion of the available light, traveling at specified angles, to pass through A .

A Dark Pixel: The crystals, suspended in an oily fluid, naturally orient themselves in a helix B . Microgrooves on the inner surface of the surrounding glass plates control the beginning rotation of these spirals C . As the light beam travels through this helix, its angle is redirected, thereby preventing the light from passing through the second polarizing filter D . A dark pixel is created on the face of the screen E .

A Light Pixel: To allow filtered light to pass all the way through the display, a charge is applied to the crystals by passing a current from a vertical electrode F to a horizontal electrode G . This charge reorients the crystals. Instead of forming a helix, most of them straighten out parallel to the light beam H . Without a helix to pass through, the light's angle is unchanged and the light passes through the second polarizing filter D . A light pixel is created on the face of the screen I .

Area of detail

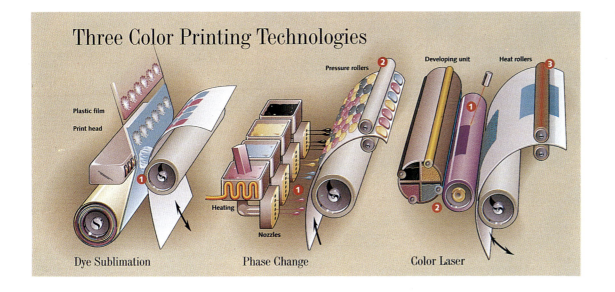

Three Color Printing Technologies

Plastic film
Print head

Pressure rollers

Developing unit   Heat rollers

Heating

Nozzles

Dye Sublimation   Phase Change   Color Laser

Diagram showing how liquid crystal displays work. From Macworld magazine.

「マックワールド・マガジン」より、液晶画面の仕組みについての図解。

U.S.A.   1991
I: Arne Hurty
Captions: Lisa Weiman
CL: Macworld Inc.

Three color printing technologies. From Macworld magazine.

「マックワールド・マガジン」より、3通りのカラー印刷技術を表した図説。

U.S.A.   1992
I: Arne Hurty
Captions: Charlie Piller
CL: Macworld Inc.

Diagram illustrating containerisation of mail, from a Royal Mail-Rail Express Systems publication.

ロイヤル・メール・レール・エキスプレス・システムズ社の発行物より、郵便のコンテナ化を表すイラスト。

U.K.
AD: David Bone
I: Michael Robinson
CL: Four IV

Containerisation

Considerable improvements in customer service through time saving and security can be achieved through containerisation. Royal Mail has designed a container operation which is specific to mail and is fully compatible with rail vehicles. Sorted mail can be loaded directly into trays at the sorting machine. The trays are stacked into containers. The containers can also carry letters and packets in bags and can move within sorting offices and through the transport network, transferring between modes without individual trays or bags being handled. The system will allow Royal Mail to achieve significant economies, reduce handling time and cut the risk of mis-routeing.

The compact wheeled containers fit well into the rail system and the rail vehicle fleet is being adapted to a container carrying role. As well as achieving manpower savings at stations, the containers enable loading times to be slashed and the train service structure to be streamlined.

Individual letters sorted into trays which then stack into wheeled containers for despatch by rail or road.

Container

Tray

Letter

Illustration of an advanced car transporter. From Chargeurs Group annual report.

シャージュア・グループのアニュアルレポートより、最新の車両輸送機のイラストレーション。

U.K.
I: Michael Robinson
CL: Wolff Olins

TRANSPORT ET SERVICES AUTOMOBILES

Walon assure le transport par route et la préparation des véhicules automobiles, depuis leurs lieux de production ou d'importation, jusqu'aux réseaux de distribution. Exploitant 70 centres et une flotte de 1 500 camions, la société occupe la première place en Europe avec 20 % du marché. En 1993, la société a transporté 2,8 millions de véhicules et assuré la préparation avant livraison de 1,2 million de véhicules.

UN RÉSEAU EUROPÉEN

Sur le marché de l'automobile, où les constructeurs et importateurs opèrent à l'échelle européenne, il est essentiel de disposer d'une organisation qui soit à leur mesure. Présent en Allemagne, en Grande-Bretagne, en France, en Espagne et au Portugal, en Hollande, en Belgique, en Italie et dans des pays de l'Europe de l'Est, Walon offre à ses clients un réseau logistique européen.

UNE SEULE SIGNATURE

En mettant un même nom et la même signature, "Walon", sur l'ensemble de ses sociétés, de ses camions et de ses services en Europe, Walon a voulu montrer qu'il s'engageait à offrir partout la même qualité de service. Présence locale, mais standard européen : deux garanties complémentaires pour les clients de Walon.

LA DISTRIBUTION INTELLIGENTE

La gamme des services offerts par Walon évolue. A la simple prestation de transport s'est ajoutée la préparation des véhicules avant leur livraison : pose d'accessoires, finitions, personnalisation... Walon va plus loin maintenant dans son partenariat avec ses clients en assurant pour leur compte le stockage et la livraison "juste à temps" : de la distribution physique à la distribution "intelligente".

WALON

Containerisation speeds the
flow of mail within the rail
network. Giving faster and
more reliable distribution.

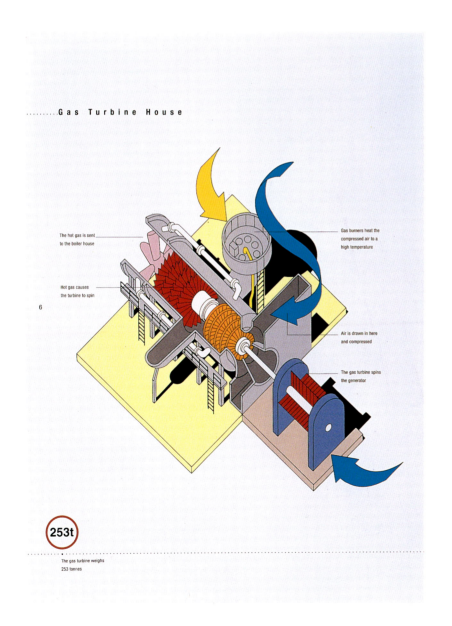

.........Gas Turbine House

The hot gas is sent
to the boiler house

Hot gas causes
the turbine to spin

6

Gas burners heat the
compressed air to a
high temperature

Air is drawn in here
and compressed

The gas turbine spins
the generator

253t

The gas turbine weighs
253 tonnes

パワージェン社の発行物より、一般の人に
も理解してもらえるように描かれた発電所の
解説図。

Diagram to help the public understand
the workings of a power generating
station. From a Powergen publication

U.K.
I: Michael Robinson
CL: Uffindell & West

Cutting through

"This is actually an easy tunnel. It's just a long, long way," Peter Bermingham, an engineer on the project, said. The tunnel boring machines did the heavy work, digging two running tunnels and a service tunnel. Each TBM operated as a self-contained tunnel-processing plant. As it burrowed through rock, it simultaneously moved spoil back to cars and lined the hole with precast concrete segments. Boring took three and a half years.

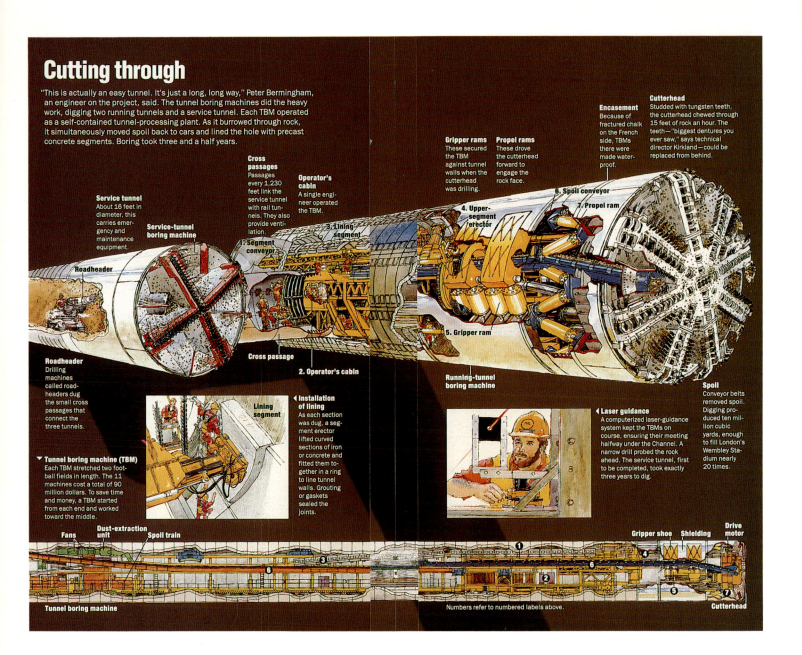

Service tunnel
About 16 feet in diameter, this carries emergency and maintenance equipment.

Service-tunnel boring machine

Roadheader

Cross passages
Passages every 1,230 feet link the service tunnel with rail tunnels. They also provide ventilation.

1. Segment conveyor

Operator's cabin
A single engineer operated the TBM.

3. Lining segment

Gripper rams
These secured the TBM against tunnel walls when the cutterhead was drilling.

Propel rams
These drove the cutterhead forward to engage the rock face.

Encasement
Because of fractured chalk on the French side, TBMs there were made waterproof.

Cutterhead
Studded with tungsten teeth, the cutterhead chewed through 15 feet of rock an hour. The teeth—"biggest dentures you ever saw," says technical director Kirkland—could be replaced from behind.

4. Upper-segment erector

6. Spoil conveyor

7. Propel ram

5. Gripper ram

Roadheader
Drilling machines called roadheaders dug the small cross passages that connect the three tunnels.

Cross passage

2. Operator's cabin

Running-tunnel boring machine

Spoil
Conveyor belts removed spoil. Digging produced ten million cubic yards, enough to fill London's Wembley Stadium nearly 20 times.

Lining segment

▼ Tunnel boring machine (TBM)
Each TBM stretched two football fields in length. The 11 machines cost a total of 90 million dollars. To save time and money, a TBM started from each end and worked toward the middle.

◀ Installation of lining
As each section was dug, a segment erector lifted curved sections of iron or concrete and fitted them together in a ring to line tunnel walls. Grouting or gaskets sealed the joints.

◀ Laser guidance
A computerized laser-guidance system kept the TBMs on course, ensuring their meeting halfway under the Channel. A narrow drill probed the rock ahead. The service tunnel, first to be completed, took exactly three years to dig.

Fans

Dust-extraction unit

Spoil train

Gripper shoe

Shielding

Drive motor

Tunnel boring machine

Cutterhead

Numbers refer to numbered labels above.

Illustration showing the tunnel boring machine used to cut the Channel Tunnel. From National Geographic magazine.

「ナショナル・ジオグラフィック・マガジン」より、イギリス海峡下にトンネルを掘るために使われたトンネル掘削機の図説。

U.S.A.　1994
AD: Mark Holmes
I: Ken Dallison
CL: National Geographic Magazine

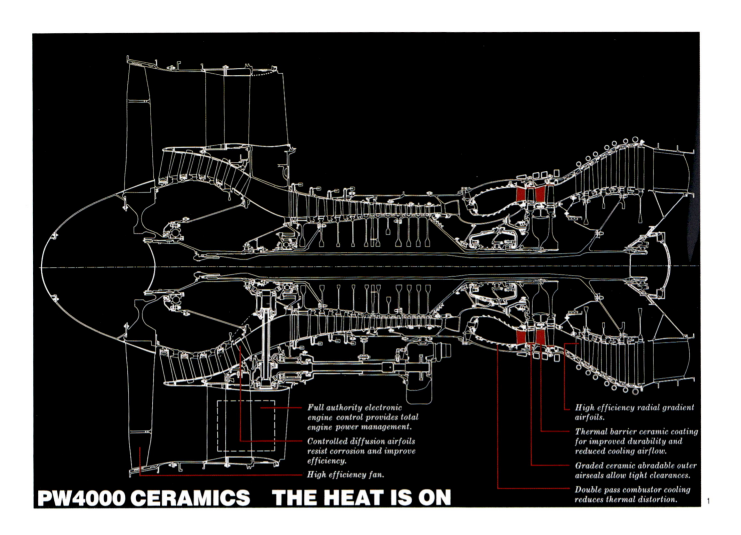

PW4000 CERAMICS   THE HEAT IS ON

Full authority electronic engine control provides total engine power management.

Controlled diffusion airfoils resist corrosion and improve efficiency.

High efficiency fan.

High efficiency radial gradient airfoils.

Thermal barrier ceramic coating for improved durability and reduced cooling airflow.

Graded ceramic abradable outer airseals allow tight clearances.

Double pass combustor cooling reduces thermal distortion.

1

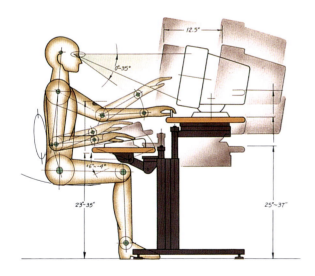

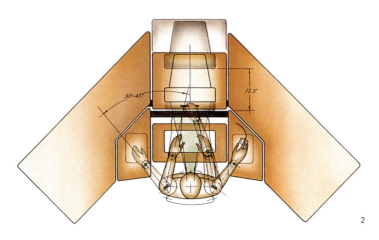

2

1

Illustration of the use of ceramics in a jet engine. From a United Technologies publication.

ユナイテッド・テクノロジー社の発行物より、セラミック素材がジェット・エンジンにどの様に使われているのかを表したイラストレーション。

AD: Derek Birdsall
I: Michael Robinson
CL: United Technologies Corporation

2

Illustrations showing ergonomic design of furniture, from a Watson Flex III brochure.

ワトソン・フレックスⅢのパンフレットより、人間工学の観点からデザインされた家具の説明図。

U.S.A.   1993
AD: Jack Anderson
D: Jack Anderson/Mary Hermes/
Leo Raymundo
I: Yutaka Sasaki
DF: Hornall Anderson Design Works
CL: Watson Furniture Company

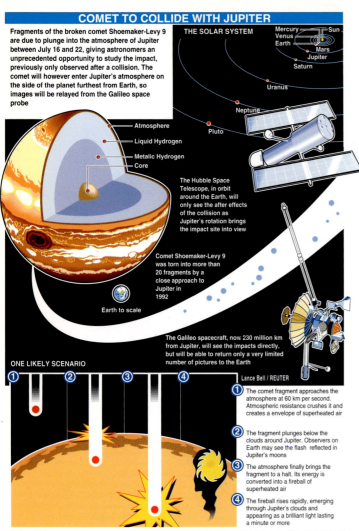

COMET TO COLLIDE WITH JUPITER

Fragments of the broken comet Shoemaker-Levy 9 are due to plunge into the atmosphere of Jupiter between July 16 and 22, giving astronomers an unprecedented opportunity to study the impact, previously only observed after a collision. The comet will however enter Jupiter's atmosphere on the side of the planet furthest from Earth, so images will be relayed from the Galileo space probe

THE SOLAR SYSTEM

Mercury   Sun
Venus
Earth
Mars
Jupiter
Saturn
Uranus
Neptune
Pluto

Atmosphere
Liquid Hydrogen
Metalic Hydrogen
Core

The Hubble Space Telescope, in orbit around the Earth, will only see the after effects of the collision as Jupiter's rotation brings the impact site into view

Comet Shoemaker-Levy 9 was torn into more than 20 fragments by a close approach to Jupiter in 1992

Earth to scale

The Galileo spacecraft, now 230 million km from Jupiter, will see the impacts directly, but will be able to return only a very limited number of pictures to the Earth

Lance Bell / REUTER

ONE LIKELY SCENARIO

① ② ③ ④

① The comet fragment approaches the atmosphere at 60 km per second. Atmospheric resistance crushes it and creates a envelope of superheated air

② The fragment plunges below the clouds around Jupiter. Observers on Earth may see the flash reflected in Jupiter's moons

③ The atmosphere finally brings the fragment to a halt. Its energy is converted into a fireball of superheated air

④ The fireball rises rapidly, emerging through Jupiter's clouds and appearing as a brilliant light lasting a minute or more

Sources: Smithsonian Institute, Oxford University, The Cambridge Encyclopedia of Space

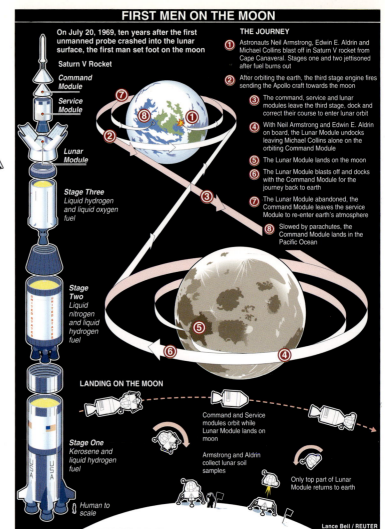

FIRST MEN ON THE MOON

On July 20, 1969, ten years after the first unmanned probe crashed into the lunar surface, the first man set foot on the moon

Saturn V Rocket

Command Module

Service Module

Lunar Module

Stage Three
Liquid hydrogen and liquid oxygen fuel

Stage Two
Liquid nitrogen and liquid hydrogen fuel

UNITED STATES

Stage One
Kerosene and liquid hydrogen fuel

USA   USA

Human to scale

THE JOURNEY

① Astronauts Neil Armstrong, Edwin E. Aldrin and Michael Collins blast off in Saturn V rocket from Cape Canaveral. Stages one and two jettisoned after fuel burns out

② After orbiting the earth, the third stage engine fires sending the Apollo craft towards the moon

③ The command, service and lunar modules leave the third stage, dock and correct their course to enter lunar orbit

④ With Neil Armstrong and Edwin E. Aldrin on board, the Lunar Module undocks leaving Michael Collins alone on the orbiting Command Module

⑤ The Lunar Module lands on the moon

⑥ The Lunar Module blasts off and docks with the Command Module for the journey back to earth

⑦ The Lunar Module abandoned, the Command Module leaves the service Module to re-enter earth's atmosphere

⑧ Slowed by parachutes, the Command Module lands in the Pacific Ocean

LANDING ON THE MOON

Command and Service modules orbit while Lunar Module lands on moon

Armstrong and Aldrin collect lunar soil samples

Only top part of Lunar Module returns to earth

Lance Bell / REUTER

Source: The Cambridge Encylcopedia of Space

Diagram of the planet Jupiter, with predictions of the effects of the collision with Jupiter of the comet Shoemaker-Levy 9. From Reuters news agency.

シューメーカーレヴィ第9彗星と木星との衝突の結果予測を解説するダイアグラム。

U.K.   1994
CD: Lance Bell
AD: Lance Bell
D: Lance Bell
I: Lance Bell
DF: Reuters News Graphics Service

Diagram describing the first manned mission to land on the moon. From Reuters news agency.

人類が月面着陸に初めて成功した時の様子を表したダイアグラム。

U.K.   1994
CD: Lance Bell
AD: Lance Bell
D: Lance Bell
I: Lance Bell
DF: Reuters News Graphics Service

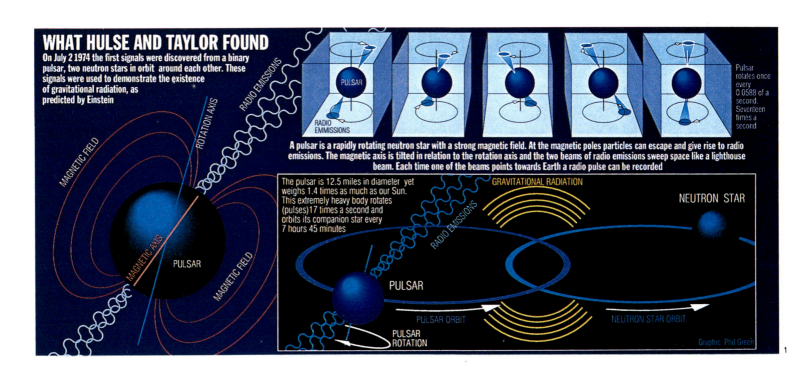

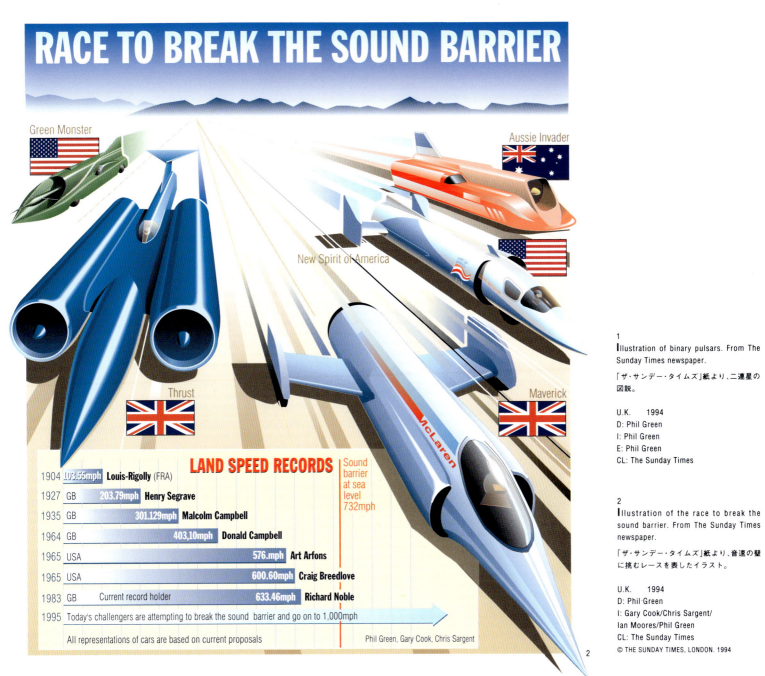

1
Illustration of binary pulsars. From The Sunday Times newspaper.

「ザ・サンデー・タイムズ」紙より、二連星の図説。

U.K.　1994
D: Phil Green
I: Phil Green
E: Phil Green
CL: The Sunday Times

2
Illustration of the race to break the sound barrier. From The Sunday Times newspaper.

「ザ・サンデー・タイムズ」紙より、音速の壁に挑むレースを表したイラスト。

U.K.　1994
D: Phil·Green
I: Gary Cook/Chris Sargent/
Ian Moores/Phil Green
CL: The Sunday Times
© THE SUNDAY TIMES, LONDON. 1994

Diagram comparing the sizes and orbits of the planets. From a Monadnock Paper Mills promotional poster.

モナドノック製紙会社のプロモーション用ポスターより、惑星の大きさと軌道を比較したダイアグラム。

U.S.A.　1993
CD: Joel Katz
D: Joel Katz
I: Steven Lyons
DF: Paradigm:design
CL: Monadnock Paper Mills, Inc.

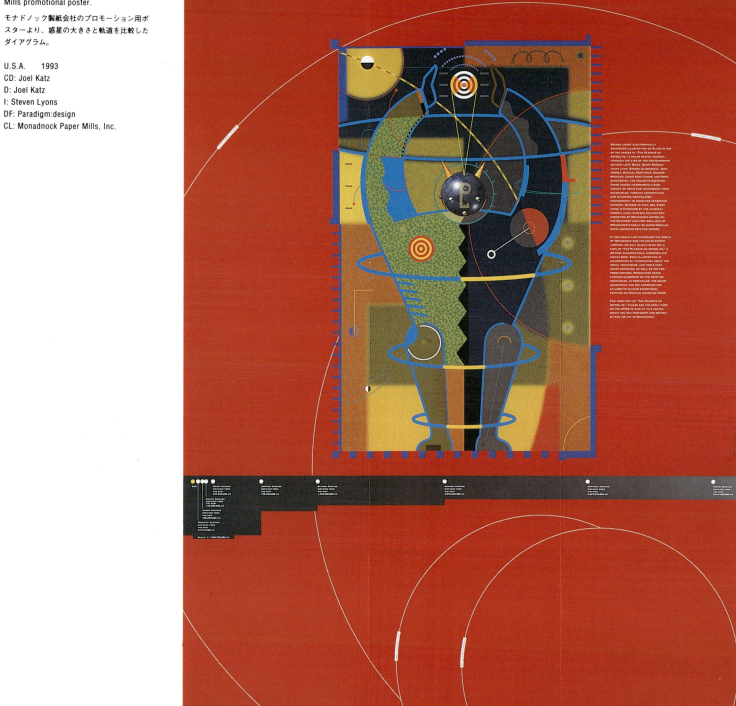

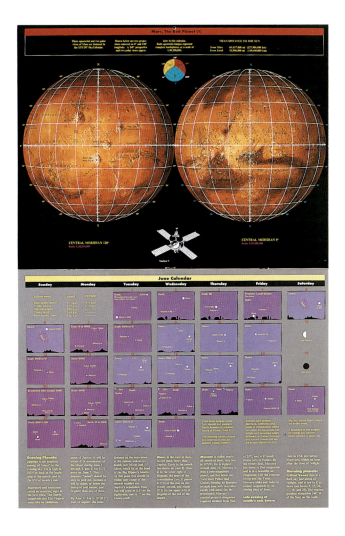

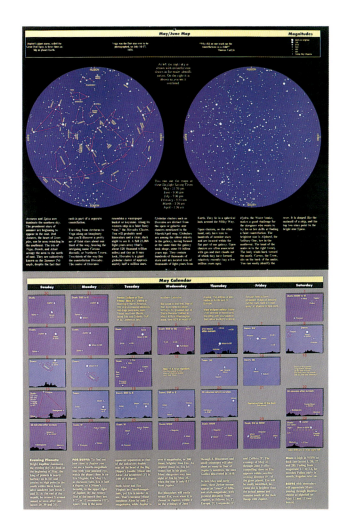

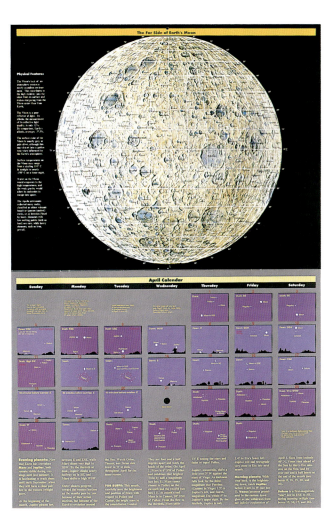

A stronomy calendar charting celestial events for every day of the year. From Epcot Sky Calendar 1993

1993年エプコット・スカイ・カレンダー より、毎日の天体の動きを記した天文カレン ダー。

U.S.A.   1993
CD: Stephan Van Dam
AD: Stephan Van Dam
D: Stephan Van Dam
P: Scott Snow/The Image Bank
DF: Van Dam, Inc.
CL: Walt Disney Company

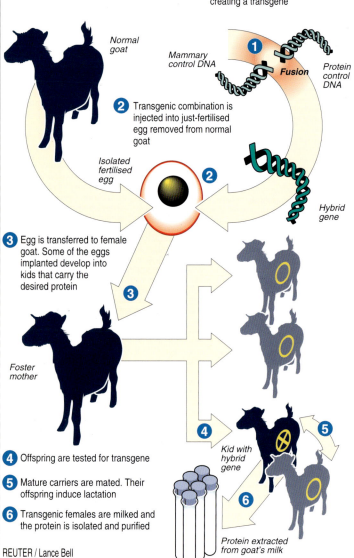

MEDICINES FROM GOAT'S MILK

Scientists have developed a method of inducing animals to produce valuable drugs in their milk. The genetically engineered animals have their DNA (the genetic building blocks of life) spliced with an extra gene that will produce proteins valuable in combating illnesses such as heart disease

1 Goat DNA that produces proteins in milk is spliced with DNA that makes desired protein for drug use creating a transgene

Normal goat

Mammary control DNA

Fusion

1

Protein control DNA

2 Transgenic combination is injected into just-fertilised egg removed from normal goat

Isolated fertilised egg

2

Hybrid gene

3 Egg is transferred to female goat. Some of the eggs implanted develop into kids that carry the desired protein

3

Foster mother

4

4 Offspring are tested for transgene

5 Mature carriers are mated. Their offspring induce lactation

6 Transgenic females are milked and the protein is isolated and purified

5

6

Kid with hybrid gene

Protein extracted from goat's milk

REUTER / Lance Bell

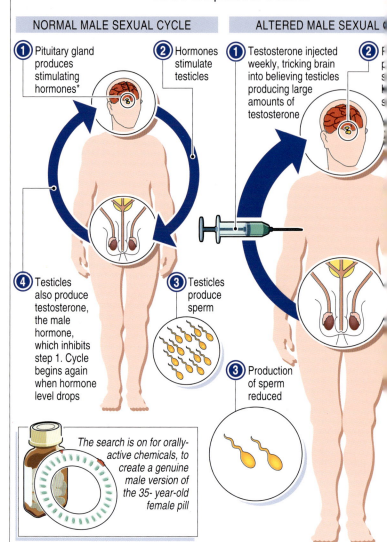

NEW CONTRACEPTIVE FOR MEN

Scientists working on a series of trials involving 700 [...] in nine countries believe they have cracked most o[...] problems of producing a contraceptive pill for m[...]

The trials, which began in 1980, involved weekly injections of th[...] hormone testosterone. A second, bigger series of tests [...] will be completed in October

NORMAL MALE SEXUAL CYCLE

1 Pituitary gland produces stimulating hormones*

2 Hormones stimulate testicles

4 Testicles also produce testosterone, the male hormone, which inhibits step 1. Cycle begins again when hormone level drops

3 Testicles produce sperm

The search is on for orally-active chemicals, to create a genuine male version of the 35- year-old female pill

ALTERED MALE SEXUAL [...]

1 Testosterone injected weekly, tricking brain into believing testicles producing large amounts of testosterone

2 [...]

3 Production of sperm reduced

Diagram illustrating how goats are genetically engineered to produce medicines in their milk. From Reuters news agency.

山羊が生まれつき自分のミルク中に薬を作り出す仕組みについての解説図。

U.K.　1994
CD: Lance Bell
AD: Lance Bell
D: Lance Bell
I: Lance Bell
DF: Reuters News Graphics Service

Diagram illustrating how a new contraceptive for men works. From Reuters news agency.

ロイターズ・ニュース・エージェンシーより、
新しい男性用避妊剤の作用についての解説図。

U.K.　1994
CD: Liz Gould
AD: Liz Gould
D: Liz Gould
I: Liz Gould
DF: Reuters News Graphics Service

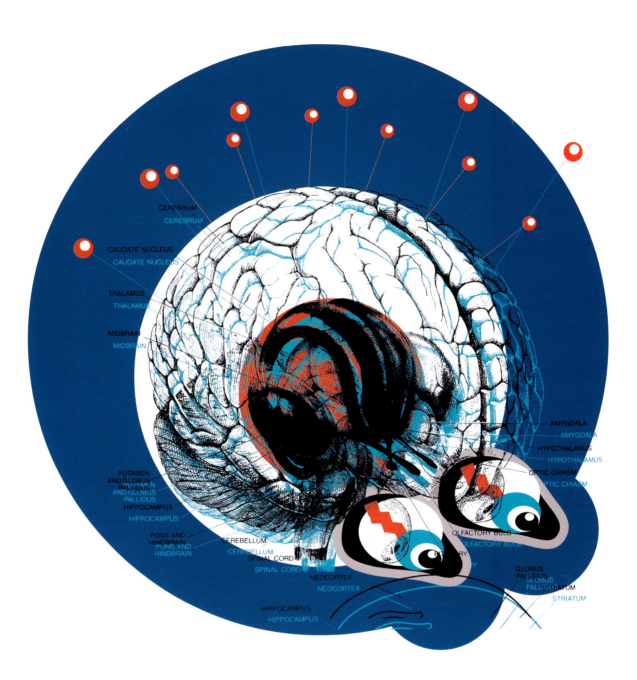

Illustration of the brain. From Esquire magazine.

「エスクワイヤー・マガジン」より、脳の
イラストレーション。

U.K.   1994
AD: Christophe Gowans
I: Andy Martin
CL: National Magazine Co.

1
Illustration showing how seals are attacked near the surface by white sharks rising from the bottom. From American Scientist magazine.

「アメリカン・サイエンティスト・マガジン」より、ホオジロザメがどのように浮上して海面付近のアザラシを襲うのかを説明するイラストレーション。

U.S.A. 1994
AD: Linda K. Huff
D: Linda K. Huff
I: Linda K. Huff
CL: Sigma Xi

2
Charts showing one interpretation of the ancestry of modern dog breeds. From American Scientist magazine.

「アメリカン・サイエンティスト・マガジン」より、現代の犬の血統解釈の一例を表した図解。

U.S.A. 1994
AD: Linda K. Huff
D: Linda K. Huff
I: Linda K. Huff
CL: Sigma Xi

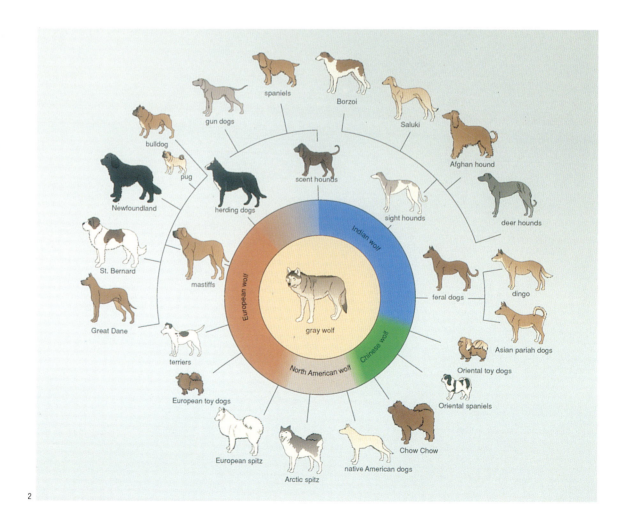

Invasion of the influenza virus

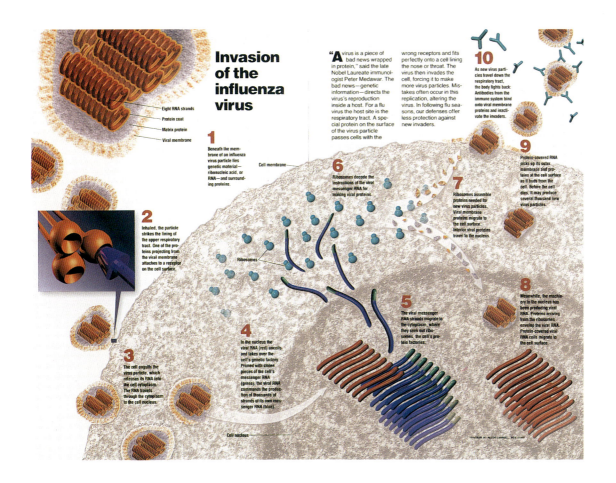

"A virus is a piece of bad news wrapped in protein," said the late Nobel Laureate immunologist Peter Medawar. The bad news—genetic information—directs the virus's reproduction inside a host. For a flu virus the host site is the respiratory tract. A special protein on the surface of the virus particle passes cells with the wrong receptors and fits perfectly onto a cell lining the nose or throat. The virus then invades the cell, forcing it to make more virus particles. Mistakes often occur in this replication, altering the virus. In following flu seasons, our defenses offer less protection against new invaders.

Eight RNA strands
Protein coat
Matrix protein
Viral membrane

1 Beneath the membrane of an influenza virus particle lies genetic material—ribonucleic acid, or RNA—and surrounding proteins.

Cell membrane

2 Inhaled, the particle strikes the lining of the upper respiratory tract. One of the proteins projecting from the viral membrane attaches to a receptor on the cell surface.

Ribosomes

3 The cell engulfs the virus particle, which releases its RNA into the cell cytoplasm. The RNA travels through the cytoplasm to the cell nucleus.

4 In the nucleus the viral RNA (red) uncoils and takes over the cell's genetic factory. Primed with stolen pieces of the cell's messenger RNA (green), the viral RNA commands the production of thousands of strands of its own messenger RNA (blue).

Cell nucleus

5 The viral messenger RNA strands migrate to the cytoplasm, where they seek out ribosomes, the cell's protein factories.

6 Ribosomes decode the instructions of the viral messenger RNA for making viral proteins.

7 Ribosomes assemble proteins needed for new virus particles. Viral membrane proteins migrate to the cell surface. Interior viral proteins travel to the nucleus.

8 Meanwhile, the machinery in the nucleus has been producing viral RNA. Proteins arriving from the ribosomes envelop the viral RNA. Protein-covered viral RNA coils migrate to the cell surface.

9 Protein-covered RNA picks up its outer membrane and proteins at the cell surface as it buds from the cell. Before the cell dies, it may produce several thousand new virus particles.

10 As new virus particles travel down the respiratory tract, the body lights back: Antibodies from the immune system bind onto viral membrane proteins and inactivate the invaders.

DIAGRAM BY ALLEN CARROLL, NGS STAFF

National Geographic magazine illustrations showing the creation of the universe from the 'big bang' (above), and how the influenza virus invades the cell lining of the respiratory tract and replicates (below).

「ナショナル・ジオグラフィック・マガジン」より、ビッグバンに始まる宇宙創造のダイアグラム（上）、及びインフルエンザのウィルスが、いかに呼吸器官の細胞膜内に侵入して増殖するかを表したダイアグラム。

U.S.A.　1994
AD: Allen Carroll
I: Chuck Carter/Allen Carroll
CL: National Geographic Magazine

Diagram showing the sky as viewed through different wavelengths of the electromagnetic spectrum. From National Geographic magazine.

「ナショナル・ジオグラフィック・マガジン」より、電磁スペクトラムの異なる波長を通して見た、空のダイアグラム。

U.S.A. 1994
AD: Allen Carroll
I: William H. Bond
CL: National Geographic Magazine

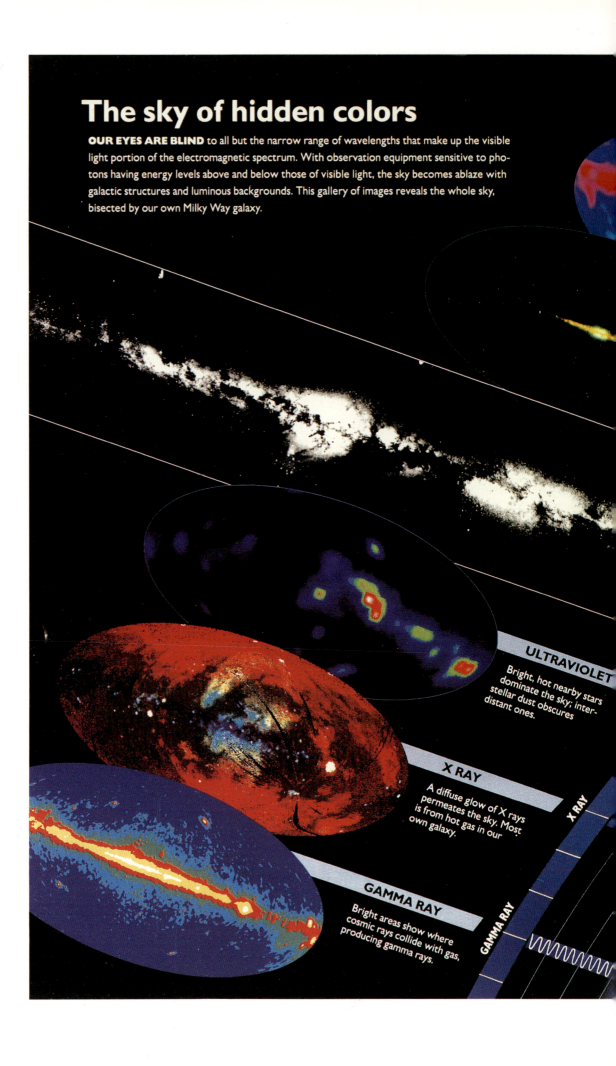

The sky of hidden colors

OUR EYES ARE BLIND to all but the narrow range of wavelengths that make up the visible light portion of the electromagnetic spectrum. With observation equipment sensitive to photons having energy levels above and below those of visible light, the sky becomes ablaze with galactic structures and luminous backgrounds. This gallery of images reveals the whole sky, bisected by our own Milky Way galaxy.

ULTRAVIOLET
Bright, hot nearby stars dominate the sky; interstellar dust obscures distant ones.

X RAY
A diffuse glow of X rays permeates the sky. Most is from hot gas in our own galaxy.

GAMMA RAY
Bright areas show where cosmic rays collide with gas, producing gamma rays.

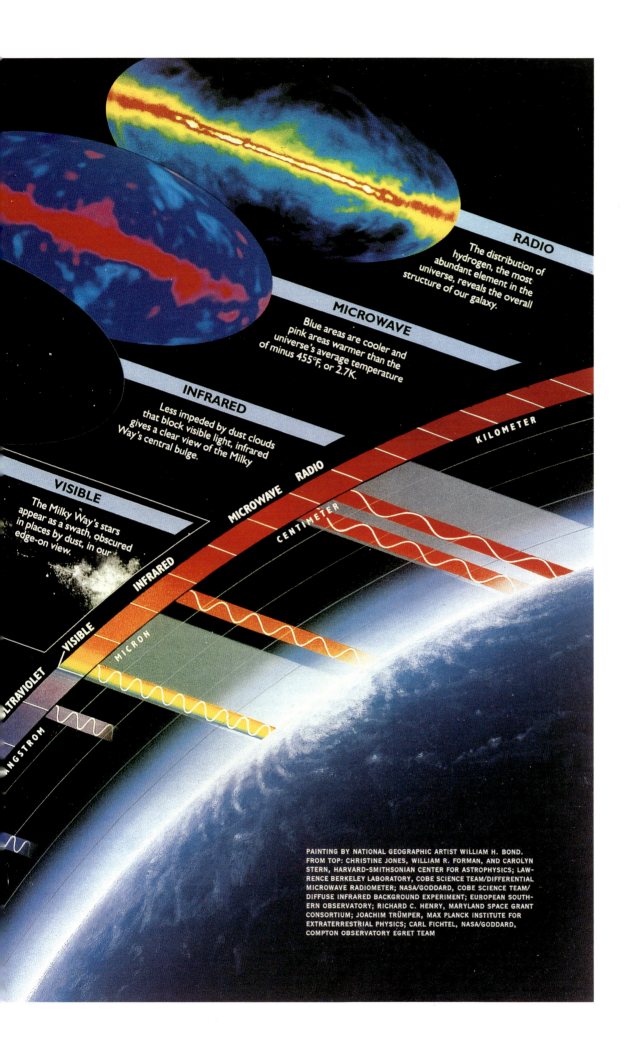

RADIO

The distribution of hydrogen, the most abundant element in the universe, reveals the overall structure of our galaxy.

MICROWAVE

Blue areas are cooler and pink areas warmer than the universe's average temperature of minus 455°F, or 2.7K.

INFRARED

Less impeded by dust clouds that block visible light, infrared gives a clear view of the Milky Way's central bulge.

VISIBLE

The Milky Way's stars appear as a swath, obscured in places by dust, in our edge-on view.

KILOMETER

MICROWAVE RADIO

CENTIMETER

INFRARED

VISIBLE

MICRON

ULTRAVIOLET

ANGSTROM

PAINTING BY NATIONAL GEOGRAPHIC ARTIST WILLIAM H. BOND. FROM TOP: CHRISTINE JONES, WILLIAM R. FORMAN, AND CAROLYN STERN, HARVARD-SMITHSONIAN CENTER FOR ASTROPHYSICS; LAW-RENCE BERKELEY LABORATORY, COBE SCIENCE TEAM/DIFFERENTIAL MICROWAVE RADIOMETER; NASA/GODDARD, COBE SCIENCE TEAM/ DIFFUSE INFRARED BACKGROUND EXPERIMENT; EUROPEAN SOUTH-ERN OBSERVATORY; RICHARD C. HENRY, MARYLAND SPACE GRANT CONSORTIUM; JOACHIM TRÜMPER, MAX PLANCK INSTITUTE FOR EXTRATERRESTRIAL PHYSICS; CARL FICHTEL, NASA/GODDARD, COMPTON OBSERVATORY EGRET TEAM

The big blow

At midnight on June 14, the mountain began to spew deadly clouds of 1500°F gas and ash (below). Columns of ash blasted into the atmosphere, eventually reaching 25 miles high. Earthquakes came so fast and strong that they appeared on seismometers as one. At dawn on June 15 a huge blast blew out the side of the mountain. By 2 p.m. the sky was black with ash and falling chunks of pumice. More pyroclastic flows swept down the slopes, filling 650-foot canyons and spreading outward as far as 11 miles. The new ash from Pinatubo (depicted at right in a painted microscopic view) was a jumble of bits of old volcano, bubbly pumice and glassy shards from new lava, sulfur-rich anhydrite, and crystals of hornblende from deep inside the magma chamber. The 1991 eruption shut down in early September, but the loose ash will remain a deadly threat for years to come—every time rain turns it into unstable slurry.

MAGNIFIED 125 TIMES

How volcanoes become killers

Majestic cones can turn into lethal monsters. Towering columns of ash collapse (1), raining hot rock on the mountain, burying whatever lies below, as at Vesuvius. Unexpected landslides, like the one at Mount St. Helens in 1980, unleash devastating lateral blasts (2). Lava domes cave in, releasing 1500°F pyroclastic flows (3), as at Unzen. Lahars, rivers of water-soaked ash (4), smother towns and fields, as they did at Pinatubo and Nevado del Ruiz, in Colombia. A cone can build so steeply that it can't support itself and so collapses in huge landslides (5) that send debris miles downslope—a process discovered in Hawaii. Flowing lava rarely kills, but it can cause widespread property loss.

PYROCLASTIC FLOW

PYROCLASTIC FLOW

Pinatubo's plumbing

What caused the eruption? Scientists believe that an earthquake in July 1990 allowed buoyant basalt from the upper mantle to squeeze into the magma chamber, which was filled with viscous dacite. That injection energized the simmering reservoir and created a fluid, gas-charged magma called andesite. This magma soon rose toward the surface, building a new dome on the northeast slope that corked the system. Pressure in the magma chamber built up rapidly. Remelted dacite rose after the andesite but ran into a clot of older domes. Probing its way to the surface, the magma finally found a clear conduit. Gas exploded from the lava, and the volcano blasted skyward, destroying the newest dome.

MAGMA CHAMBER

PAINTINGS BY NATIONAL GEOGRAPHIC ARTISTS
WILLIAM H. BOND AND CHRISTOPHER A. KLEIN

Ember on the Ring of Fire

The Philippines originated as huge volcanoes built up from the ocean floor. The island of Luzon alone has 13 active volcanoes, some only a short drive from Manila, a city of 6.7 million people. The pattern of volcanoes around the rim of the Pacific Ocean is called the Ring of Fire.

Ring of Fire
NORTH AMERICA
ASIA
PACIFIC
PHILIPPINES
EQUATOR
OCEAN
AUSTRALIA
Plate boundary

South China Sea
Luzon
Philippine Sea
Mt. Pinatubo
Manila
PHILIPPINES
Mindanao

0   300
MILES
NGS CARTOGRAPHIC DIVISION

SUBMITTORS' INDEX

DIAGRAM GRAPHICS 2

Editorial Consultant
Nobuo Nakagaki

Jacket Design
Ichiro Higashiizumi
Hiroshi Nakajima

Designer
Yutaka Ichimura

Editor
Yuko Yoshio

Business Manager
Masato Ieshiro

Photographer
Kuniharu Fujimoto

Coordinators
Chizuko Gilmore (San Francisco)
Sarah Phillips (London)

English Translator and Consultant
Sue Herbert

Publisher
Shingo Miyoshi

1995年 5月25日初版第1刷発行

定価 16,000円 （本体15,534円）

発行所　ピエ・ブックス
〒170 東京都豊島区駒込4-14-6-301
TEL: 03-3949-5010 FAX: 03-3949-5650

印刷/製本　エバーベスト・プリンティング（株）
Printed and bound by Everbest Printing Co., Ltd.

Ko Fai Industrial Building, Block C5, 10th Floor,
7 Ko Fai Road, Yau Tong, Kowloon, Hong Kong
Tel: 852-2727-4433 Fax: 852-2772-7908

ISBN 4-938586-74-6 C3070 P16000E

THE P·I·E COLLECTION

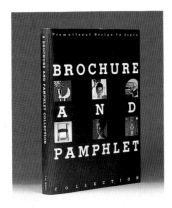

BROCHURE & PAMPHLET COLLECTION 1
Pages: 224(144 in color) ￥15,000
業種別カタログ・コレクション
Here are hundreds of the best brochures and pamphlets from Japan.
This collection will make a valuable sourcebook for anyone involved in corporate identity advertising and graphic design.

LABELS AND TAGS
Pages: 224(192 in color) ￥15,000
ファッションのラベル＆タグ・コレクション
Over 1,600 garment labels representing 450 brands produced in Japan are included in this full-color collection.

COVER TO COVER
Pages: 240(176 in color) ￥17,000
世界のブック＆エディトリアル・デザイン
The latest trends in book and magazine design are illustrated with over 1,000 creative works by international firms.

BUSINESS STATIONERY GRAPHICS 1
Pages: 224(192 in color) ￥15,000
世界のレターヘッド・コレクション
Creatively designed letterheads, business cards, memo pads, and other business forms and documents are included this international collection.

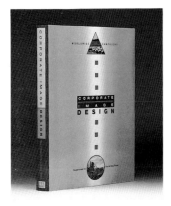

CORPORATE IMAGE DESIGN
Pages: 336(272 in color) ￥16,000
世界の業種別ＣＩ・ロゴマーク
This collection presents the best corporate identity projects from around the world. Creative and effective designs from top international firms are featured in this valuable source book.

POSTCARD GRAPHICS 3
Pages: 232(208 in color) ￥16,000
世界の業種別ポストカード・コレクション
Volume 3 in the series presents more than 1,200 promotional postcards in dazzling full color. Top designers from the world over have contributed to this useful image bank of ideas.

GRAPHIC BEAT London / Tokyo 1 & 2
Pages: 224(208 in color) ￥16,000
音楽とグラフィックのコラボレーション
1,500 music-related graphic works from 29 of the hottest designers in Tokyo and London. Features Malcolm Garrett, Russell Miles, Tadanori Yokoo, Neville Brody, Vaughn Oliver and others.

BUSINESS CARD GRAPHICS 2
Pages: 224(192 in color) ￥16,000
世界の名刺＆ショップカード、第２弾
This latest collection presents 1,000 creative cards from international designers. Features hundreds of cards used in creative fields such as graphic design and architecture.

T-SHIRT GRAPHICS
Pages: 224(192 in color) ￥16,000
世界のＴシャツ・グラフィックス
This unique collection showcases 700 wonderfully creative T-Shirt designs from the world's premier design centers. Grouped according to theme, categories include sports, casual, designer and promotional shirts among others.

DIAGRAM GRAPHICS
Pages: 224(192 in color) ￥16,000
世界のダイアグラム・デザインの集大成
Hundreds of unique and lucid diagrams, charts, graphs, maps and technical illustrations from leading international design firms. Variety of media represented including computer graphics.

SPECIAL EVENT GRAPHICS
Pages: 224(192 in color) ￥16,000
世界のイベント・グラフィックス特集
This innovative collection features design elements from concerts, festivals, fashion shows, symposiums and more. International works include posters, tickets, flyers, invitations and various premiers.

RETAIL IDENTITY GRAPHICS
Pages: 208(176 in color) ￥14,800
世界のショップ・グラフィックス
This visually exciting collection showcases the identity design campaigns of restaurants, bars, shops and various other retailers. Wide variety of pieces are featured including business cards, signs, menus, bags and hundreds more.